# HUMAN RIGHTS
# IN
# SOUTH ASIA

# HUMAN RIGHTS
# IN
# SOUTH ASIA

Editor
Pramod Mishra

**KALPAZ PUBLICATIONS**
Delhi-110052

Human Rights In South Asia
*(Sociology, Human Right, International Studies)*



ISBN: 81-7835-008-4



Published in 2000 in India by
Kalpaz Publications
C-30, Satyawati Nagar
Ashok Vihar Phase-III
Delhi-110052
E-Mail: kalpaz@hotmail.com

Laser Typeset at A.S. Printers
Printed at Mehra Offset Printers, New Delhi

# Contents

# Preface

The concept of human rights is necessarily evolving in nature apace with the evolution of human civilization in the context of a changing social, political, economic and cultural milieu. It is, therefore, a daunting task for anyone to assess the state of implementation of human rights in a society.

Respect of human rights makes freedom meaningful. Human rights are meaningless in an environment of poverty and deprivation. Human rights are above politics. They are part and parcel of life in society and they concern humanity. Human rights necessarily signify human values in an absolute senses: but they have greater relevance to the real wellbeing of the individual if they are applied in the context of society.

The basic problem that arises concerning human right relates to their proper enforcement and this aspect varies today from State to State. This is indeed so because the first initial step in the direction of enforcement of human rights is very much confined to the national frontiers of the state where the individual resides. The liberal democratic concept of human rights in the second half of the twentieth century has come to mean defence of the rights of the human being against abuses of power committed by the organs of the state with the help of institutionalized means. It also involves the promotion of the establishment of human living conditions and the overall development of the human personality.

This book aims is to present a general overview of the human rights situation in South Asia. The ethos and problems of a developing ancient oriental society like India must first be understood before an acceptable standard of rights performance assessment is evolved. Indeed, the non-dirigible rights to life and dignity do provide a universal bottom line. Yet, to look at a society purely through that looking glass is to ignore the ground realities in the midst of which the human rights culture has to nurture.

*Editor*

1

# HUMAN RIGHTS IN INDIA

On 15th August, 1947 when we the people of India became independent the Constituent Assembly was already engaged in the task of framing a Constitution for us. The teeming millions of this country were suffering from deprivation, exploitation and social and economic injustices for centuries under a colonial rule when we enacted the Constitution.

We the people in our Constitution made a promise to ourselves to build a new socio-economic and political order in which people would enjoy real justice social, economic and political. This was a document of hope.

There was a promise contained in the preamble and part IV in Directive Principles of State Policy, The promise contained was to be redeemed by legislators we would elect, the judges we would select and the executive we would nominate. Directive Principles exhort the state to ensure that citizens have an adequate means of livelihood, that the operation of the economic system and the ownership and control of the material resources of the country subserve the common good, that the health of the workers, including children is not abused and that special consideration be given to pregnant women. Workers, both agricultural and industrial are to have a standard of living that allows them to enjoy leisure and social and cultural opportunities. Among the primary duties of the state is the raising of the level of nutrition and the general standard of living of the people. The principles express the hope that within ten years of the adoption of the Constitution, there will be compulsory primary education for children up to the age of fourteen years. The other provisions of the Principles seek equally to secure the renovation of Indian society by improving the techniques of agriculture, husbandry, cottage industry, etc.

It was expected that we should have, achieved these objectives within a reasonable time, say within two decades or roughly say by 1970. But there has been a breach of faith by those who were elected by us to redeem this promise.

Since 1971 we have allowed politicians to define the national agenda, be it Garibi Hatao, Su-raaj, or social justice. No other nation in the world has been held to ransom by politics and politicians as relentlessly as India has been. And all along, we have depended upon our politicians to represent us, seeking false comfort in the thought that we are, after all, the largest democracy in world. Till 1989, the people in this country had an urge, an impatient urge to participate in events and processes that could shape their lives. This urge was manifesting itself consistently and persisted as a regular feature from 1947 till 1971 in all walks or life. In 1971 corruption started in public life. In 1967 elections there were large number of M.Ps. and M.L.As., who had won election without spending much money Politics was an instrument of public service and a person in politics had to respond to the aspirations and impatient urge of the people of this country.

The peoples' urge was marred and sought to curb during emergency, but it re-emerged with greater force in 1977. Till 1989, poverty, unemployment, right to work, corruption high prices, etc. were issues and there was an impatience in the people but if it had been properly nurtured in the national frame work, it could have become a source of tremendous vitality and innovation for the creation of a dynamic and just society. But that impatience of the people was marred by the impatience of those who were in the waiting to come into power. Development must be woven around people, not people around development and it should empower the citizens with an awareness of the issues to participate in the development and politics and not to make them share the corruption of the politicians.

We have raw materials and natural resources of all types in abundance and this country is perhaps the only one where we have skilled labours of all types, like potters, weavers, shoe makers, carpenters, candle stick makers and so on, and also unskilled labour. This skilled and unskilled labour was to be brought up and engaged in building up a prosperous social order by using our raw material and natural resources by a sustainable development.. The sustainable development is the key to a social order based on equality, prosperity and security. It is a process in which development can be sustained for many generations to come.

The fundamental norm governing the concept of human rights is that of the respect for human personality and Its absolute worth, regardless of colour, race, sex, religion or other considerations. These are essential for other considerations. These rights are essential for the adequate development of the human personality and for human happiness and progress. That a general election in 1971 was fought and won on the single slogan of 'Garibi Hatao' with huge majority was symptomatic of the people's expectations. Lack of people's mandate could no longer be invoked to explain inaction. But in 1971 the children of those who were in power started attaining adulthood. Politics ceased to be an instrument of service and started becoming a hereditary profit; oriented huge business and corruption in public life made the things worst. If those in power are corrupt, the relevant consideration for them in taking major policy decisions is not the interest of the country that their own personal narrow interest at the cost of even losing political and economic sovereignty of the country. The people gave a massive mandate to the political leadership to act but the grim reality is that those to whom we elected had not planned for the poor. The super powers took full advantage of corruption in politics in India and with a nexus of corrupt political leadership with those super powers, we followed the western industrial path. Through the instrumentality of World Bank and I.M.F. the corrupt politicians of this country have made us to enter an era of liberalization and globalisation. Now poverty has ceased to be important on the political agenda. It has become a technical matter for experts and planners to handle. The rheotic, however, is being kept alive as it has tremendous appeal for the Vote Bank.

Mr. M.A.O. Oaman, a scientific fellow of Institute for Social Science, New Delhi who is presently co-ordinating research on IMF/World Bank Conditionalities and its Impact on Growth and Social Justice in India has made a recent survey in which he says.

"Look at where we are as nation. 291 million adults are still illiterate and substantial majority of them are females whose capabilities are the key to changing the society, 45 million children were out of Primary Schools in 1995. Nearly one third of children under 16 are forced to child labour. 135 million people are denied access to primary health care, 226 million are without safe drinking water, 640 million lack basic sanitation and so on 350 million people live below a poverty line which views people only as biological entity and not as a social individual with self respect. Ironically, the same India which houses the largest number of the world's poor, was ranked first in arms India imports among the developing countries.

Mr. Ooman further says:

> "In less than 6 years, the Prime Minister, the Finance Minister, Union Ministers, Chief Minister, senior bureaucrats have gone abroad innumerable times in order to convince the capital of the world that we have given up planning in favour of market medicated regime. Freedom for capital does not mean freedom for people. Living in squalor and misery you have no real freedom of choice. True development essentially in enlarging the capabilities of the people and their choice. Looking back we have failed in this task during the last fifty years of independence."

These visits of Prime Minister, Union Finance Minister, Chief Ministers and Senior bureaucrats created a nexus between corrupt politicians and bureaucrats and the super powers and the result is the acceptance of the policy of Liberalization and reliance on free global market. A key element in the present development strategy is reliance on a 'Free' global market. It needs to be recognized that conceding supremacy to the freemarket in economic affairs makes the very concept of a society's development strategy meaningless. For development or lack of it brings in its wake the outcome of the interplay of market forces, too complex, impoundable and un-predictable to be brought within a policy frame. What is produced how, how much and for whom sold out, at what price, all gets determined by free competition in the market and by competitive profitability.

Investment also follows the signals put out by market. Thus even at a conceptual level dependence on a free global market does not appear consistent with any definite strategy even for economic development, much less so for development in the full sense of the term.

We take loan from the World Bank even for infrastructure, roads, bridges, etc. Central Government, State Governments and even Local Self Governments take such loans. The result is total dependence upon loan and no desire to build up our own economy in accordance with our necessities. All the institutions at all levels including at the level of Local Self Government have been destroyed. We must come out of it. Otherwise we are bound to be ruined completely.

The Globalisation is nothing but losing our economic and political sovereignty by entering into unequal treaties like GATT and becoming member of WT.O. There are clauses in these Treaties that our Parliament will have to enact laws in tune with some of it's provisions and if our Parliament does not do so the W.T.O. can take cross retalitory measures. We are not free to decide what to export, or import. The consequence is that we can never even imagine of having an economy of self reliance. These unequal treaties suit either the developed countries who have surplus production, or those under developed countries who have an economy of self restraint like China.

Market hunger of Americans and their blind admiration for the glamorous life at the expense of World's happiness has been demonstrated and remonstrated in a book "On Third World Legs" by a well known author Willson who says in that book about United States of America.

> "This country consumes more than 40% of the world's production of natural resources with about 6% of the population, a disparity that is both practically and morally indefensible."

This globalisation is creating unemployment, recession, scarcity of raw materials and a haphazard industrial growth and making this country economically bankrupt and it has put us in the cobweb of multinationals with total loss of sovereignty, both political and economic, on account of liberalization and globalisation of W.T.O

The people's Commission on GATT consisting of Mr. Justice V.R. Krishna lyre, Mr. Justice O. Chinnappa, Reddy, Mr. Justice D.A. Desai, Mr. Justice Rajendra Sacchar submitted its report in which it came to the conclusion, after hearing large number of eminent experts and organizations who made their submissions to that commission that the treaty constituted a 'Surrender of India's sovereignty' and was inimical to the fundamental rights of the citizens guaranteed under the Constitution.

Although on account of twin social diseases, institutional corruption and consumer culture, which have been aggravated by our membership of W.T.O. and loan of World Bank total apathy has been created in the minds of India, yet there are still some people and the organisers left in this country who are mobilising public opinion against this treaty. These include Mr. Justice V.R. Krishna Iyer, Mr. Justice O. Chinnappa Reddy, Mr. Justice D.A. Desai, Mr. Justice Rajendra Sachchar and few organisations like Azadi Bachao Andolan Rabi Ray's Lok Sakti Abhiyan, Sunder Lal Bahuguna's Himalaya Bachao Andolan and Medha Patekar's Narmada Bachao Andolan. U.P., PUCL will make an appeal to all such distinguished citizens and N.G.O's approach National Human Rights Commission by filing petitions and to urge on the inevitable adverse effect of signing of the treaty to become member of W.T.O. on the:

1. Fundamental rights of the citizens of India and specially the right to food, livelihood, health, self governance and democracy.
2. Sovereignty and integrity of India in as much as sovereignty and integrity is part of the basic structure of the Constitution; and
3. Federal structure of the constitution as a consequence of which the exclusive powers of the State would be lost to the Union without the consultation and consent of the States.

If the N.H.R.C. is satisfied with the submissions, then the Commission may also be persuaded to file a writ petition on behalf of people of the country in the Supreme Court as P.I.L. in exercise of its powers U/S 18(2) of the Protection of Human Rights Act. No doubt judges are not expected to examine the desirability of entering into a particular treaty obligation. That is another matter altogether. But if the direct and inevitable effect of the treaty is that it will infringe fundamental rights. The judiciary has constitutional obligation to interfere. Nor can the judiciary stand by to witness a treaty simply riding rough shod over the very basic structure of the Constitution including, democracy, sovereignty and social justice.

Old timers of our country confine the concept of Human rights only to civil liberties and not the economic social and cultural rights. Mr. Justice H.R. Khanna in a recent article published in March part of AIR has said that Civil Liberty and Human Rights are two faces of the same coin. His whole article is based on the belief and assumption that Human Rights have to remain confined to the question of Civil Liberties only, PUCL Uttar Pradesh begs to differ. In the Indian context, particularly in the context of globalisation at the dictates of W.T.O. and under the debts of World Bank and I.M.F. there has to be an emerging concept of Human Rights which affects the lives and liberty, natural resources and cultural aspects of the people of the country.

The corrupt politicians of this country have also divided us on caste and communal lines. The human right activists of this country are terribly upset and shocked at the brazen increase of caste and communal violence, atrocities, harassment and hate campaign that has been unleashed by all types of politicians against one community or the other. It suits the arithmetic of all the political parties. There are criminals in the game of power politics in all the political parties. These criminals are encouraging religious fundamentalism which leads to large scale violence like Bombay riots and these days oppression of the Christian minorities in Gujrat and else where in the country.

The National Human Rights Commission in its Annual Report of 1996-97 in the summary of that report and principal recommendations has observed "In recent years there has teen growing concern in the country that the process of governance have, on occasion, been corroded by a nexus between criminals, lees then scrupulous political elements and members of the executive lacking in integrity. The deleterious effects on human rights resulting from such a nexus can be ganged from the nature of the petitions received by this Commission.

True democracy is built on restraint, on the excise of moderation both by the majority and by minority groups. When such restraint snaps and society yields of ethnic, religious and caste entrepreneurs who garner support for opportunistic ends even at the cost of inciting violence against those belonging to other groups, the citizens of this country pay the price in the destruction of their right to life and in assaults on the dignity and worth of the human person. It is time that the leadership of this nation untidily turned away from the politics of expedience and established clear code of Conduct of govern their behaviour".

This shows that the National Human Rights Commission recognizes that corruption in politic, criminalisation of politics, communal and caste politics are issues directly related to questions of violation of Human Rights and the concept of Human Rights can not be confined only to Civil Liberties.

Any democratic set-up of society should ensure equality to its constituents. Democracy without equality would be incomplete. It was, therefore, proper for the makers of the, Indian Constitution to assure principles of equality in the Preamble of the Constitution. The Preamble promises "to secure to all its citizens equality of status and opportunity".

Besides, Articles 14 to 18 guarantee right to equality. All these rights fall under Chapter III on Fundamental Rights.

Article 14 guarantees equality before law and equal protection of laws. Article 15 prohibits discrimination on grounds of religion, race, caste, sex etc. Article 16 guarantees equality of opportunity in matter of employment. Articles 17 and 19 abolish untouchability and titles respectively.

In a classic statement on rule of law as operating in England, Dicey has said that one of the three attributes of this rule is that no one is above law, and everyone is subjected to the same law irrespective of his rank or status. The Fourteenth Amendment to the U.S. Constitution guarantees the same right.

Article 7 of the U.D.H.R. says: "All are equal before the law and are entitled without any discrimination to equal protection of the law." Article 10 guarantees him "full equality to a fair and public hearing by an independent and impartial tribunal, in the determination of his rights and obligations and of any criminal charge against him." Article 14 of the International Covenant says: "All persons shall be equal before the courts and tribunals." Article 14 of the Constitution guarantees that the "State shall not deny to any person equality before the law or equal protection of the laws." Article 14 of the Constitution also fulfils the promise given in the Preamble that the Constitution shall secure to its people equality of status and opportunity. The object of this Article is to see that no one is above the law and every one is entitled to equal protection of his rights. This was aptly put by Justice Subba Rao in the case of State of U.P. vs. Deoman Upadhyay when he said:

> Equality before law is a negative concept; equal protection of law is a positive one. The former declares that every one is equal before law, that no one can claim special privileges and that all classes are equally subjected to the ordinary law of the land; the latter postulates an equal protection of all alike in the same situation and under like circumstances.

Every person, therefore, shall be treated alike in India. Negatively, no person shall be subjected to prejudicial procedure in any proceeding against, or in respect of, him. It is on this account that everyone shall be entitled to procedural safeguards, irrespective of serious allegations against him. This was held by the Punjab High Court in the case of Gouri Shanker vs. Union of India. As it held:

> I agree that at the present juncture our national security is linked with the elimination of the evil

> and no one can look at it with indifference, and that persons who indulge in these prejudicial activities are wittingly or unwittingly doing irreparable injury to the cause of the defence of the whole country. But, however anti-national and distasteful to this court the activities of these unpatriotic persons, who callously indulge in illegal smuggling of gold or, who trade in smuggled gold. . . so long as their activities do not clearly fall within the mischief of law, imposing personal penalty, they must be held entitled to the protection guaranteed by our constitution.

It is said that there can be no absolute equality. Nor should equality be confused with uniformity. Equality only means that same law is applicable to the given class of people. Absolute equality is impossible. Aristotle's concept of justice also implied that equals should be treated equally; unequals unequally. This was echoed by Chief Justice Subba Rao while he was Chief Justice of Andhra Pradesh High Court in the case of Pichayya vs. Government of Andhra. As he said:

In a society of unequal basic structure, it is well-nigh impossible to make laws suitable in their application to all the persons alike.

It is argued that what Article 14 purports to achieve is to avoid unequal treatment for persons who are similarly situated. The Article is designed to protect persons against discrimination among equals. In the case of Sri Kisan vs. Dutta, the Nagpur High Court approved the concept of equality as given by Sir Ivor Jennings in his book on Constitution. He said:.

> Equality before the law means that among equals the law should be equal and it should be equally administered and that like should be treated alike.

In the case of Devadsam vs. Union of India, Justice Madholkar, while giving the majority judgment, declared:

> What is meant by equality in this Article is equality among equals. It does not provide that what is aimed at is an absolute equality of treatment to all persons in every conceivable circumstance, in utter disregard of the differences such as age, sex, education and so on and so forth, as may be found in people in general. Indeed the aim of the article is to ensure that invidious distinction or arbitrary discrimination shall not be made by the State between a citizen and a citizen who answer the same description.

In view of the above observations, while the concept of equality is maintained among equals, reasonable classification has been permitted, and sometimes it has been found imperative to do so, as Chief Justice Subba Rao has rightly said:

A reasonable classification is not only permitted but is necessary if society should progress. But such a classification cannot be arbitrary but, must be based upon differences pertinent to the subject in respect of and the purposes for which it is made.

Reasonable classification is, therefore, permissible. The Supreme Court has also upheld reasonable classification. In the case of Charanjit Lal vs. Union of India, Justice Das declared:

> The inhibition of the Article that the State shall not deny to any person equality before the law or the equal protection of the laws was designed to protect all persons against legislative discrimination against equals and prevent any person or class of persons from being singled out as a special subject for discrimination and hostile legislation. It does not, however, mean that every law must have universal application for all persons who are not by nature, attainment or circumstances in the same position. The varying needs of different classes of persons often require separate treatment and, it is, therefore,

> established by judicial decisions that the equal protection clause of the Fourteenth Amendment of the American Constitution does not take away from the State the power to classify persons for legislative purposes. This classification may be on different basis. It may be geographical or according to objects or occupations or the like. If a law deals equally with all of a certain well-defined class, it is not open to the charge of denial of equal protection.

The sum-total of the decisions has been that, although Article 14 guarantees equality before law, it does not mean uniform law for all. This is not possible. There has got to be reasonable classification and the court will not declare such laws as ultra vires the Constitution and its Article 14 so long as there is reasonable and rational classification made on some basis. Naturally, diplomats cannot be touched by law. It will, therefore, be wrong on the part of others to say that there is inequality between them and diplomats. Similarly, minors cannot claim that because they are not allowed to enter into valid contracts, they are denied equality before law. Again, exemption of military personnel from the application of any laws of Prohibition is not a denial of equality. However, people are assured equality with respect to basic laws.

While it may be conceded that there cannot be absolute equality and there can be reasonable and rational classification, it may be emphasised here that there should not only be a semblance of equality but working equality. This is particularly essential in criminal cases. It has been noticed that inequality becomes too apparent in criminal cases when the State can engage the most competent lawyer for the prosecution, while the poor suspect is either denied the services of a competent lawyer of his choice or he is given a none-too-competent lawyer. This makes the principle of equality a sham.

It is, therefore, essential that in order to make the

phrase "equality before law" meaningful, Article 39A of the Constitution should be scrupulously implemented and competent legal aid given to the suspect, so that he can put his defence well, against the almighty prosecution. It is heartening in this respect to find in the Supreme Court a zealous mistress who had declared free legal aid as part and parcel of fundamental right Of personal liberty.

The phrase—equality before law—should mean that law should equally treat as well as protect the indigent suspect who cannot afford to produce a surety to secure his release pending trial nor can he put up a desirable defence due to the lack of services of a competent lawyer who can prepare his defence. The poor suspect cannot enjoy life with his family as guaranteed to him under Article 21 because money is the measuring rod for getting release on bail. Fortunately, the Supreme Court has come to the rescue of the indigent undertrials by executing their release against personal bond.

**Prohibition of discrimination**

Article 14 of the Constitution guarantees equality in general terms. Articles 15 to 18 deal with particular aspects of equality. Article 15 prohibits discrimination on grounds of religion, race, caste, sex, or place of birth. As the Article says:

1) The State shall not discriminate against any citizen on grounds only of religion, race, caste, sex, place of birth or any of them.

2) No citizen shall, on grounds only of religion, race, caste, sex, place of birth or any of them, be subject to any disability, liability, restriction or condition with regard to:

   a) access to shops, public restaurants, hotels and places of public entertainment; or

b) the use of wells, tanks, bathing ghats, roads and places of public resort maintained wholly or partly out of State funds or dedicated to the use of the general public.

3) Nothing in this article shall prevent the State from making any special provision for women and children.

4) Nothing in this article or clause (2) of Article 29 shall prevent the State from making any special provision for the advancement of any socially and educationally backward classes of citizens or for the scheduled castes and scheduled tribes.

While clauses 1 and 2 prohibit discrimination on grounds of religion, race, caste, sex or place of birth only, clauses 3 and 4 are exceptions to clauses 1 and 2, thus permitting some discriminatory treatment in favour of women, children and, socially and educationally backward classes, scheduled castes and scheduled tribes.

Articles 15(1) and (2) prohibit discrimination on ground of only religion, race, sex, caste or place of birth. The word "only" is significant because while discrimination is prohibited solely on ground of religion etc., the State may resort to discriminatory treatment due to combination of grounds, if that is based on reasonable classification.

It was because of Article 15(1) that the Supreme Court considered the notification of the Government of Rajasthan as contravening the Article on the ground that it discriminated against some residents of the village on account of their religion. The notification in question purported to impose penalty tax towards reimbursement of expenses incurred on posting of extra police in the village whose residents were suspected to harbour dacoits. Some sections of society were exempted from such penalty tax.

In the case of Girdhar Gopal vs. State, it was held by the Madhya Pradesh High Court that Section 354 of the Indian Penal Code which discriminates in favour of women does not become invalid because such discrimination is not solely based on sex but other grounds of propriety, public morals, decency and decorum as well.11 On the same grounds, Section 497 of the same code which exempts women from being an accused in an adultery case was held to be valid by the Bombay High Court.12 This was later upheld by the Supreme Court.13

In a case, where capitation fee was challenged on the ground that residents of the State of Madhya Pradesh were exempted, while applicants from outside Madhya Pradesh were to pay the same, the Supreme Court did not consider it as contravening.

Article 15(1) because the place of birth was different from residence.14 Similarly, where admissions were given only to applicants domiciled in the State, it was held that there was no discrimination on grounds of place of birth.

Article 15(3) permits special protection to women and children. This kind of protection to women and children is universally recognised. Observations in the case of Muller vs. Oregon may be relevant in this connection. As it was observed:

— It is impossible to close one's eyes to the fact that she still looks to her brother and depends upon him. Even though all restrictions on political, personal and contractual rights were taken away, and she stood, so far as statutes are concerned, upon an absolutely equal place with, him

— It would still be true that she is so constituted that she will rest upon and look to him for protection; that her physical structure and a proper discharge of

> her maternal functions -having in view not merely her own health, but the well being of the race, justify legislation to protect her from the greed as well as the passion of man.16

Clause 4 of Article 15 makes special provision for the protection of the interests of socially and educationally backward classes as well as of scheduled castes and tribes. This clause was added by the First Amendment of 1951, one year after the Constitution came into force. It was thought that although equality is guaranteed under Article 14, it will remain a dream unless socially and educationally backward classes as well as scheduled tribes and castes are given some support to achieve equality with other sections of the society. Clause 4, therefore, is Meant to give a real shape to the concept of equality. The Kerala High Court has aptly remarked:

> It has, however, been realised in a country like India where large sections of the people are backward ~socially, economically, educationally and politically. These declarations and guarantees will be meaningless unless provision is also made for the uplift of such backward classes who are in no position whatever to compete with the more advanced classes. Thus, to give meaning and content to the equality guaranteed by Arts. 14, 15, 16 and 29, provision has been made in Articles 15(4) and 16(4), enabling preferential treatment in favour of the weaker sections.

### Equality of opportunity in public employment

As stated, the Preamble promises to secure equality of opportunity. Article 16 is in fulfilment of this promise. The Article runs as follows:

1) There shall be equality of opportunity for all citizens in matters relating to employment or appointment to any office under the State.

2) No citizen shall, on grounds only of religion, race, caste, sex, descent, place of birth, residence or any of them, be ineligible for, or discriminated against in respect of, any employment or office under the State.

3) Nothing in this Article shall prevent the Parliament from making any law prescribing in regard to a class or classes of employment or appointment to an office under the Government, or any local or other authority within a State or Union Territory, any requirement as to residence within that State or Union Territory prior to such employment or appointment.

4) Nothing in this Article shall prevent the State from making any provision for the reservation of appointments or posts in favour of any backward class of citizens, which in the opinion of the State, is not adequately represented in the services under the state.

5) Nothing in this Article shall affect the operation of any law which provides that the incumbent of an office in connection with the affairs of any religious or denominational institution or any member of the governing body thereof, shall be a person professing a particular religion, or belonging to a particular denomination.

Equality of opportunity does not mean for any job. Naturally, each job demands its own set of qualifications which the candidates must fulfil before applying. Nor, does it mean that, because, the given candidates' fulfil the required qualifications they necessarily get taken. It is impossible to select all the candidates who meet the required qualifications. As it normally happens, there are always more candidates than there are vacancies. Therefore, it is wrong to expect that all qualified persons can be appointed. Naturally, the best among the qualified candidates get selected and the rest remain rejected.

Equally, fixation of higher qualifications does not mean denial of equal opportunity. This was held in the case of All Station Masters Association vs. General Manager, Central Railway.

It has been held that clause 1 of Article 16 is the governing clause having wider scope than clause 2 of the same Article. If there is discrimination on any ground which is in contravention of the spirit of clause 1 of the Article, such discrimination is to be considered as invalid.

The Supreme Court has held that equality of opportunity of employment does not only apply to initial appointments but subsequent promotions or dismissals as well.

Clause 3 permits some restrictions to be made on ground of residence for employment under the state. However, the power to restrict employment to residents of the State can be assumed under an Act of Parliament and not under the Act of State Legislature.

In pursuance of the power, the Indian Parliament passed the Public Employment (Requirement as to Residence) Act in 1957 which permitted requirement of residence in erstwhile centrally administered States of Himachal Pradesh, Manipur and Tripura. Exception was also made in respect of Telangana, part of State of Andhra Pradesh, where residential qualifications were required, but the Supreme Court declared the exception as void. The reasoning of the Court was that residential requirement cannot be made in respect of part of a State only.

Clause 4 of the Article permits the State to make provision for reservation of some appointments in favour of backward classes who, in the opinion of the State, are not adequately represented in the services. This is in order to give a fillip to economically, educationally and socially backward classes in order to assure them due representation and eventual equality in the real sense.

The reservation has to be made in advance on the basis of which selection may be made. However, if candidates of backward classes are given preference to other classes, despite their having scored less qualifying marks, the Supreme Court has held that in the absence of notification of provision for reservation, such selection will violate Article 16(1) and will not be saved by clause 4 of the Article.21

While making provision for reservation of the backward classes, the State has to take into consideration that in the services efficiency is of utmost importance and that cannot be compromised at any cost. Besides, any provision of reservation should not make a sham of Article 16, clauses 1 and 2. Clauses 1 and 2 are the guiding rules and clause 4 an exception. Exception should not be the general rule, and the general rule an exception. Any such step will contravene the Preamble, Article 14 and Article 16 clauses 1 and 2. This was held in the case of A. Rajendran vs. Union of India."

**Abolition of untouchability**

Untouchability has been a great social stigma in India. Untouchability means a person who is identified as the so-called "'low caste" and is treated as a social outcast. Until recently the "upper caste" Hindu refused to inter-relate in any way with the "Harijan". The Harijan was even prohibited from entering a temple.

Article 17 aims at the abolishment of untouchability. Its practice in any form is forbidden and made punishable. Emphasis is on equality between man and man as enshrined in Article 14 and to maintain the dignity of an individual as, promised in the Preamble. This Article heralds a classless society in India, thus heralding equality and fraternity. However, this does not vouchsafe absolute equality which is yet to be achieved.

**Abolition of titles**

Article 18 purports to prohibit the conferring of titles on Indians by the government. The abolition of titles assures equality of status as promised in the Preamble. Article 18, however, does not prohibit military and academic distinctions.

The Government does however, also confer non-military and non-academic titles like Padma Shri, Padma Bhushan, Padma Vibhushan and Bharat Ratna.

**Civic Rights**

Every person should have some rights in a society where he is born and brought up. The most important in this connection may be the right to citizenship and the franchise. Both these rights are inter-related. Normally, only citizens are allowed the right to vote in any political set-up of a State. But citizenship is determined by State law, although in most of the cases, it is automatic in the sense that people get citizenship by dint of their birth.

***1) Right of Citizenship***

Article 15 of the U.D.H.R. says that every one has a tight to nationality and he cannot be arbitrarily deprived of it. The article gives an additional right to a person to change his nationality if he so voluntarily desires. Article 24 of the International Covenant gives the right to every child to acquire a nationality.

Nationality or citizenship is a link between the individual and his State. He is recognised in the international community through the State of his nationality.

A State has a right to champion the cause of its nationals in a foreign country. A person may go around foreign countries, and do business there with the assurance that in case any of his rights is violated or denied by any agency of the foreign country, remedy will be secured to him through his State. It is the States duty to receive back its nationals on their return, expulsion or deportation from a foreign country. While it is one of the sovereign rights of a State to grant or refuse entry within its territory, such a right cannot be exercised in respect of its own nationals who return from a foreign country either voluntarily or otherwise.

Citizenship in India is governed by Article 5 of the Constitution and Citizenship Act of 1955. Article 5 of the Constitution provides:

At the commencement of this Constitution, every person who has his domicile in the territory of India and-

a) who was born in the territory of India; or
b) either of whose parents was born in the territory of India; or
c) who has been ordinarily resident in the territory of India for not less than five years immediately preceding such commencement, shall be a citizen of India.

Article 5 grants Indian citizenship to any person who is domiciled in India and fulfils one of the three other requirements as given in clause a, b or c of the Article. There is no discrimination on any ground in the granting of citizenship under the Constitution. Any person can claim Indian citizenship irrespective of his race, religion, caste or sex, provided he fulfils the requirement of domicile and one of the three conditions stated. The "Constitution has adopted a territorial basis for citizenship and not a racial or religious one".

Domicile is an essential element under Article 5. It is a technical word in Private International Law which has defied exact definition at the hands of courts and publicists. Nevertheless, there have been a few definitions which may be given here to understand the connotation and concept of domicile. Dicey has defined domicile' as follows:

> The notion which lies at the root of the concept of domicile is that of permanent home. A person may be said to have his home in a country if he resides in it without any intention at present of moving from it permanently or for indefinite period. But a person does not cease to have his home in a country merely because be is temporarily resident elsewhere; and a person who has formed an intention of leaving a country does not cease to have his home in it until he acts according to that intention.

Elsewhere he has said:

A person who determines to spend the rest of his life in a country, clearly has the necessary intention, even) although, he does not consider his determination to be irrevocable. It is, however, rare for the *animus menedi* to exist in this positive form; more frequently a person simply resides in a country without any intention of leaving it, and such a state of mind suffices for the acquisition of domicile by child.

In the case of Graiguish, Judge Chitty said:

> That a place is properly the domicile of a person in which his habitation is fixed without any present intention by removing therefrom.
>
> The Indian Supreme Court had the occasion to adjudicate on domicile in the case of the Central Bank of India vs. Ram Narain.
>
> While holding that it is impossible to give any absolute definition of domicile, it said that it had

> two essential constituents of residence and intention which may be called as *factum* and animus. According to the Supreme Court, the "residence need not be continuous but it must be indefinite, not purely fleeting. The intention must be a present intention to reside for ever in the country where the residence has been taken up."'

As it further said:

> It is also a well established proposition that a person may have no home but he cannot be without a domicile and the law may attribute to him a domicile in a country where, in reality he has not. A person may be a vagrant as when he lives in a yacht or a wanderer from one European hotel to another, but, nevertheless, the law will arbitrarily ascribe to him a domicile in one particular territory. In order to make the rule that nobody can be without a domicile effective the law assigns what is called a domicile of origin to every person at his birth. This prevails until a new domicile has been acquired, so that if a person leaves the country of his origin with an undoubted intention of never returning to it again, nevertheless, his domicile of origin adheres to him until he actually settles with the requisite intention in some other country.

Domicile may, therefore, be defined as residence of a person in a particular country with an intention to reside there permanently. Every person has his domicile of birth which is acquired at the time of his birth. That domicile continues until domicile of choice is acquired in another country. There can be only one domicile at one time. A person cannot have two domiciles, a domicile by birth and a domicile of choice simultaneously.

There is Article 6 of the Constitution which confers Indian citizenship on refugees who migrated from Pakistan to India immediately after the establishment of the two States. Under Article 6, refugees who migrated to

India before 19th July, 1948, and have been ordinarily residing in India since then, acquire Indian citizenship automatically. However, in case of refugees who have come to India on, or after 19th July, 1948, they can acquire Indian citizenship by registration provided they have been resident in India for at least six months immediately preceding their application for registration as citizens. In both cases, either he or any of his parents or grandparents must have been born within united India of pre-independence days.

There is no arbitrary deprivation of nationality in India as enjoined by Article 15(2) of the U.D.H.R. There are two articles in the Indian Constitution which seek to deny Indian citizenship. Article 7 denies Indian citizenship to such persons who would have been entitled to the citizenship under Article 5 but who have migrated to Pakistan after March 1, 1947. This has been done on the presumption that persons who have migrated to Pakistan have decided to settle down there and, there fore, have given up their Indian citizenship. The articles can be better understood with the background knowledge of events which led to the partition of India on 15th August, 1947 into the States of India and Pakistan. Article 6 is the reverse of Article 7 giving Indian citizenship to those who have migrated from Pakistan to India. It is, therefore, clear that Article 7 can not be said to amount to arbitrary deprivation of Indian citizenship as proscribed under Article 15(2) of the Universal Declaration of Human Rights. It is rather voluntary change of citizenship as envisaged under Article 15 of the Declaration and Article 24 of the Covenant.

The word 'migration' is important in Article 7. It means that the person must have left India without any intention to return. Any casual visit to Pakistan does not deprive the man of his Indian citizenship. Nor, can a person lose his citizenship if migration is involuntary or under compulsion.

It may, however, be said in fairness that the Supreme Court's decision in the case of Kulathil Mammu vs. State of Kerala,8 giving wide interpretation to the word 'migration' requires rethinking. Migration should mean leaving the country with the intention of not returning; otherwise, it would lose the meaning which is ordinarily attributed to it.

Article 9 of the Constitution denies Indian citizenship to such persons who have voluntarily acquired citizenship of a foreign country. This loss of Indian citizenship is based on the sound principle that, if a person has acquired foreign citizenship, it is presumed that he is no more interested in the earlier citizenship. There are such provisions in many other national legislations. While Article 7 is applicable to cases of migration to Pakistan, Article 9 is more general and relates to acquisition of foreign citizenship of a country other than Pakistan. Both result in loss of Indian citizenship.

*2) Right of Franchise*

Right of franchise is the most important right in any democratic society. Any denial or deprivation of this right would indeed be negation of democracy. Article 21(3) of the U.D.H.R. provides for such right. As it says:

The will of the people shall be the basis of the authority of government; this will shall be expressed in periodic and genuine elections which shall be by universal and equal sufferage and shall be held by secret vote or by equivalent free voting procedures.

Article 25(b) of the International Covenant on Civil and Political Rights confirms the above right. It gives the citizen the right "to vote and to be elected at genuine periodic elections which shall be by universal and equal sufferage and shall be held by secret ballot, guaranteeing the free expression of the will of the electors."

The Indian Constitution fulfils these aspirations by giving the right to vote to every adult? Because of this, India is considered the largest democracy at work in the world. Every Indian citizen having attained the age of twenty-one years is entitled to vote for the State legislature as well as for the Parliament.

There is one general electoral roll for every territorial constituency and no person will be declared ineligible because of religion, race, caste, sex or any such cause." There are no political minorities, or second class citizens in India. Every Indian citizen has equal rights, irrespective of his race, religion, caste or sex. This is an extension of Article 14 which guarantees equality in the generic sense. Articles 325-26 maintain secularity and equality in respect of elections.

Articles 330-33 had initially permitted reservation of some seats for scheduled castes and tribes and Anglo-Indian communities in the Parliament and State legislature for 30 years from the date of commencement of the Constitution, 26th January, 1950, because of the backwardness of scheduled castes and tribes and the microscopic minority status of Anglo-Indians. The date has since then been extended.

No one can be denied the right to vote in an election for which he is qualified to vote. There is no provision for defranchise in India. This is a healthy sign for democracy.

A person can be disqualified under Indian Election Law from contesting for any elective post if he has been found guilty of corrupt practices by a competent judicial organisation and the order is appealable. The process is judicial and not political.

Indians have the right to participate in political institutions, contest elections and participate as members in parliamentary or legislative debates of the country as envisaged under Articles 21 and 25 of the U.D.H.R. and the International Covenant on Civil and Political Rights respectively.

Any person who is duly elected as a member of a given House should not be deprived of his membership of the said House. Only the people who elected him earlier have the right to reject him at the following election.

The Parliament or the Legislature cannot assume the right to expel its members on the basis of privileges and powers of the House. Any such expulsion by legislative Houses is denial of representation of the people who had earlier elected him. Such practice should stop in future.

It may be mentioned here that election procedures have discouraged technocrats and experts from participating in elections and therefore, in the governance of the country by placing a condition that they must become members of any House within a period of six months. This restriction should be relaxed.

Technocrats or experts may be appointed as ministers without being member of a House for a period of two to three years. This may reduce the predominance of politician administrators and bring in expertise in the governance of the country.

**Political Rights**

A man is entitled to some basic rights, like freedom of speech, expression, assembly, association, ideology and movement. These freedoms reflect man's feelings on the political fabric of the society of which he is a member.

1) Freedom of Speech and Expression

Article 19 of the U.D.H.R. as well as that of the International Covenant on Civil and Political Rights guarantee the right to freedom of opinion and expression. The Indian Constitution confers this right on its citizens under Article 19(1)a. Freedom of speech is one of the primary and inseparable conditions of democracy. The concept of democracy will be a sham if it does not permit freedom of speech or expression. These are essential for the successful functioning of democracy. Every human being has a right to express his opinion on a matter of public interest. This right corresponds to the First Amendment of the U.S. Constitution which says that "Congress shall make no law ... abridging the freedom of speech. . . ."

In the words of Thomas Emerson, freedom of speech fulfils four democratic functions: personal self-fulfilment which reflects his potentialities as a human being; advancement of knowledge and discovery of truth; participation in public decision-making; and securing social change without resort to violence.'

Freedom of speech and expression has a wide connotation. It is not only the liberty to say what one wants but to be free to express one's feelings, opinions and convictions. The word "expression" has wider implications than "speech". Expression not only includes speech but any process which reflects feelings, Classes will be hauled convictions and opinions. This can be done by word of mouth, speech in writing, by action or visual projections having a similar effect. Expression would also include propagation of ideas and ideology. Otherwise expression would be incomplete. Demonstration, picketing or specific form of public behaviour are different 2 forms of expression. However, since these actions could interfere with the rights of others', there could be no unlimited right of demonstration or picketing.

**Restrictions on freedom of speech and expression**

Article 19 clause 2 imposes some reasonable restrictions on the right to freedom of speech and expression. These restrictions may be imposed in the wider interests of sovereignty, integrity and security of State, maintenance of friendly relations with foreign States, public order, decency or morality, or in relation to contempt of court, defamation or incitement to an offence.

All these grounds for putting reasonable restrictions on the freedom of speech are well recognised throughout such countries where the rule of law prevails. No State can afford to give unlimited right of freedom of speech which is abused or which threatens the sovereignty , integrity and security of the State. Nor would a State like its relations with foreign countries to be jeopardised, because of any irresponsible concept of freedom of speech or behaviour.

Maintenance of public order is equally important. The word "Public order" was discussed by the Supreme Court in the case of Madhu Limaye vs. District Magistrate Monghyr. It was observed that:

> It means what the French designate order *publique* defined as an absence of insurrection, riot, turbulence or crimes I of violence. The expression "public order" includes absence of all acts which are a danger to the security of State and also acts which are comprehended by the expression "order publique" explained above but not acts which only disturb the security of others.

Any person who seeks to disturb public order or does anything which is likely to cause enmity between two-or, more up for misuse of the right of, freedom of speech. At the same time the Government cannot impose arbitrary restrictions on the plea of maintenance of, public order. The restrictions cannot be "far-fetched, hypothetical, problematic or too remote in the chain of its relation with public order." This was held in the case of Superintendent Central Jail vs. Dr. Lohia. As the Supreme Court held in that case:

> We cannot accept the argument of the learned Advocate General that instigation of a single individual not to pay tax or dues is a spark which may in the long run ignite a revolutionary movement destroying public order. We can only say that fundamental rights cannot be controlled on such hypothetical and imaginary considerations. It is said that in a democratic set-up there is no scope for agitational approach and that if a law is bad the only course is to get it modified by democratic process and that any instigation to break the law is in itself a disturbance of the public order. If this argument without obvious limitations be accepted it would destroy the right to freedom of speech which is the very foundation of democratic way of life. Unless there is a proximate connection between the instigation and the public order, the restriction, in our view, is neither reasonable, nor is it in the interest of public order."

Decency and morality would check the utterance and exhibition of obscenity. There is a ban on obscene exhibition in many countries, although the standards of determining obscenity may differ from country to country and from time to time. But that does not diminish the reasonableness of putting restrictions to avoid obscenity according to individual standards.

Freedom of speech does not mean that a person may be allowed to speak whatever he wants. His freedom is circumscribed in such a way that he does not commit contempt of court, defame someone or incite others to commit an offence.

Article 19(3) of the International Covenant on Civil and Political Rights also envisages some restrictions. It says that freedom of expression carries with it special duties and responsibilities. It may therefore, be necessary to impose some restrictions for respect of the rights and reputations of others and for the protection of national security, public order, public health and morals. It may as such be noted that restrictions, as arc put under the Indian Constitution are identical with those given under the International Covenant. Article 20 of the Covenant goes further and says that f here can be no propaganda for war nor advocacy for national, racial or religious hatred.

*2) Freedom of Press*

It must be said at the outset that there is no separate freedom Of press in India. Nor, is it specific, as in the United States of America. First Amendment of the American Constitution enjoined that "Congress shall make no law abridging the freedom of speech or of the press." However, it would be wrong to assume that there is no freedom of press in India.

In India, freedom of press is part of freedom of speech and expression. Indeed, freedom of speech will be insignificant if what one says is not printed and disseminated. In 1787, Thomas Jefferson said that people are the only censors of their governors and newspapers are the media to let them know as to what their governors are doing. He preferred newspapers without government rather than government without newspapers.

Freedom of press would mean freedom of dissemination of information from diverse and antagonistic sources for the welfare of the public. It is the foundation of a free Government of a free people. It is to feed the public and thus prevent the government from assuming guardianship of public mind.5 In 1974, Justice Lewis F. Powell spoke of the social purpose of the First -Amendment. I would prefer the societal mission of the press. In a democratic society, press has a dual function. It has to feed the public appetite for news and views from different sources, sometimes from diagonally opposite sources. This amounts to freedom of information.

The press has also to function as a watchdog to oversee the functioning of the government of the day, so that it does not indulge in arbitrary or antipeople actions. In the process, it may expose the corrupt practices, if any, of the government. Instances would not be wanting where scandals have come to surface due to exposure of government malpractices by the investigative and inquisitive press.

Governments or Powers-that-be have not taken kindly to press exposures of their malpractices or acts of malfeasance. Freedom of press being part of freedom of speech is subject to same limitations. Government can, therefore, impose reasonable restrictions in the interest of sovereignty, security and the integrity of the county maintenance of friendly relations with foreign States, public order, decency or morality. The press can be hauled up for contempt of court, defamation or incitement to an offence if that can be Proved. These restrictions and limitations arc fairly far-reaching and cause enough limitations to the freedom of press.

**Freedom of assembly**

Article 20(1) of the U.D.H.R. guarantees the right of peaceful assembly. Article 21 of the Covenant recognises the right of peaceful assembly. Right of assembly includes right of Procession and public demonstration." But all these rights are valid so long as they not violate or infringe upon anyone else's specific right to use the streets and highways as well as other general rights. The right relates to peaceful assembly and not to an assembly which disorderly or violent. Thus, any legislation which aims at outlawing demonstration by bank employees which cause inconvenience to the customers has been considered as constitutional Such reasonable restrictions can well be imposed by the legislation under Article 19(3) which permits limitation on the rig of assembly in the interest of the sovereignty and integrity India. Such restrictions are permitted even under Article 21 the International Covenant in the interests of national security, public safety, public order, protection of Public health or moral or the Protection of the rights and freedom of others.

*4) Freedom of Association*

Freedom of association is an essence of democratic life Democracy is ascertained in a particular country by the extent of freedom granted to its people to form associations. Formation of Political parties is one form of association. Article 20(1) of the Universal Declaration of Human Rights and Article 22(2) of the International Covenant recognise this right. Article 19(1-c) of the Constitution guarantees the right of association to its citizens. This is a supplementary right to the two rights of freedom of speech and assembly as both would be incomplete without the freedom of association.

It has been held by the Supreme Court that the freedom of association includes the freedom not to join an association. No person, therefore, can be compelled to join a given association. The right of association does not also include the right to strike. Nor can it include the right to raise funds for the promotion of an association.

The right of association permits the formation of professional and trade unions, including the union formed by government servants. Since professional unions are permitted, traders as we as industrialists can form their own associations. The Indian Chamber of Commerce is a typical organisation established to promote the welfare of persons engaged in trade and commerce.

The right of association however, is not unrestricted. The International Covenant recognises some restrictions in the interests of national security, public order, protection of public health or morals, or protection of the rights and freedom of others. Article 19(4) puts similar restrictions in the interest of sovereignty and integrity of India, public order or morality. Association may be discouraged in sensitive jobs like military, intelligence and police establishments where there is a likelihood of the security of State or public order within the territory being adversely affected.

### *5) Freedom of Ideology*

There can be no democracy if there is no freedom of ideology. In these days of competitive ideologies, it would be a negation of democracy if a person has no choice of ideology and has to subscribe compulsorily to State-dominated ideology. Article 19 ,of the Universal Declaration of Human Rights and International Covenant give the right to hold opinion without interference. This implies that people should have the right to hold any political opinion and subscribe to any political ideology.

There is no such specific right under the Indian Constitution. But it can be fairly implied from the conjoint effect of Article 19(1-a) which gives the right of freedom of expression and Article 19(1-c) which gives the right of freedom of association. The right of freedom of expression may be expressed in any form, including the right to hold a particular opinion and -subscribe to a particular ideology and to join an ideology-dominated political party or group.

It is, perhaps, because of this right of having any ideology that all political parties thrive in India and so far, no political party has been banned. Freedom of subscribing to any ideology may be inferred from Article 25 which gives the "freedom of conscience" which may also mean freedom of ideology. This proposition is not likely to get much support because the Article appears under the subhead of freedom of religion. Therefore, freedom of ideology may not be claimed in India under Article 25(d) but under Article 19(1-a) and 19(1-c). In the case of State of Madras vs.

V.G. Rao, it was held by the Supreme Court that the petitioner has a right to form an association, and no association can be declared illegal by the executive without judicial scrutiny."

In a Gujarat case, the Gujarat High Court gave a verdict against an order of the State Government which sought to ban a Gujarati book titled Quotations from Mao Tse-Tung. The court observed that if the people wanted to read or follow the philosophy of Communism as expounded by Mao Tse-Tung, confiscation of a book would not stop them. The court observed:

> To condemn them (quotations) as seditious would be to close the doors of knowledge, to ostracise a philosophy because it challenges the most cherished values of society and heralds for the acceptance of a new way of life, vastly different from that to which our people were presently accustomed. It is not for the government of the day nor for the judges presiding over the courts to decide what doctrine or philosophy is good for our people. It is for the people to choose what is best for them, and to help them to make a wise and intelligent choice, free propagation of ideas is an essential requisite.

Freedom to hold any ideology is the basic ingredient of any democratic society. Ideas cannot be fought by banning the publication of such ideas or by confiscating the published material. Such an action will only force the material to go underground. Ideas must be matched or challenged by ideas. People should be free to decide for themselves which ideology is good or bad for them.

Of course, there can be no absolute right of freedom of ideology. As discussed freedom of ideology is subject to reasonable restrictions in the interests of sovereignty, integrity and security of the State, maintenance of friendly relations with foreign States, public order and morality.

*6) Freedom of Movement*

Article 13 of the Universal Declaration of Human Rights gives the right of freedom of movement within the State and also the right of leaving, and returning to, one's country. Article 12 of the International Covenant on Civil and Political Rights guarantees similar rights. Article 19(1-d & e) gives the right of movement within the country and of residence at any place.

It has been held that freedom of movement of an Indian is not violated by any watch kept over his movements. This does not prohibit or prevent him from moving from one place to another. The mere fact that there is psychological inhibition entertained by a person, does not violate his right. However, it does not appeal to reason to monitor anyone's movements, particularly of politicians. Criminals and bad characters may be shadowed to prevent commission of crimes.

The right of movement is guaranteed throughout India. An Indian citizen may also choose to reside anywhere in India. Unlike some States, where there are two domiciles, one of the Centre and the other of the State, there is only one domicile in India and, therefore, no Indian can be prevented from going to any part of the country or from making residence at any place of his liking within the country. A person may, however, be prohibited from entering a given town or State if his presence is likely to cause a problem of law and order or if his security is endangered. Any reasonable restriction on any person in such circumstances would be permissible under the Constitution and would indeed be justifiable.

Freedom of movement is guaranteed not only inside India but outside India as well. It is on the basis of this freedom that many Indians have been permitted to emigrate to England, Canada and other countries. There is no bar on migration of any Indian to a given country if the latter has no objection to his entry into that country and to settle therein. The Supreme Court has also facilitated easy issue of passports.

It is indeed an irony of fate that a man has to subscribe to the "ism" of the country whose national he is. There is hardly any choice for him to deviate from his country's "ism". It has been found that either there is ban on such deviation or some stigma is attached to such deviation. In the circumstances, the only alternative is to let him settle at a place where he can breathe freely according to his conscience.

It is equally necessary to allow a person to return to his original country if he is disillusioned with his adopted country. The right to leave, or return to his country, are very important for a person. Article 13 of the U.D.H.R. gives every person this right. In this connection, the Jammu and Kashmir Bill of 1982 which allows a person who had migrated after I March, 1947, to return, is not a bad Bill. The only criterion is that he or she must prove that he was a Kashmiri subject on May 14, 1954. However, the Bill is to be considered in the totality of circumstances. On one hand, there are about half-a-million refugees from Pakistan living in Kashmir, since 1947-48. But they have not been made Kashmir nationals, nor allowed to acquire property in the State. On the other hand, people may come to the valley on pretext of returning to their homeland, when in fact, the object may be to spy. Others may have worked against Indian interests prior to their entry into India. Naturally, such unwanted persons cannot be allowed to return. For this, there has got to be some screening of prospective entrants. There should be no serious objection to it if it is done along with making the local refugees of yester-years from Pakistan as subjects of Kashmir with all consequent rights.

**Rights Relating to Person**

The sanctity of life and liberty is the most important right that man can aspire for. He needs to be sure that he cannot be deprived of his life and liberty arbitrarily. No one has the right to take anyone's life or his personal liberty. Not even the State. Article 3 of the Universal Declaration of Human Rights states ,that "Every one has the right to life, liberty and security of person." Article 6(1) of the International Covenant on Civil and Political Rights, 1966 declares "Every human being has the inherent right to life. This right shall be protected by law. No one shall be arbitrarily deprived of his life." Article 21 of the Indian Constitution upholds the above right when it says that: No person shall be deprived of his life or personal liberty except according to procedure established by law.'

**Right to life**

Article 21 guarantees the most important right: the right to life. As Justice Field of the U. S. Supreme Court once said:

By the term 'life' something more is meant than mere animal existence. The inhibition against its deprivation extends to all those limbs and faculties by which life is enjoyed. The provision equally prohibits the mutilation: of the body by amputation of an arm or leg or putting out an eye or the destruction of any other organ of the body through which the soul communicates with the outer world. The deprivation not only of life but of whatever God has given to everyone with life, for its growth and enjoyment, is prohibited by the provision in question if its efficacy be not frittered away by judicial decision.'

The Supreme Court of India upheld the above observation in the case of Kharak Singh vs. State of U.P.2 The Supreme Court held that the word "life" as it occurs in 5th and 14th Amendments of the U.S. Constitution corresponds to Article 21 of the Indian Constitution. It means not only continuance of a person's animal existence, but a right to the possession of each of his organs, his arms, legs, etc.3

It may, therefore, be safely assumed that the word 'life' does not mean animal or physical existence. "Right to life" as given in Article 21 would mean right to decent life, life with human dignity, otherwise, there is nothing to guarantee. Right to life would include the following rights-Basic necessities of life, life with human dignity, freedom from police or other atrocities and freedom from torture. In the process, the validity of death penalty is also be discussed.

***a) Basic Necessities of Life***

Life is worth living only when a person has access to the basic necessities of life. How can a person be said to have right to life when he cannot be assured basic necessities which are vital to his very existence? While there may be controversy regarding basic necessities of life, they must essentially include food, clothing and shelter. These are the bare minimum requirements for human living. This has been upheld by the Supreme Court in the case of

Francis Mullin, where it was said that right to life would "include the right to basic necessities of life and also the right to carry on such functions and activities as constitute the bare minimum expression of the human-self.

Government has, of course, not assured these necessities to the Indian society. However, it has undertaken some measures in that direction. Regulation of essential supplies of sugar and wheat at a reasonable price from fair price shops is motivated to cater to the needs of the society. Maintenance of Essential Commodities Act aims at preventing black marketing and unfair practices in the supply of essential articles. The Government has also sought to control the price of inferior cloth so that, it would be made available to the weaker sections of society at a reasonable price that they can afford to pay. Government has encouraged various housing schemes with soft housing loans so that people could own their houses. State Governments have also introduced old age pensions for destitute persons. Tamil Nadu and some other State Governments have started mid-day meals to poor sections of society.

The various measures adopted by the Central or State Governments in order to provide basic necessities of life to various sections of society have either been misused or have not been adequate. It is desirable to plug all the loopholes for misuse of welfare funds and make adequate funds available so that basic necessities of life are made available to people' at reasonable prices.

There is also an urgent need to check population explosion. It is impossible for any Government to feed and clothe millions of unplanned newly born children, when existing population is already inadequately fed. Thus, while one should impress upon the Government to have more plans for the welfare of the weaker sections of society, it is equally the duty of society to discipline itself and show healthy growth. Family planning and population control are a "must" for Indian society.

### b) Human Dignity

As stated, life does not mean mere physical or animal -existence. Life means to live with human dignity. It is no use living a wretched life where human dignity is an abyss. Human worth and dignity need not be lost even in prison setting.

Right to life under Article 21 has been interpreted to mean the right to live with human dignity. In the Sunil Batra case, Justice Krishna Iyer approved the words of Justice Douglas that prisoners are still persons and also the words of Justice White that there is "no iron curtain between the Constitution and prisons of this country."" As Justice Desai said in the same case, treatment of a human being which offends human dignity reduces the man to the level of a beast. It was thus held that use of bar fetters on a prisoner for unusually long time is an "anathema to the spirit of the Constitution."

In Francis Mullin's case, the court observed that "fundamental right to life which is the most precious human right and which forms the core of all other rights must therefore be interpreted in a broad and expansive spirit so as to invest it with significance and vitality which may endure for years to come and enhance the dignity of the individual and the worth of the human person."8 As the court explained:

> Right to life includes the right to live with human dignity and all that goes along with it, namely, the bare necessities of life such as adequate nutrition, clothing and shelter over the head and facilities for reading, writing and expressing oneself in diverse forms freely moving about, mixing and co-mingling with fellow human beings.

It was further observed that any act which offends or impairs human dignity would constitute deprivation protanto of this right to life unless it is done by reasonable, fair and just procedure established by law which stands the test of other fundamental rights.

The Court observed that right to life would also ınply the right of a detenue to have interviews with members of his family and friends and any prison rules which regulate such a Tight should be fair, reasonable and just.

Prisoners do not cease to be persons even in prisons. Nor is a prison a totalitarian territory beyond the pale of the law. Justice Krishna Iyer said that human dignity is equally applicable to prisoners and it cannot be bartered away by jail officers. The right to human dignity has been upheld again in the cases of Agra Protective Home and Delhi Nari Niketan. Detenues under preventive detention are equally entitled to treatment consistent with human dignity.

***c) Freedom from Police Atrocities (Zulum)***

The right to life would mean right to peaceful life. There is no charm of life without it being peaceful. However, many are not able to lead a peaceful life. Poverty and illiteracy are predominant in the Indian society. Law-enforcing authorities take advantage of the poverty and illiteracy of people by harassing them in several ways. They are sometimes fleeced merely on suspicion. At other times, they are fleeced by implication in false charges if they dare to challenge their authority or illegal activities. Women are molested. People are often known to have been killed in fake police encounters. Others have died while in police custody due to third degree methods of torture used by the police. It was rightly observed by the court that police should better depend on its wits than on fists for their investigation. It advised the Government to re-educate the constabulary, to wear them out of their sadistic tendencies, and inculcate in them respect for the human person and punish those who are found to have misconducted. The Court hoped that police cruelty would receive Government's serious attention. "Otherwise, who will police the police?"

Late Prime Minister Shrimati Indira Gandhi had expressed her concern at police violence by exhorting upon "the need for new orientation to their (the police's) training so that they should not treat everybody as guilty." The police personnel are to be freed from the *lathi* wielding attitude. The police assault on V.M. Tarkunde at Madurai in November, 1982 exhibited the callousness of police units. The attitude has to be one of respect towards people and toughness with criminals. Police personnel must be oriented towards public service. In India, there is always a tiff between police and public. This tiff must be removed to make police service worthy. Perhaps, it is necessary to frame a code of conduct for law-enforcing officials on the lines of the Code of Conduct for Law Enforcement officials adopted by the U.N. General Assembly on December, 17, 1979.

Sometimes, people resist police harassment successfully. At other times, when they resist, they are implicated further with the result that either they succumb or are destroyed in the process. The Indian society is aware of it. Steps are, taken sometimes to check such police malpractices. While the courts readily come to the rescue of group harassment, sometimes it is too late. The Bhagalpur blindings are a constant reminder of the extreme excesses which the law-enforcing authorities are capable of perpetrating on people, without much redress to its victims. This is despite the fact that there is inhibition against deprivation of all those limbs and faculties by which life is enjoyed. The right prohibits mutilation of body or amputation of an arm or leg, gouging of an eye or destruction of any other organ of the body. Private police version of such incidents is that several persons have become professional criminals or criminal *dadas* (leaders), sonic of them with political patronage. They "reign" over the localities where no one dares to give evidence for fear of reprisals against themselves, their families or relations. The only language these criminals know, is liquidation or physical disablement. This version is -not absolutely false. Something needs to be done in this respect to make the life of a person worth living without making the job of the law-enforcing authorities more difficult in matters of suppressing crime and punishing the criminals. Criminals must be made to fear the law. Yet innocent people should not be made to suffer. Mutual respect and trust between the citizens and the law-enforcing authorities is essential. Witness-protection measures may be legislated as is presently done in the United States, although, it is not free from complications also.

***d) Freedom from Torture, Inhuman and Cruel Punishment***

Article 5 of the U.D.H.R. prohibits cruel, inhuman or degrading treatment. It is reaffirmed by Article 7 of the International Covenant on Civil and Political Rights which became effective in 1976 and which the Government of India ratified in 1979. It is prohibited under the European and Inter-American Conventions on Human Rights. Although, there is no specific prohibition of degrading treatment under the Constitution, Article 21 has been interpreted to include immunity from cruel, inhuman and degrading treatment. The Supreme Court has held in Mullin's case that any form of torture or degrading treatment would be offensive to human dignity and would therefore violate Article 21.16 In an earlier case, Justice Krishna Iyer observed that courts should come to the rescue of detenues who are tortured in prisons.

Torture has emerged as a worldwide phenomenon. State torture has become a fashion with a number of authoritarian governments. Amnesty International Reports indicate that about seventy States practice torture against their political activists or enemies. Bokassa's Central Africa, Amin's Uganda, Macia Ngvema's Equatorial Guinea, Shah's Iran followed by Khoemeni's Iran or Pol Pot's Khemr Republic have been a few typical centres of State torture which have surpassed almost all past records of torture. Unfortunately, excesses have been resorted to by the very functionaries who are entrusted with the responsibility of maintaining law and order within the society.

Torture seeks to turn the victim into a wornout wreck, often irreparably damaged in body and mind. In some countries, torture is a regular mode of governing the country and overawing its people into silence.

The United Nations became greatly concerned over the increased incidence of torture in the mid-seventies. There is a U.N. Declaration of 1975 against torture. In 1977, the U.N. General Assembly asked the Human Rights Commission to prepare a Draft Convention against torture. Sweden and the International Commission of Jurists have submitted drafts to the Human Rights Commission which is seized of the matter.

Torture is proscribed by legal systems all over the world. About fifty States have banned torture under their national constitutions. Unfortunate part of the story is that while States condemn torture in public, they practice it quietly within their borders as an effective instrument to eliminate dissidents from within. Some States maintain regular torture cells within their borders for political opponents and criminals.

Perpetrators of crime of torture should be severely punished. The effort should be to take to task such State functionaries who instigate, encourage or condone the torture when it is resorted to extract information, false confessions or to intimidate. State functionaries accused of torture should be summarily dismissed irrespective of judicial proceedings. At the same time, victims of torture should be rehabilitated and compensated according to the gravity of the damage done to them.

***e) Capital Punishment***

Capital punishment is one aspect of cruel, inhuman and degrading treatment, except, that it is sanctioned by law. It is argued that it is against the spirit of Article 2 1, which gives right to life, to condemn any person to death. But the Indian provision says that no one shall be deprived of life except by procedure established by law. In this case, if the law condemns someone to death, nothing can be done, nor is the Constitution violated.

There has been quite a debate around the world regarding the abolition of death penalty and the opinion is greatly divided. Amnesty International which monitors violations of human rights throughout the world exhorted upon the abolition of capital punishment through its Stockholm Declaration of 1977.

Article 3 of the U.D.H.R. says, everyone has right to life. Life has been given by God who alone can take it back. Man-made machinery cannot deprive a man of his life. Since man is not the creator of life, he cannot destroy it either. Death sentence is man's inhumanity to man.

Article 5 of the U.D.H.R. says that no one shall be subject to torture or to cruel, inhuman or degrading treatment or punishment. Death sentence is categorised as cruel and inhuman punishment. This was held by 'he U.S. Supreme Court in 1972. Justice Thurgood Marshall cited society's evolving, standard of decency as "perhaps the most important principle in analysing the cruel and unusual punishment questions." Justice William Douglas considered it to be unconstitutional because it was selectively applied, feeding prejudices against the accused if he is poor, despised and lacking in political clout or, if he is a member of a suspect or unpopular minority. The five judges thought that, capital punishment was arbitrary, capricious and freakish. Although the punishment was sanctified and restored by the U.S. Supreme Court in 1976, Justice Marshall has in his dissenting opinion said that execution is a total denial of human dignity and worth.

Constitutionality and legality apart, death sentence often appears to be freakish and arbitrary depending on the good luck or bad luck of the accused who is tried by a given court. A judge may be known as a convicting or acquitting judge depending upon his environment or prejudices. In most cases, death penalty appears to be imposed on the poor and misfits. Prosecutions fall unequally on the ignorant, under-privileged, minority and opposition groups.

There is also the problem of political sentences passed in case of political opponents or dethroned functionaries. While it is difficult to say that all political opponents are awarded political sentences, the possibility of such sentences cannot be ruled out. Indian legal history already knows of the judicial murder of

Nand Kumar in the days of British rule. Bhutto's execution is a modern example of judicial murder of a political adversary.

The United Nations Economic and Social Council, which deals with human rights, recommended in 1971 progressive decrease in several offences for which death sentence may be awarded. This was reaffirmed by the U.N. General Assembly resolution 2857 (XXVI) in 1971.

While there is a trend toward the eventual abolition of death sentence, world practices reveal a confusing picture. There are twenty States which have totally abolished death sentence. Venezuela was the first country to have abolished death sentence in 1863. There is another set of 17 States which have abolished death penalty for ordinary crimes.

On the other hand, some States which had abolished death penalty earlier have reintroduced the same later on. The Soviet Union had abolished death penalty in 1947 but reintroduced it in 1950 for traitors and spies. France reintroduced it in 1960 in the wake of the Algerian war. Brazil and Argentina did the same in 1969 and 1971 respectively due to increasing activities of urban guerrillas.

There is also visible change in the attitudes of people in regard to offenders. While the number of ordinary crimes carrying death penalty is decreasing, death penalty is being increasingly imposed for State crimes like terrorism, drug-trafficking, economic offences, corruption and security of State. Professional offenders may be another category which may be sought to be wiped out through death sentence.

The Supreme Court of India had the opportunity to dwell upon the validity of the capital punishment in 1979-1980. It held that death penalty is not an unreasonable, cruel, unusual or degrading punishment.19 Nor is it violative of Article 21. Justice Bhagwati gave a dissenting opinion after two-and-half-years on the lines of Justice Marshall. The Supreme Court has however, emphasised that award of death sentence is valid in rare cases only.

The International Covenant on Civil and Political Rights, 1966 which India ratified in 1979 also does not prohibit death penalty. Relevant Article 6(1) states:

> Every human being has the inherent right to life...
> No one shall be arbitrarily deprived of his life.

There is a ban only on the arbitrary deprivation of anyone's life. Thus if any one is deprived of his life in accordance with a fair, just and reasonable procedure established by law, Article 21 of the Constitution and Article 6 of the International Covenant will be deemed to have been complied with.

**Right to privacy**

There is no specific right to privacy under the Indian Constitution. But it is inconceivable to enjoy many facets of life, as guaranteed under Article 21 of the Constitution, without having the right to privacy. According to common law, every home is a castle which cannot be intruded into without the authority of law. Nor is it ethical to interfere in the affairs of others.

As Justice Subba Rao observed in Kharak Singh's case, personal liberty means freedom "from encroachments on his private life".As he further observed:

> If physical restraints on a person's movements effect his personal liberty, physical encroachments on his private life would affect it in a larger degree.

Surveillance affects personal liberty and privacy of man and as such is violative of Article 19(1-d) and 21. But that was a minority judgement then.

In the United States also, there is no specific right to privacy but nevertheless the right has been invoked under the First, Fourth and Fifth Amendments.

Article 12 of the Universal Declaration of Human Rights and Article 17 of the Covenant on Civil and

Political Rights gives a person the right of privacy and non-interference in relation to his family, home and correspondence. Article 8 of the European Convention of Human Rights does the same thing.

In Govind vs. State of Madhya Pradesh, the Supreme Court has held that amalgam of fundamental rights constitutes the right to privacy. The matter came under consideration again before the Supreme Court in the case of Malak Singh vs. State of Punjab. The Supreme Court held that surveillance may be intrusive and may seriously encroach upon the privacy of person and infringe personal liberty under Article 21 and 19(1-d) of the Constitution."

However, the right to privacy Is not absolute. Public interest or State security may affect the right to privacy. Section 26 of the Indian Post Office Act, 1898 permits interception of letters on grounds of public safety or State security. Tapping of telephones may be done on the same grounds. But any law which affects privacy must be fair, just and reasonable.

There is some attempt to differentiate between the privacy of an individual and that of a public person. It is claimed that while an individual has the right to privacy, a public man has no such right. All his life is an open book. This is stretching the point too far. Even a public man has the right to privacy vis-a-vis his life at home. But, since a public man remains under constant public gaze what may be legally possible may be practically impossible. It may be difficult for a public man to maintain secrecy about his affairs, however private these may be.

**Personal liberty**

Article 21 of the Constitution prohibits deprivation of personal liberty. Dicey has defined it as a right not to be subjected to imprisonment, arrest or physical coercion of any kind that does not admit of legal justification. This definition was approvingly cited by Justice Mukherjee when he said that personal liberty means "liberty relating to, or concerning the person or body of the individual .... . and it is antithesis of physical restraint or coercion."

However, a wider meaning could be attributed to the word "personal liberty". Chief Justice Kania and Justice Fazal Ali thought that "personal liberty" not only includes liberty of the person but also rights attached to the person. As the Chief Justice observed:

> Deprivation (total loss) of personal liberty. . *inter alia* includes the right to eat or sleep when one likes or to work or not to work as and when one pleases and several such rights."

In a later case, Kharak Singh vs. State of Uttar Pradesh, the majority view regarding the phrase "personal liberty" was reiterated. It was remarked:

> "Personal liberty" is used in the Article as a compendious term to include within itself all the varieties of rights which go to make up the personal liberties of man other than those dealt with in the several clauses of Article 190).

In another case, Satwant Singh vs. Assistant Passport Officer, Chief Justice Subba Rao interpreted the phrase as, including the right of locomotion and travel abroad. The Supreme Court held in that case that no Indian would be arbitrarily denied the issue of a passport which is a necessary document for travelling abroad.28 After this judgement, the issue of passport to Indians has been liberalised and the law regarding the procedure for issue of passport simplified and further enacted in 1967. In Maneka Gandhi's case, it was held that the phrase—personal liberty—"is of the widest amplitude and it covers a variety of rights which go to constitute the personal liberty of man."

The Court reaffirmed the statement of Chief Justice Tambe in the case of A.G. Kazi that personal liberty under Article 21 not only means freedom from physical restraint but "includes a full range of conduct which an individual is free to pursue within the law, for instance, cat or drink whatever he likes, mix with people whom lie likes, read what he likes, sleep when and as long as he likes, travel whenever he likes, go wherever he likes, follow a profession, vocation or business as be likes, of course, in the manner and to the extent permitted by law."

Justice Iyer cited Justice Douglas to show that the right to travel is a part of liberty which cannot be denied without due process of law. According, to him, "personal liberty makes for the worth of a human person. Travel makes liberty worthwhile. Life is a terrestrial opportunity for unfolding personality. The spirit of Man is at the root of Article 21. Absent liberty, the other freedoms are frozen."

Personal liberty is indeed the essence of all rights. Some of them are given in Article 19(1). The residue are enjoyed under Article 21. The phrase "personal liberty" should mean freedom of action for a person to do what he wants to do or not to do what lie (toes not want to do within the precincts of the law. It should give him the freedom to make his choice. Thus, it is left to him to emigrate and settle abroad or return to his country as lie may desire.

The right given to a person to leave his country and to return to his country under Article 13 is implied under Article 21 of the Constitution. So also, the right given to the person to seek and enjoy asylum elsewhere under Article 14 of the U.D.H.R.

In Francis Mullin's case, it was held that personal liberty would include the right of person including prisoner or detenue, within limited circumstances, to socialise with members of his family and friends.' It was further stated by Justice Bhagwati in the same case that under Article 21 the detenue would have the right to consult a legal adviser of his choice for the defence or for securing his release from preventive detention as part of living with human dignity and personal liberty. Earlier, in Sunil Batra's case, it was held that bar fetters on a prisoner deprive him of "locomotion which is one of the facets of personal liberty."

**Procedure established by Law**

Article 21 of the Constitution says that no one shall be deprived of his life or personal liberty, except, according to procedure established by law. Article 31 of the Japanese Constitution says the same thing. So also, Article 9(1) of the International Covenant on Civil and Political Rights.

What is the meaning of "procedure established by law"? It has been held in the Maneka Gandhi case that there cannot be semblance of procedure which may otherwise be arbitrary and fanciful. The procedure which seeks to deprive man of his life or personal liberty must be fair, just and reasonable." Justice Bhagwati further applied the rules of natural justice in such cases and held that the principle of *audi alteram partem* (no one shall be condemned unheard) will be applicable and judiciary will supply the omission made by the legislature. All functionaries which discharge judicial or quasi-judicial functions must observe' rules of natural justice. Justice Bhagwati remarked that there is no distinction between quasi-judicial action and administrative action. Therefore, rules of natural justice will be applicable to administrative actions as well.

Law, which affects life or personal liberty, must be fair, just and reasonable. This was reiterated in Francis

Mullin's case. It has further been held that free legal aid is an essential ingredient of reasonable, fair and just procedure under Article 21.

**Right against arrest**

Liberty of a person is sacrosanct. He cannot be arrested unless there is some charge against him or he is suspected to be involved in anti-social acts or is likely to do such acts. Therefore, a person may be arrested under a procedure established by law under Article 21 of the Constitution as well as under Article 9 of the International Covenant on Civil and Political Rights.

The Maneka Gandhi and Francis Mullin cases have established that law which sanctions physical restraint must be fair, reasonable and just.

The Indian Constitution has ironical contradictions. On the one hand, no one can be deprived of his life or personal liberty except by procedure established by law which must be fair, just and reasonable. On the other hand, a person can be arrested under preventive detention, under Article 22 of the Constitution.

Preventive detention is justified in the interests of security of State and welfare of its people to avoid communal disharmony, caste conflicts, atrocities against Harijans and other weaker sections of society, social tensions and extremist activities.

Yet, preventive dentention is labelled as a Draconian law which confers extraordinary powers on the Government to physically restrain any person according to the subjective satisfaction of the officer concerned. To this extent, preventive detention certainly neutralises the right of personal liberty. Because of these implications it is considered to be a black spot in the Constitution and on Indian democracy. Undoubtedly, preventive detention is justified in times of emergency, as in England and the

United States of America. But there is no such thing as preventive detention during peacetime in England and the United States of America.

When Sardar Patel piloted this provision, he promised to use it very sparingly and, he so did. However, it appears to have become almost a regular feature of the Indian Constitution ever since its inception in 1950. Preventive detention can be invoked by the Central as well as State Governments. In some cases, it has been used against political adversaries which was not the intent of Article 22.

Abolitionists of the provision argue that there is no needfor preventive detention, since, there is enough provision in Section 41 of the Criminal Procedure Code which enables a police officer to arrest any person without 'Warrant if a complaint is received against him or credible information or reasonable suspicion exists against him. However, there remains a basic difference between Section 41 and Article 22. Under the former, reasonable suspicion or credible information is justiciable in a court of law. Under the latter, subjective satisfaction has to be sustained before the Advisory Board only. While the provision of preventive detention may not be entirely desirable, in developing democracies when people are unfortunately more conscious of their rights than their duties, preventive detention becomes necessary. But ideally it must disappear with the development of a mature democracy. As was aptly remarked by Justice Patanjali Shastri in A.K. Gopalan's case when he observed:

> This (preventive detention) sinister looking feature so strongly out of place in a democratic Constitution which invests personal liberty with the sacrosanctity of a Fundamental Right, and so incompatible with the provisions of its Preamble is doubtless designed to prevent an abuse of freedom by anti-social and

> subversive elements which might imperil the national welfare of the infant republic.

As long as the law of preventive detention is found necessary during peacetime, it has to be ensured that it is used to the minimum and with safeguards against misuse of the same against political adversaries or out of vendetta.

Article 9 of the Covenant which envisages arrests according to procedure established by law requires supply of reasons to the suspect for his arrest; his right of challenging the validity of the arrest; the right of defence through a lawyer of his choice; prompt production of the detenue before the magistrate; speedy trial and compensation for the detention if held to be illegal.

Article 22 provides some safeguards against arbitrary arrests. Clauses 1 and 2 of the Article provide similar safeguards as given in Article 9 of the Covenant. They are: the need to supply grounds of arrest; the right to consult a lawyer of his choice, production before a magistrate within twenty-four hours and no further detention without the magistrate's order. There are some in-built safeguards against arbitrary preventive detention. Any preventive detention beyond two months must be approved by an Advisory Board which must consist of a sitting judge as chairman and two other members who are either sitting or retired judges of the High Court. Preventive detention cannot be beyond twelve months. Normally, the detenue can not be shifted from his usual place of residence. His family members must be informed when he is arrested, and also of the place of his detention. Grounds of detention should be communicated to the detenue within 5 to 10 days. The whole procedure should be fair, just and reasonable in order to fulfil the requirements of Article 21. Article 21 is the guiding article in respect of all types of detentions, preventive as well as punitive. The detenue has a right to consult legal counsel of his choice to defend him before the court. He can also seek assistance of his friend before the Advisory Board. He may secure the services of competent lawyer under the free legal aid system.

Regarding treatment of detenues under preventive detention, the Supreme Court has held that they should be given all reasonable facilities for an existence consistent with human dignity. For this, they may be allowed to wear their own clothes, eat their own food, socialise with family and friends and get reading material. Above all, they should be separated from ordinary criminals. If an earning member of family is arrested under Article 22, his family should be provided with a maintenance allowance.

# 2

# Refugee Situation in South Asia

The Human Development Index ranking in terms of longevity, knowledge and standard of living also places most of the South Asian countries in the very low echelons. Except Sri Lanka, all the countries in South Asia have a very low HDI value and rank towards the bottom quartile of the ranking among the listed 175 nations.

*Table I*
*HDI Ranking of South Asian Countries*

| | *HDI Value* | *HDI Rank* |
|---|---|---|
| Bangladesh | 0.368 | 145 |
| Bhutan | 0.338 | 155 |
| India | 0.446 | 138 |
| Maldives | 0.611 | 111 |
| Nepal | 0.347 | 154 |
| Pakistan | 0.445 | 139 |
| Sri Lanka | 0.711 | 91 |
| Best Achieved (Canada) | 0.960 | 1 |
| Total number of countries | | 175 |

A regional organisation viz., South Asian Association for Regional Cooperation (SAARC) was initiated in 1985 and have made some progress in many areas of regional issues including trade. Despite the fact that none of the South Asian countries have signed the 1951 UN Conventions and, 1961 Protocol on Refugees, this region has some interesting success stories in refugee management. One can cite the example of Tibetans in India and Nepal where over 150,000 Tibetan refugees -have been quietly and tightly integrated into these societies.

The management of East Pakistanis (Bangladeshis) in India is still afresh when over 10 million refugees came to Eastern and North, Eastern India on the eve of Liberation War in Bangladesh. After a massive relief operation most of them were voluntarily repatriated within a year of their arrival.

> During the peak months of January and February 1972 the repatriation effort placed great pressure... encouragement was hardly needed. Visitors to the camp areas during that period marvelled at the unending streams of people on the trek, walking, riding bicycles or rickshaws, standing on truck platforms, with the single purpose in mind of reaching as soon as possible their native places in East Bengal. In January, a daily average of 210,000 persons crossed the Bangladesh Border."

Given the magnitude of the exodus of Afghan refugees to Pakistan, it can be said that the refugee situation in this country has been successfully managed by both the host and the participating humanitarian and other international agencies. Despite many odds, the fact remains that the repatriation did take place in a well designed and regular manner for a particular period of time. The refugee population in South Asia constitutes roughly about 12 per cent of the world's total refugees.

Some of the South Asian States like Bangladesh, Bhutan and Sri Lanka are gradually coming under the category of principal sources of World's refugees and asylum seekers.

On the other hand, countries like Afghanistan (1.2 million), Sri Lanka (0.90 million) and India (0-25 million) have substantial number of people who have been displaced within their homeland [also known as internally displaced persons (IDPs)] as a result of persecution, war, human conflict or forced relocation. Although they share many characteristics with refugees who cross international borders, they are not eligible for protection under international refugee law as they remain inside their own countries. Equally alarming has been the case of more than half a million people spread over in Pakistan, Bangladesh, India and Nepal who are considered to be in refugee like situation. These include people who are in constant fear of persecution or harm if returned to their home countries and thus who may be refugees, are not recognised by governments as refugees. Some are given temporary refuge or allowed to remain on humanitarian grounds whereas others remain undocumented.

### *Why these Exodus?*

*Bangladesh :* The Rohingyas from Myanmar are mostly Muslim farmers and labourers from Rakhine region of Myanmar who have taken shelter in the adjoining towns like Teknaf-Cox's Bazar of Bangladesh because of rampant human rights abuses both by the State and other communities in Myanmar. Along with this the system of excessive unpaid community labour, denial of citizenship rights, arbitrary taxation and extortion, concept of model villages, forced relocation, restriction on freedom of movement and poor level of food security led to their massive exodus in 1992. By 1994, there were over

116,000 Rohingya refugees in Bangladesh. A fresh lot of refugees came again in 1996. Prior to this the Operation Nag Min (King Dragon) in Burma spurred over 200,000 Rohingyas to flee to Bangladesh in 1978 but were repatriated back within sixteen months following the agreements between the Governments of Burma and Bangladesh.

*Table 2*

*South Asia Refugees and Asylum Seekers in need of protection and/or assistance 1996*

| | *Numbers* | *Principal sources* |
|---|---|---|
| Bangladesh | 30,578 | Myanmar |
| | (1.92) | |
| Pakistan | 1,200,000 | Afghanistan, Iraq |
| | (75.48) | |
| Nepal | 106,801 | Bhutan |
| | 20,005 | Tibet (China) |
| | (7.97) | |
| India | 18,607 | Afghanistan |
| | 53,500 | Bangladesh |
| | 98,000 | Tibet (China) |
| | 62,226 | Sri Lanka |
| | (14.61) | |
| World Total | | 13,199,646 |
| South Asia Total | 1,589,717 | |
| & As % of World | 12,04 | |

India has been a host nation of refugees originating from various neighbouring countries which include Lhotsampas from Bhutan, Tamils from Sri Lanka and Chakmas from 11 Bangladesh. Sri Lankan Tamils constitute about 12.6 percent of the total population of Sri Lanka as against 74 percent Sinhalese. The Tamils after prolonged complaints of systematic deprivations in all walks of life by the majority Buddhist Sinhalese started its armed uprising soon after the communal clash that rocked the capital city Colombo in 1983.

In the after math, large-scale killings by the extremist force like the Liberation Tigers for Tamil Elam (LTTE) was retaliated by the armed forces killing and displacing thousands. In the course of last fifteen years of protracted violence, over 50,000 people have been killed and top notches of both Tamil and Sinhalese politicians have been wiped out. The LTTE wants an independent homeland for the Tamils of Sri Lanka comprising mainly the Tamil inhabited areas in the North and the East. There have been bouts of exodus to India which stand today at 63,000 Sri Lankan refugees in various camps in Tamil Nadu and 40,000 refugees outside the camps.

*Table 3*

*South Asia People who are in Refugee like Situation*

| | | |
|---|---|---|
| Pakistan | Afghanistan | 300,000 |
| Bangladesh | Pakistan (Biharis) | 238,000 |
| India | Burma | 40,000 |
| Nepal | Bhutan | 18,000 |

Many persons are similarly situated to refugees, but for various reasons do not meet the narrow refugee definition. Some refugee-like populations are tolerated or ignored; others are allowed to remain on humanitarian grounds. Some are stateless, denied the protection afforded by the citizenship. Many are regarded by the host governments simply as illegal aliens.

In many such cases, and often in the absence of credible refugee determination procedures, it is difficult to determine who among them might be bonafide refugees. The 1964 abrogation of the special "excluded area" status extended to this hill tracts during the British days like in many parts of the North East India opened the flood gates for the Bengali migrants (Samtalbashees) form the plains. After Bangladesh got its Independence from Pakistan in 1972, the then Prime Minister Mujibur Rehman declared Chakmas so as Bengalis' with an aim to crush their protracted demand of' autonomy. This brought about a serious identity crisis among the Chakmas d deepened the process of their alienation. Being Buddhist they also d genuine fears on account -of the Islamisation drive. This was followed by a conscious attempt by the Bangladesh Government to make these Chakmas a minority in CHT by massive human settlements of *Samtalbashees* particularly from the districts of' Comilla, Noakhali, Barisal and Patuakhali. This Included distribution of free lands amongst the new settlers and deployment of military to enforce this objective.

The net result was a sharp change in the demographic composition in the CHT region. The hill people constituted 90.9 percent of the total population in CHT in 1951 as against 9.1 percent Bengalis. This drastically changed to 51.5 percent of Hill people and 48 percent Bengalis in 1991. This injected a severe pressure on land and violation of basic rights including detachment from their common property resources. As a consequence, fierce fighting has been taking place between Chakmas military outfit "Shanti Bahini" and Government forces some times leading to literal massacres of Chakmas as happened in Karkhail 1980, Dewan Bazar 1986 and Logang in 1992. This led to a large-scale exodus of Chakmas to the adjoining Indian State of Tripura where they remained for long in the camps set up by the Indian Government.

*Nepal :* Last seven years Nepal has been a host to the Lhotsampas refugees from Bhutan. The Nepali speaking Bhutanese known as Lhotsampas who migrated to Bhutan over the last few centuries have mostly settled in the Southern belts also known as the granary of

Bhutan.. The Lhotsampas are more enterprising with lot of exposure across the border both in terms of economic exchange and democratic aspirations. Though there has been a huge gap in the population figures given by the Bhutanese official and the international agencies, it is widely believed that the Lhotsampas constitute about 50 percent of the total Bhutanese population. Out of the remaining 50 percent the lesser known eastern Bhutanese *viz., Sarchops* have a majority followed by the ruling elites known as the *Drukpas.* Bhutan has been an absolute monarchy with no democratic system in its background meaning an absence of: a proper constitution, court of justice, elected representatives, human, civil and political rights and freedom.

Since 1952 the Lhotsampas are fighting for a democratic rule as advocated by the Bhutanese State Congress. In 1958 most of the Lhotsampas were given proper citizenship. The 1985 Citizenship Act and 1988 Population Census, declared at least 100,000 Lhotsampas as illegal immigrants. Most of them were uprooted with brutal forces by 1993. Top Lhotsampa officers and *Tshogdu* (National Assembly) members were also uprooted. Prior to this the traditional *Drukpa* code of conduct had been imposed which made the wearing of *Kho and Kira,* the traditional Bhutanese dress compulsory for all the Lhotsampas also. Whoever was seen to be fighting for democracy was declared as 'anti -national'.

The setting up of multi-party democracy after 33 years of excruciating absolute monarchy based on Panchayati system in neighbouring Nepal in 1991 further deepened the crisis as the Lhotsampas thought that it was the most opportune time for them to pressurise the Bhutanese Monarch to introduce certain democratic principles. The questions of nationality of the Lhotsampa the most thorny issue. Bhutanese authorities have from the very outset of the refugee outflow maintained that, they are 'illegal, immigrants'. In fact the prime reason behind their both forced expulsion and voluntary movement has been their nationality issue purportedly triggered by the 1985 Citizenship Act and the census exercise of 1988. Prior to this at two points of time (1958 and 1977) the controversy had erupted though in a much subdued form. This strict adherence of the authorities to nationality clauses in the representation in *Tshogdu* (National Assembly) set up in Bhutan in 1953 and the right of the Nepali speaking Bhutanese in Southern Bhutan to own property in 1950s created both resentment and confusion mainly because the authentic documentation of citizenship had never been in vogue in Bhutan.

This was heightened by some serious political initiatives taken by Bhutan State Congress (BSC) set up in Assam in India to bring a democratic system in Bhutan in the wake of India's Independence in 1947, freeing of Nepal from the clutches of autocratic Rana regime in 1951 and similar attempts towards democratisation in the Indian protectorate of Sikkim ruled by the Chogyal. The oath of loyalty in the Bhutanese politico-cultural context meant something much larger than a simple commitment to the Constitution. It meant an emotional integration with the mainstream *Drukpa* community both in terms of accepting their politico-economic superiority and in strictly abiding by their socio-cultural norms. This also indicated an acceptance and aiding the process of consolidation of an only surviving traditional Buddhist monarchy. These perceptions have been the guiding principles of Bhutanese nationality.

These Lhotsampas refugees first fled to India in hordes, but were chased away to Nepal by the local authorities in the adjoining districts of Darjeeling and Jalpaiguri. As they entered into the eastern parts of

Nepal, refugee camps were set up by the Nepalese Government and the UNHCR was invited to manage the camps and other contingencies.

*Pakistan:* The heightened Cold War and the Soviet invasion of Afghanistan in 1979 and 18 years of civil war have altogether made Pakistan as the most vulnerable refugee host in South Asia. The birth of resistance movement and the subsequent violent clashes between the Afghan forces and the resistance groups led to a large scale refugee influx into Pakistan. Massive US arms supply ($ 630 million annually) to the Mujahiddin to fight the Soviet forces and indiscriminate rocketing and shelling on civilians with 10 million land mines scattered around the country side uprooted almost 6 million Afghans (1\3rd of its total population) in the 1980s.

The repatriation process which had started after the withdrawal of Soviet forces was abruptly halted by the capturing of Kabul and 2/3rds of Afghanistan by Taliban in September 1996 (reportedly supported by Pakistan, Saudi Arabia and the US). Taliban essentially a Sunni force with large scale support from the Pashtuns has created jitters among other northern neighbours like Tajikstan and Iran. This ultra fundamentalist force has brought about a total realignment of forces in Afghanistan. Fightings have been intensified between Taliban and the Northern alliance led by Uzbek General Dostum. However, contrary to expectation that these infightings would generate another fresh exodus of refugees, there has not been any major increase in Afghan refugee population in Pakistan. In fact, more people have been internally displaced.

### *Geographical Destinations*

Most of the South Asian refugees are absorbed in the region. Their geographical destinations are determined mostly by :

i) easy physical accessibility like Chakmas going to neighbouring Indian State of Tripura, Tibetans arriving in India and Nepal via Sikkim and Nepal-Tibet border, Afghans in North West Frontier Province (NWFP), Rohingyas of Burma crossing over to the nearest Bangladeshi frontiers. It has been observed that over 80 percent of the Afghan refugees in Pakistan hailed from within 250 kms of the border and all Bhutanese Lhotsampas are from Southern Bhutan belt adjoining India.

ii) cultural and linguistic affinity which could be easily observed in case of the exodus of Pashtuns from Afghanistan to Pakhtun dominated NWFP regions in Pakistan, Nepali speaking Lhotsampas refugees from Bhutan in Nepal, Rohingyas with Muslim background in Bangladesh and Sri Lankan Tamils in the Tamil Nadu State of India.

iii) political support of the host government as shown -by the overt and covert support to the liberation struggle in East Pakistan and to the cause of Sri Lankan Tamils by India and the subsequent flow and acceptance of refugees by- India.

***Why India does not produce refugees?***

India has always been a host to refugees coming from many comers of the world including the Vietnamese, Ethiopian and the Somalian. It has been in the centre stage of South Asian refugee management. Many scholars have started asking as to why India does not generate the kind of refugees that fit into complex at times intriguingly defined format refugees. This question assumes more significance particularly because of the fact that India has been one of the most violence-porn States in South Asia. India has had and continues to reel under variety of violent movements like Naxalites in West Bengal, Bihar and Telengana region of Andhra Pradesh,

Caste and Communal cauldrons, Punjab agitation, movements in the North-East (Assam, Gorkhaland, Nagaland, Mizoram) and the violent turmoil in Jammu and Kashmir. Despite the severity of protracted violence there has been no noticeable exodus of people to any of the neighbouring countries from India.

The possible reasons that could be attributed are large size of the country with accommodative federal structure where the constituent States have more independence and political space. More than this each State has a pluralistic ethnic and communal composition thereby insulating themselves from the violence that occur in the places of origin of the displaced/fleeing persons. This enables them not only to accommodate the fleeing people but also remain unaffected by the violence. For example, the atrocities against the Kashmiri Pandits in Jammu and Kashmir by the militants have led to large scale exodus of this community from Kashmir but most of them have been accommodated and absorbed by neighbouring States like Delhi and unaffected region like Ladakh.

Similarly during the height of Assam agitation in the beginning of 1980s most of the fleeing "illegal immigrants" were given shelter in North Bengal which remained totally unaffected despite its close physical proximity to Assam and noticeable presence of "illegal immigrants' in this region also. This is an indicative of the fact that the absorptive capacity of shocks and tensions in the Indian societies has been quite high. As a result, normalcy is restored in no time. For the displaced persons to enter into the neighbouring countries, the physical and political conditions should be congenial at the basic minimum level which has not been the case among potential hosts in India's neighbourhood. In other words, the displaced people in India have always found the possibility of taking shelter in the neighbouring countries less attractive both because of the politico-economic situations and human acceptability and politico-social adaptability in the neighbouring countries.

More than this, except Pakistan most South Asian countries have so far remained aloof from India's internal problems despite a long and mostly porous physical border. This is both because of "big brother" image of India and their own internal compulsions which keep them away from the internal bickerings in India. In a way, India produces a hordes of internally displaced people sometimes in large scale, who are scattered in many comers of the country depending upon the nature, magnitude and place of violence.

***Repatriation***

The 1990s has been to a large extent a decade of repatriation for South Asia. Except in the case of the Lhotsampas refugees from Bhutan, there has been a chain of repatriation activities both under the aegis of the host government and the international organisations like the UNHCR. The Rohingyas began returning home on a limited scale in 1992 after the bilateral agreement between Myanmar and Bangladesh Governments and UNHCR's Memorandum of Understanding with Burma in 1993. By January 1998, some 230,000 persons were repatriated thus reducing the camp population to just over 21,000.

The entire repatriation operations arc conducted by the UNHCR. In the case of the Afghan refugees, after the 1989 withdrawal of' Soviet forces and fall of the Communist Government of Najibullah in 1992, over 3.9 million people have been repatriated till the beginning of 1997. Similarly, since July 1992 over 54,000 Sri Lankan Tamils have been repatriated from India. The UNHCR which was consistently denied any role in the refugee management by the Government of India since their participation in the 1972 East Pakistani crisis, has been for the first time given the right to decide the voluntariness of repatriation by the Indian Government.

However, since April 1995 repatriation has literally stopped as the Sri Lankan army launched its final war to recapture the LTTE bastions: Jaffna, Vavuniya, Mannar, Trincomalee, Kilinochi, Mallaivatu (all in the north and east). Though the process of repatriation of the Chakmas to their places of origin in the CHT region of Bangladesh had already set in with some attractive package for the rehabilitation programmes, it really got a major boost after the Chakma movement leaders and the Bangladesh Government signed an accord giving the CHT region an autonomous status. By May 1998, almost all the Chakma refugees had been repatriated from the camps in Tripura.

*Cost of refugees to host countries*

The question of security/instability framework brings In a host of issues that have turned out to be adverse to the refugee receiving countries. At times they have acquired the dimension of serious threat to both security and stability of the host nations. These situations are said to have set in when refugees are seen as a political risk, ii) perceived as a threat to cultural identity and iii) are considered as a social and economic burden.

The Sri Lankan Tamil refugee-induced Indian action in Sri Lanka known as the "IPKF Operation" of 1987-90 was not only an utter failure but is now considered as a major diplomatic misadventure. It actually strengthened the ever belligerent LTTE as it could at a later stage mobilise support from the Sri Lankan Government itself.

A major fall out of this Operation was the dastardly killing of former Prime Minister of India Rajiv Gandhi allegedly by the LTTE in May 1991 on the home ground of Tamil refugees in Tamil Nadu. It is this southern State of India which had provided the Sri Lankan Tamil refugees with political asylum and physical shelter.

A landlocked economy like Nepal already has the highest deforestation rate (4 per cent) in South Asia. The large scale intrusion into forest areas by the Lhotsampa refugees for both fuel and timber purpose have started getting manifested in the protests and clashes with the locals and the authorities. The armed groups from among the refugees have caused severe dislocation in the repatriation activities in Nayapara and Kutupalong camps in Bangladesh, These elements who are opposing "forced repatriation" have links with some of the right wing political forces in Bangladesh and have refused access to any Bangladeshi officials to the camp sites thereby creating a serious law and order problem. In the management of Afghan refugees the UNHCR alone has spent 1 billion in its Pakistan Programme.

However the most vital fall out for a fragile economy like that of Pakistan has been the sharp rise in drug addicts in Pakistan (from a few thousands in 1977 to 1.9 million in 1987 and the jump in the number of people involved in the complex narcotics trade. By 1985 over 33 per cent of the total heroin seized in the world was from Pakistan. Afghanistan's main cash crop poppy was all diverted to Afghan-Pakistan border where they processed into heroin. The UN Drug Control Program Report mentions that 50 percent of the World supply and 80 percent of the European supply of heroin comes from Afghanistan with a street value of $30-40 billion. This has put a tremendous pressure on Pakistan as it has both domestic and international implications. In its recently concluded 8th Plan period, Pakistan spent $82 million on drug demand reduction programme.

More serious has been the crystallisation of nexus between politicians and drug barons. It has been reported that US State Department sent a list of 14 drug barons of Pakistan to its Ministry of Interior which appallingly also included few well known ministers. Large chunk of this drug money allegedly goes to support cross-border insurgences. A significant portion of the arms supplied to the Mujahiddins to fight the Soviet forces by the US made its way into the 'arms hungry mafia. As a result Pakistan has now been infested with open arms bazaar.

The Afghan refugees injected "Kalashnikov Culture" with lethal arms like land mines, rocket launchers and missiles, grenades and machine guns freely available. Its impact on violence in Karachi and Punjab distinctly visible in the 1990s. There has been an apprehension that the Afghan Mujahiddins along with the LTTE have spread their pernicious designs in Kashmir with Harka-tul-Ansar, in Nagaland with NSCN and in Assam with ULFA in India has been substantiated by the recovery of 19000 AK-47 rifles, 5,500 anti-tank missiles, 29000 hand grenades in Kashmir during the period 1988-97. On the height of their exodus, the Afghans came along with 3 million heads of livestock and literally exhausted the grazing land in NWFP and Baluchistan in Pakistan.

This has been often cited by the local inhabitants as the reasons behind price rise, scarce supply of essentials, pressure on both cultivable land, agriculture, livestock, forest resources and the limitations in the employment opportunities. This is where we find unequivocal expressions and symptoms of 'compassion fatigue' finally leading to a show down with the refugee population. A study done by the a Peshawar based research institute concluded that i) local population benefited from the food aid which entered into local markets form the donor network. As a result Peshawar registered the lowest increase in the prices of basic commodities of consumption compared to Karachi, Lahore and Rawalpindi, ii) It was also found that the refugees entered into the local unskilled labour market and reduced the wage level because they were also getting a living stipend from the donor agencies. This depressed the local wage rate and was strongly resented by the traditional local labourers and iii) Refugee traders took a sizable portion of local trade particularly as general merchants, carpets and antiques, cloth, leather and shoes. They made huge investment in the prime areas including construction and business.

**Plight of the Returnees**

Even after the voluntary repatriation, the returnees in many cases are not able to acquire the normal life situation. They continue to have their own plights. More noteworthy aspect has been the fact that in most of the cases, the repatriations have been made without any substantial change in the circumstances under which these refugees left their homeland. In other words, the conflicts that led to exodus of refugees have mostly remained unresolved in most parts of South Asia.

This brings in the moot question of voluntariness of the process of repatriation. For example, the ultra conservative Interpretation of Islam and the harsh regulations imposed by the Taliban particularly on women have made the life of returnees miserable. They have pronounced edicts like: no education for girls, no employment for women, no music, no kite flying, no photography of living creatures and compulsory visits of Mosques on Friday.

The large scale "executions and amputations" of the persons not adhering to these inhuman dictats of the Talibans have been amply highlighted by the latest report of the Amnesty International. The Islamic militia defends these actions as the penal code for social peace and order. This is further heightened by the largest deposits of land mines (over fifty varieties) contaminating more than 550 square km in which grazing land accounted for 75.6% and agriculture land 20.2% of the mined areas as reported by the ICRC making the resettlement a herculean task. However, despite the harsh working conditions for the UN Agencies and other humanitarian organisations which included detention of even the European Commissioner for Humanitarian Affairs, many quick impact projects are operationalised with the help of NGOs like OXFAM and Swedish Committee for Afghanistan. In Sri Lanka the "last round of battle" between the government forces and the LTTE known as "Operation Jayasukur" (Sure of Victory) to capture the strategic 88 krn Vavuniya-Killinochi Highway has been going on for the last eight months.

A large scale bombing and fierce fighting continues leading to mass displacement. The repatriated refugees are kept in Transit Camps and Open Relief Centres to give them better feeling about the real security situations and both pre-settlement assistance and reintegration assistance are extended by the UNHCR. In Myanmar, refugees are returning to seven townships of the Rakhine State close to the border of Myanmar and Bangladesh-with more than 99 percent returning to just three townships viz,. Maungdow, Buthidaung and rathedaung.

A large-scale integration programme under the direct supervision of the UNHCR with UNICEF, WFP, UNDP, Myanmar Red Cross society, Action Centre La Faim, Bridge Asia Japan and other NGOs on skill development, health care, education, rural infrastructure and food for work have been undertaken. But the Rohingyas continue to feel insecure as most of them have not been given citizenship by the State implying no entitlement to lands which they previously owned. They are living in a state of "legal limbo". The hunger strikes and the violence in the Rohingya refugee camps in Bangladesh against the "forced repatriation" in very recent months is a clear manifestation of the poor reception of the returnees in the country of their origin. Under the bilateral agreement between India and Bangladesh refugees are rehabilitated in a congenial manner.

Multinational companies like United Meridens of US has been encouraged to hire only Tribals in its Oil and Gas Exploration project in the CHT region to ensure improvement of economic and employment situations in the region. The much talked about political solutions giving the CHT region and the tribals an autonomous status in development and administration has brightened the chances of the proper absorption of the returnees.

*Future Scenario*

There seems to be no immediate solution to the refugee intrigues in South Asia in the foreseeable future. Among other reasons this could be attributed to i) the intricacies and complexities involved in the situations under which they were forced to leave their birth places, ii) the low priority given by the host governments to the refugee issues and the withdrawal syndrome shown by the international agencies and iii) protracted political instability in both the country of origin and the host. Even a less complicated issue of Lhotsampa refugees from Bhutan which otherwise could have been solved—if a neighbouring country like India shows some kind of political sagacity—has evaded solution for the last seven years now.

In the case of Afghanistan, except Pakistan, Saudi Arabia and UAE no other States have so far recognised the Talibans. Meanwhile in the course of eighteen years of fierce civil war and violence, a new generation of people have emerged with little education, strong weapons training and no memory of life in a peaceful state as their background. This along with the distinct failure of the State, makes the future direction of Afghan politics and the fate of refugees and displaced persons more fragile and uncertain. Equally disturbing phenomenon has been the irreversible process of social disintegration that has taken roots in the post Cold War Afghanistan. The opposing approaches of US-Pakistan-Saudi Arabia on the one hand and Iran-India-Russia and other Central Asian States mainly on strategic grounds on the other hand in observing and playing with the Afghan situation give no solace to the suffering mass.

The vested interests of the drug barons leave no stone unturned in injecting further instability. However, of late the UN effort to mobilise regional countries and Security Council Members to find some sort of lasting solution and the call by the US for a multi-ethnic Government bring about some semblance of hope. For the first time, the student militia had a long negotiations with the Northern Alliance in Islamabad in April 1998. Though the negotiation failed on the ground of setting up of Ulema Commission, the Taliban leadership had, very strong reservations on the role of the United Nations as a mediator. The declaration of the LTTE as a terrorist outfit by the US is likely to have a considerable impact on funds, arms and propaganda by the Tamil diaspora.

The European countries another bastion of Tamil diaspora—are likely to follow the suit. On the other hand, the Defence Minister Ratwatte declared that 80 percent of the battle is over. This has put a tremendous pressure on the LTTE to come to the negotiating table. Despite the fierce opposition from the Buddhist Monks, much hope has been pinned on the now famous "Devolution Package" announced by the President of Sri

Lanka. This gives Autonomous Regional Councils to Tamil speaking areas in the North and the East. The LTTE has so far vehemently opposed any negotiated settlement based on this package. Sri Lankan Government's new policy of restoring civil administration in the war ravaged areas like Jaffna and attempt to politically marginalise the LTTE by encouraging moderate Tamil parties like Tamil United Liberation Front (TULF) have resulted into fresh spate of violence including the bomb attack on Tooth Temple in Kandy and the killing of Mayor of Jaffna, Sarojini Yogeswaran. The Inter-Ministerial Meetings between Nepal and, Bhutan have taken place seven times but no solution can be sighted as the latter wants to go by its own strict categorisation Bhutan has strictly categorised 4 varieties of refugees, viz, a) Bonafide Bhutanese if they have been evicted forcefully, b) Bhutanese who emigrated, c) Non-Bhutanese people and d) Bhutanese who have committed criminal acts. This will allow hardly 10,000 Lhotsampas to return. It is by now very clear that there is a significant presence of terrorists mostly belonging to the dreaded group of United Liberation Front of Assam (ULFA) in the thick jungles Southern Bhutan.

The recent operations by Unified Command Structure in Assam to flush out these terrorists who has been demanding independence form India since late 1980s has led to their relocation in the Bhutanese jungles just across Assam-North Bengal-Bhutan border. Some of them had fled from their reported training camps located in Bangladesh, after the present government led by Hasina Wajed came down heavily on them. The Bhutanese Government is fearing the ULFA reprisals against the royal forces that could fuel trouble in the Kingdom and lead to a nexus between the extremists and the pro-democratic activists in case of any precipitate action against the extremists. Though Nepal has been demanding India's intervention in finding a lasting solution to the Lhotsampa refugee issues, India has consistently kept itself aloof saying it is bilateral issue between Bhutan and Nepal. There are ample evidences to prove India's consistent apathy towards the refugee problems as demonstrated by literal driving away of the refugees to Nepalese border in the most crucial phase of refugee exodus, the complete absence of Indian relief participation in refugee camps even on humanitarian grounds; arrest and imprisonment of refugees going back to Thimphu via India under the banner of Appeal Movement Coordinating Council during the last two years and finally the arrest and detention of Rongthong Kuenley Dorji, Chairperson of the United Front for Democracy in Bhutan and Chairman of the Druk National Congress in Delhi in April 1997.

*Regional Approach*

None of the South Asian nations have ratified the 1951 UN Convention and the 1967 Protocol, though at least three of them are the members of the EXCOM of the UNCHR. In the process, they have reduced the status of fleeing humanities to political arbitrariness. The grant of refugee status has been at the discretion of the political authorities. For example, Pakistan gives refugee status only to Afghans. Others are mostly declared as illegal immigrants not eligible for work permits or public education.

The refusal of entry into Bangladesh by its agencies to fresh asylum seekers and denial of refugee status to those who have entered is indicative of both aid and compassionate fatigues of the host and poor checks and balance prompted, by the absence of standard national instruments. By not ratifying these instruments, they are rejecting refugees on narrow political -grounds. For instance, the Sri Lankan Tamil refugees are taken as refugees depending upon which party is there in power in Tamil Nadu. Bhutan and Nepal do not have a common border. So the first country of asylurn for the fleeing Bhutanese Lhotsampas was only India and the refugees did come and tried to reside in bordering Indian districts of Jalpaiguri and Darjeeling. They were physically removed\chased away by the security forces of West Bengal because the Bengal government thought it will add fuel to the Gorkhaland Movement which has been fighting for a separate statehood within the constitutional framework of India.

There are quite a number of unanswered questions that go to show both violation of international norms and parochialism of the ruling elites in West Bengal. Here the refugees were purely a local issue. No South Asian countries have any constitutional provisions to deal with the refugees. As a result most of them deal with them on an adhoc basis. In many cases the refugees have been used as pawns In regional geo-politics. Each country has different arguments to offer for not ratifying the 1951 UN Convention and 1967 Protocol. For instance, India does not agree with the very definition of the refugees and wants these convention and Protocol to have strong provisions for insulating the refugee influx-prone developing countries against massive influx. In other words, it wants the affluent developed nations to share at least equitably the increasing refugee burdens. It is worried at the closing down of gates by the developed market economies.

On the other hand, Pakistan feels that without ratifying these international instruments also, it has been able to host and manage refugees in a scale much larger than the developed market economies. Many scholars have now started focussing on enabling national laws and organisation like Indian Centre for Humanitarian Laws and Research has even drafted Model National

Law on Refugees. At the regional level, the SAARC can play an instrumental role in formulating), a regional convention on refugee management. The SAARC already has two major conventions viz., Agreement on Establishing the SAARC Food Security Reserve (SFSR - 1987) and SAARC Regional Convention on Suppression of Terrorism (1987).

The later Convention embodies and gives a regional focus to many of the well established principles of international law in this respect. Under its provisions, member States are committed to extradite or prosecute alleged terrorists thus preventing them from enjoying safe havens. This Convention also envisages preventive action to combat terrorism. The exchange of information, intelligence and expertise are among the areas identified for mutual cooperation. Taking the lessons from other regional arrangements like that of Organisation of African Unity (1969) and Cartagena Declaration (1984), some kind of debate has been initiated in South Asia also towards a comprehensive regional convention. This could incorporate the aspirations of the regional member countries in a more forthright and nondiscriminatory manner. This can in fact be realised through the SAARC forum using the SAARCLAW as the pressure group.

The SAARCLAW is an Association for persons of the legal communities of the SAARC countries, established in 1991 and is the first body (SAARC Chamber of Commerce and Industry—SCCI, 1992 was the second one recognised by SAARC as a regional apex body. The success brought about by the consistent pressure of the SCCI on the SAARC member countries in introducing South Asian Preferential Trading Arrangement (SAPTA) and South Asian Free Trade Are (SAFTA) by 2001 can be cited as a major breakthrough in the thinking process in South Asia. Only a couple of years back it was beyond the thinking of the member countries of SAARC to have trade regime of this nature. Therefore, the offices of the SAARCLAW stand to be most effective instrument in trying to evolve a regional convention on the refugees. This has three distinct immediate advantages.

Firstly, this will pave the way for the member States in designing their own national laws. Secondly, it will also expedite the process of ratifying the 1951 UN Convention and the 1967 Protocol by the South Asian nations. And thirdly, regional approach may persuade the other nations in the UNHCR to make the definition more comprehensive. In fact some of these countries are yet to examine the benefits these non-signatory nations have foregone as compared to the signatory nations and the price these non-signatory nations have to pay in not ratifying these instruments.

**Refugees in South Asia**

South Asia, like other parts of the world, is faced with the growing humanitarian, political and economic challenges posed by movements of forcibly displaced persons. It is estimated that: the South Asian region hosts around 1.5 million Refugees who have fled across international borders due to war, persecution and human rights violations in their countries of origin. These refugees are largely cared for by Governments and the Office of the United Nations High Commissioner for Refugees. In addition, the SAARC region hosts large numbers of Internally Displaced Persons who have also fled their homes but remain within the boundaries of their homeland in refugee-like conditions. As well, Stateless persons are another distinct group who have been subjected to forced movement across international borders, but may be unable to find acceptance and durable solutions to their problems.

**Refugees in India**

The traumatic birth of modern India resulted in large scale population movements, the likes of which had never before been witnessed in this part of the world. While still recovering from the rehabilitation process, India gave refuge to Tibetans, who currently number over 100,000. In 1971, India also provided temporary refuge to over ten million refugees from erstwhile East Pakistan, until they returned home voluntarily to an independent Bangladesh. Today India hosts approximately 40,000 Chakmas from Bangladesh, 100,000 Sri Lankan Tamil refugees and over 17,000 refugees of other nationalities, including Afghans. India has also facilitated the repatriation of a large number of Chakma & Sri Lankan refugees.

**Absence of a legal framework for refugees**

Refugees in South Asia account for nearly one tenth of the global refugee population, yet there is visible lack of a refugee regime in all the SAARC countries. Although by and large South Asian countries have been generous in granting asylum to refugees despite their strained-resources, policies towards refugees have been based on ad hoc administrative decisions with no legislative framework to clearly define parameters.

The situation is further compounded by the fact that none of the SAARC countries have acceded to the 1951 UN Convention and the 1967 Protocol relating to the status of Refugees, the main international instruments for protecting refugees. There is neither a regional treaty or declaration on refugees, nor have any of the SAARC countries adopted a national legislation for the protection of refugees. The lack of an adequate legal regime to ensure the rights of refugees, who as aliens are often among the most vulnerable members of society is an ongoing problem. Having lost the protection of their country of origin, refugees often lack legal recourse in host countries to ensure their basic human rights including the right to Non-Refoulement i.e. Non-expulsion to one's country of origin. The presence of an adequate regime governing the admission, treatment and voluntary repatriation of refugees in India would serve to address various concerns regarding refugees such as:

*Identification of refugees*

International refugee law clearly differentiates refugees from other foreigners. The criteria for determining refugee status is based on the establishment of a well-founded fear of persecution on the grounds of race, religion, nationality, sex, membership of a particular social group or political opinion, followed by flight from country of origin or habitual residence, and the inability to return to one's country of origin due to the above reasons. This established regime would ensure an objective refugee status determination and persons falling outside the definition of 'Refugee' such as persons simply seeking better economic or social prospects, would not qualify for Refugee status.

*Exclusion from refugee status*

Asylum seekers found to have committed crimes against peace, war crimes or crimes against humanity; serious non-political crimes outside the country of refuge, or are guilty of acts contrary to the purposes and principles of the United Nations, do not qualify for refugee status tinder international law. During the period of asylum, a refugee should be legally entitled to the basic rights of humanitarian treatment in terms of right to life and liberty, equality, sustenance, work, health care, primary education etc., subject to certain obligations by the refugee to the host country.

The primary right of a refugee is to seek and enjoy

Asylum in another country. This right is protected by the corner stone principle of Non-Refoulement which is considered a norm of customary international law and ensures the right of non-expulsion, push-back or interdiction of asylum seekers and refugees to a place where they may face human rights violation. Other international law provisions notably the Convention Against Torture enhance this principle of non return.

*Cessation of refugee status*

Refugee status need not be permanent, it ceases when the refugee voluntarily avails the protection of his/her country of origin; voluntarily re-acquires nationality or protection of the country of origin or any other country, or when the" circumstances in connection with which the person has been recognised as a refugee have ceased to exist thereby enabling safe return.

*Durable Solutions*

Apart from provision of a cessation clause, international refugee law and practice provides for three distinct durable solutions depending upon the circumstances; these are: voluntary repatriation to country of origin, local integration in country of asylum, and resettlement to a third country. The international system of refugee protection ensures the protection of refugees, as well as the interests of the State.

However, the benefit of refugee status may not be claimed by a refugee of asylum seeker where there are reasonable grounds for regarding him or her as a danger to the security of the country or who has been convicted by a final judgement of a serious crime and constitutes a danger to the-community. It is apparent that the existence of an adequate refugee regime would deter-mine the fate of refugees by the rule of law, manner than by ad hoc administrative measures. Many other relevant provisions of international refugee law and practice could be relied upon as guiding principles in the presence of an established legislation specifically created to protect refugees. The Regional Consultations on Refugee and Migratory Movements in South Asia was initiated in November 1994 by a group of eminent persons from the SAARC countries for the purpose of providing a platform for discussing and developing strategies to address forced population displacements in South Asia.

The eminent personalities have evinced concern over the need to protect the basic human rights of refugees who have been subjected to forced movements for reasons beyond their control. As part of its deliberations, the Regional Consultations has focused on possible means of alleviating the plight of refugees to be balanced with the legitimate security concerns of States. To this end, the need for domestic legislation on refugees was unanimously deemed to be of priority in the region.

Towards that end, in 1996 a pilot group led by justice P.N. Bhagwati former Chief justice of India drafted a Model National Law on Refugees and presented it for appraisal at an earlier SAARCLAW/ UNHCR seminar held in May 1997 at New Delhi. An amended draft law was formally adopted at the Fourth Regional Consultations held in Dhaka in November 1997. Consequently, the Fifth Regional Consultations held in Kathmandu in November 1998 agreed that the draft law may be individually taken up by its members with their, respective countries for further country-specific refinement and consideration at the national level.

**SAARCLAW**

Being an association of the legal fraternity from the South Asian countries believing in the objectives of SAARC (South Asian Association for Regional Co-operation), and aware of the relevance of rule of law in contemporary society, SAARCLAW is the logical organisation to take up the issue of refugee protection in South Asia.

A UN Convention on the Status of Refugees held in 1951 defined a refugee as any person who owing to well founded fear of being persecuted for reasons of race, religion, nationality, membership of a particular social group or political opinion, is outside the country of his nationality and is unable, or owing to such fear, is unwilling to avail himself of the protection of that country.

The scope of refugee status was expanded when, following the exodus of Chinese from the Mainland to Hong Kong in 1957, the UN High Commissioner for Refugees (UNHCR) was mandated to extend his 'good offices' to assist the groups of refugees. This helped the Greek Cypriots in 1960 and the displaced persons from Indo-China in 1975, following the US defeat in Vietnam.

There were obvious ideological reasons behind symp-athies for the refugees pushed out of the Communist or 'unfriendly' states. The displaced persons from Indo-China could get the benefit of the international community's support and sympathy because in 1969, the Convention on Refugee Problem in Africa, adopted by the Organisation of African Unity, had clearly recognised a person as a refugee, who has had to flee his country as a result of external aggression, occupation, foreign domination or events seriously disturbing public order.

Similarly some Central American nations like Panama and Mexico further developed the OAU definition of refugee by adding the criteria of "massive violation of human rights" in Cartagena Declaration adopted in 1984. Without going into the debate about the legal validity of OAU and Cartagena Declaration, it may be underlined here that UNHCR in its approach to refugees, respects these provisions and hence these Conventions have acquired an international status irrespective of their regional character and narrowly defined scope.

A growing community of scholars and practitioners in the field of refugee problems tend to follow a broader framework of refugee status in order to be as helpful as possible. An important aspect of legally defining the refugee status is that such definition decides entitlement of support and protection from international community, particularly the organisations such as UNHCR and also a number of humanitarian inter-national organisations.

Here a couple of additional points need to be considered about the refugee status. This status is accorded to the people 'persecuted' by states and also to such victims who have to cross international borders in order to save themselves from the 'persecution' involved. On both these counts, broadening of the refugee status further has been urged in the debate on the issue.

Increasing number of scholars and involved persons are drawing attention to indirect and implied persecution carried out by nature, through economic deprivation and as a result of developmental process that causes uprooting and displacement of people.

Accordingly, a new category of environmental and developmental refugees as also refugees resulting from economic migration has come to be recognised. This category does not have the same international legal force to get 'entitlement' in the host state for its protection and sustenance. But it adds to the complexity of the refugee phenomenon.

However, under the thrust of post-cold war developments, a clear shift is taking place on the question of refugees where those once treated as refugees are being forced to return to their countries of origin. What is happening to the Vietnamese refugees in Southeast Asia illustrate the point. Thailand has succeeded first in persuading, and then forcing its Vietnamese refugees to return to Vietnam, with the help of UNHCR. Now other ASEAN members and Hong Kong have also joined in sending Vietnamese asylum seekers back home. And this is being done by asserting that most of them are "economic migrants" and not "political refugees". Such shift in attitude is also evident in the West.

In the post-cold war era, we have witnessed a major shift in the world's approach towards persons who are forced out of their homes because of political and ethnic violence or the threat of persecution. The international community is now generally committed to keeping would-be refugees at home, saying at once that this is for their own good and for the good of countries increasingly reluctant to host foreigners uprooted by war and persecution. We do not wish to discuss the factors behind this shift, but the end of cold war rivalry and its consequences that saw political advantage in encouraging refugees from the other 'bloc' or the rival states, is no longer relevant.

The end of the cold war has also generated a new push for the flow of refugees due to the collapse of barriers in the 'east', as a result of which, there is increased movement of people from 'east' in search of better economic prospects.

The West is not willing to accommodate this new rush as many of the industrialised countries are caught in an unhappy spiral of economic stagnation. Then there are also refugees that do not cross international boundaries and are displaced within their respective countries but away from their normal place of residence and economic activity.

Such 'internal' refugees are, primarily the responsibility of the concerned state itself, but increasingly, the UNHCR and other voluntary agencies are coming forward to extend support and protection to such 'internal' refugees as well. Basic justification for this has been the resource constraints of the affected country in looking after the displaced persons. At times, the victims of displacement neither receive any help, nor do they trust their own state to provide them succour and protection.

In view of the nature of ethnic or political conflict affecting them and the partisan character of the state in such conflicts, they perceive the State as a victimiser. Several of such examples can be seen in Africa and also South Asia.

Complexity of the refugee phenomenon is not only on account of its definitional sources and the dimensions of the size of the people involved. The end of the Second World War and the consequent beginning of the East-West cold war generated the flow of refugees from East to West, with the latter encouraging such flows to underline the attraction of its humanitarian, democratic and capitalist ideological character, as also to undermine the 'inhuman' and 'totalitarian' nature of Communist States and societies.

The extension of cold-war generated and reinforced ideological conflicts in the Third World also resulted in refugee flows from the developing countries to the industrialised world. The emergence of undemocratic and coercive state further added to such flows of refugees from South to North. Such movement from South to North also received impetus when the economic migrants joined the flow.

The most important direction of refugee flows has been within the Third World; from one South country to the other. In terms of numbers, this is the largest flow. The refugee statistics compiled for 1993, in *World Refugee Survey, 1994* by the US Committee on Refugees show that of a total of 16.25 million refugees and asylum seekers in the world, all but 2.78 million people are in the Third World.

*Table 1*
*World refugee statistics as of 31 December 1993*

| Region | Number in '000 |
|---|---|
| Africa | 5825 |
| Europe and North America | 2785 |
| Latin America and The Caribbean | 102 |
| Fast Asia and the Pacific | 468 |
| Middle Fast | 4924 |
| South and Central Asia | 2151 |
| Grand Total | 16, 255 |

Since the early sixties, the refugee flows within the South were generated by wars of national liberation as well as of ethnic and religious assertion. Significant contribution to this flow was made by the West during the late Seventies and through out the Eighties by their "strategic and political interests... to maintain pressure against and to destabilise revolutionary states in the Third World."

What has facilitated most the South-South refugee flows are the factors like contiguous and porous borders, sociocultural identities of the people across the borders and encouragement by the neighbouring states for strategic or humanitarian reasons.

*Table 2*
*Refugee in South Asia*

| Host country and source of refugees | Numbers |
|---|---|
| *Afghanistan* | 35, 000 |
| Tajikistan | 35,000 |

| | |
|---|---|
| Bangladesh | 199, 000 |
| Burma | 198, 00 |
| Others | 200 |
| *India* | 325, 600 |
| Tibet | 119, 000 |
| Sri Lanka | 106, 000 |
| Bangladesh | 53, 500 |
| Afghanistan | 24, 400 |
| Bhutan | 20, 000 |
| Burma | 1, 600 |
| Others | 700 |
| *Nepal* | 99, 100 |
| Bhutan | 85, 100 |
| Tibet | 14, 000 |
| *Pakistan* | 1,482,300 |
| Afghanistan | 1,480, 000 |
| Others | 2, 300 |
| Grand Total | 2, 140, 600 |

If we look at the South Asian refugee situation in the long term perspective, taking into account nearly twenty million refugees that crossed newly created international borders between India and Pakistan between 1947 and 1950, about 10 million refugees that came to India from the then East Pakistan in 1970-71 during the emergence of Bangladesh, and more than 3.5 million Afghans who took refuge in Pakistan during the early Eighties in the wake of the then Soviet military intervention, the region would clearly be one of the most persistently and seriously affected one.

Most of the South Asian countries have been receiving as well as generating refugees. India has been more of a refugee receiving than a generating country due to its easily accessible borders, sociocultural identities, economic opportunities and a democratic and generally soft state, in relation to almost all the neighbours.

If the flow of refugees from East Pakistan in 1970-71 is discounted, Pakistan has also been on the receiving side of the refugees, but then Pakistan does not have common borders with any other South Asian country except India. And most of the refugees received by Pakistan have not been from India but from Afghanistan, due primarily to geographical proximity and socio-cultural identities. Sri Lanka's island status has spared it from being a host to asylum seekers.

Bangladesh, which has generally been a refugee gene-rating country, and there are Bangladeshi refugees all over South Asia—in India, Nepal, and Pakistan—also had to receive Muslim refugees, Rohingyas, from Myanmar, when in 1978, the Myanmar government started cracking down on non-nationals. The Myanmar government's contention was that these people did not have any nationality certificate with them as they were, in fact the recent illegal migrants from Bangladesh.

Similarly Nepal, which has generally been a source of migrants to India and, to a much smaller extent, Bhutan, not only received refugees from Tibet, but has been complaining of large scale migrants from India, and lesser than that from Bangladesh, since the late Seventies.

In recent years, Nepal has also received nearly 85,000 persons of Nepali origin from Bhutan as a consequence of ethnic conflict between the Nepalese of Southern Bhutan and the highlander Drukpas of Tibetan origin. Bhutan refuses to accept them as its nationals and pleads that many of them were economic migrants from Nepal or India, who came to work on the Kingdom's various developmental projects even during the British period in South Asia. Bhutan also had to accept Tibetan refugees but in the mid-Eighties, it forced them out because of ethnic tensions between the Tibetans and local residents.

In the theoretical studies of refugee phenomenon,

six broad causal factors have been identified as being responsible for creating refugees. They are:

i) Anti-colonial wars and self-determination movements,

ii) International conflicts,

iii) Revolutions, coups and regime changes,

iv) Ethnic, communal and religious conflicts,

v) Creation and restructuring of state boundaries,

vi) Population transfers.

Three broad categories of refugee generating factors in South Asia may be identified.

In the first place, the breakdown of colonial rule and the rationalisation of some of the colonial legacies created refugee flows. The largest of such flows, was between India and Pakistan, resulting from the partition of British India which gave birth to the new State of Pakistan on the basis of religion. As a result, not only the Muslims of North India migrated to the newly created state but the consequent communal frenzy also pushed the Hindu residents of the newly created Pakistan to migrate to the truncated India.

This process of migration continued for nearly a decade, though the largest migrations took place in the first two years, of 1947 and 1948. No precise estimate of the exact numbers of people involved in these flows is available, but flows from both the directions put together, would not have been less than 20 million. The problems of their resettlement and rehabilitation were enormous but both India and Pakistan sorted them out administratively.

There was yet another way in which decolonisation in South Asia generated flow of refugees in the region.

Myanmar and Sri Lanka were granted independence from British rule in 1948. Soon after this, Myanmar started a vigorous process of nationalising its admini stration and public sector institutions, where a large number of the persons of Indian origin, who had migrated to Myanmar under the British patronage, were employed. All these Indians were pushed out of their jobs and since most of them were not granted citizenship, they had to come to India as refugees.

Myanmar again sent refugees to India after the dismissal of U.N's democratic regime and the establishment of military rule by Gen. Ne Win in 1962. The military rule had nationalised various economic establishments, depriving sources of livelihood to many persons of Indian origin, who were working as middlemen and money lenders since the British times. The Indian government's disapproval of the military rule in Myanmar had made the Rangoon rulers harsh towards these Indians whose position then became further vulnerable and they had to leave for India as refugees. An estimated 150,000 of such refugees returned to South India where they had their roots.

Sri Lanka had a large population of the persons of Indian origin, employed in the estate sector since the British days. The nationalist government of Sri Lanka, through newly introduced citizenship Acts in 1948 and 1949, deprived these estate workers of their voting rights. As a result, a new category of,stateless Indians' emerged in Sri Lanka, which neither India, nor Sri Lanka wanted to own.

Several attempts to resolve the problem of the persons of Indian origin in Sri Lanka, failed to yield results. The two country signed their first major agreement on the question of the 'stateless' persons in 1964, which has been revised and improved since then due to new problems of implementation. Under these various agreements and their implementation, India has repatriated some 338,000 persons of Indian origin from Sri Lanka for resettlement and rehabilitation between 1964 and 1987. The last agreement to deal with the residual problem was concluded between the two countries in 1988 and it is hoped that sincere and complete implementation of this agreement will finally eliminate this irritant between the two neighbours.

The second category of factors responsible for generating refugees in South Asia is related to state and nation-building processes which precipitated not only political, ethnic and religious conflicts but created economic and environmental conditions that forced people to migrate within or outside their respective countries

The first and also the largest refugee flow generated by factors under this category was in 1971, from the then East Pakistan to India. Some 10 million refugees from the eastern wing of Pakistan took asylum in India. As a consequence of the emergence of Bangladesh, another category of refugees was created, who had refused to support the struggle for Bangladesh. Under an agreement concluded in 1974, Pakistan accepted about 170,000 of these people, popularly known as 'Bihari Muslims'.

Pakistan is not an important aspect of the state and nation-building process in South Asia has been the changing identity, of the State and its consequent precipitation of religious, ethnic and sectarian conflicts.

In the beginning, all the South Asian states started with liberal, democratic and secular ideals, but gradually, they drifted into acquiring the identities of their respectively dominant and governing social groups. This process and its culmination in the emergence of a majoritarian and domineering state which was also undemocratic, has inflicted discrimination, deprivation and marginalisation on the minority, ethnic and religious groups.

The dominant community or the social group in control of the state has used undemocratic political structures and the state is coercive apparatus to appropriate dispro-portionate share of the state's resources for itself, denying the same to their minorities and out groups. This precipitated ethnic and other conflicts and generated refugees. This distorted state-building process has been reinforced by, and in turn contributed to, the challenge of under or unequal development.

The case of Tamils in Sri Lanka, where the state, through a gradual process beginning in 1956, acquired a Sinhala-Buddhist identity. The simmering ethnic conflict that exploded in July 1983 sent more than 220,000, refugees to India and nearly 75.000 refugees Outside the region to Europe. America. Canada and Australia.

Half of the Sri Lankan refugees in India were sent back following the conclusion of the Indo-Sri Lankan Agreement in July 1987, and subsequently through the good offices of the UNHCR. India's former Prime Minister Rajiv Gandhi's assassi-nation, in Tamil Nadu in May 1991. Suspected to be an act of the Sri Lankan Tamil extremist group, the Liberation Tigers of Tamil Eealam (LTTE), during the election campaign expedited the return of Sri Lankan refugees.

Most of the Western governments are also keen to see the return of Tamil refugees back to Sri Lanka but collapse of the peace process initiated by President Chandrika Kumaratunga and the outbreak of Eelam War-III in April 1995 make this difficult. Sri Lanka's ethnic conflict has also generated internal refugees, total number of whom, according to official Sri Lankan estimates stood by August 1993, at more than 600,000.

The newly created state of Bangladesh had imbibed the ideals of democracy and secularism but after the coup against the first representative government in 1975, a drift towards authoritarian political order and assertive Islamic identity became evident. This strengthened the traditional flow of Hindu refugees from Bangladesh to the Indian state of Assam. For instance, between 1971 and 1981, an estimated 1.8 million Hindus had migrated from Bangladesh to India, suddenly increasing demographic pressures in Assam and creating a conflict between the Assamese and Bengalis.

The changing character of the Bangladeshi state also further increased the alienation of Buddhist Chakmas, the tribal inhabitants of Chittagong Hill Tracts (CHT) of Bangladesh, and intensified their fight for autonomy and cultural, political and economic rights with the Dhaka regime. The conflict in CHT resulted in more than 50,000 Chakma refugees landing in India. The prospect of their return to Bangladesh has increased following an understanding to that effect arrived at in June 1995 between the home and the host governments. This understanding will not be vitiated by the realities on ground as has been the case with all the previous arrangements worked out on the Chakma issue.

In Bhutan, the state has been a monarchy and dominated by the Buddhist Drukpas. The Southern Bhutanese, mostly of Nepali origin who migrated from India and Nepal over the years not only lived under restrictions of movement and residence, but also were denied due share in the political and economic decision making of the Kingdom. This was mainly due to the fears of the dominant Drukpa community that demographic expansion of Nepalese would eventually lead to their marginalisation within the Kingdom. The conditions of the Southern Bhutanese of Nepali origin, further deteriorated when rigorous policies of Bhutanisation, through the imposition of cultural and dress code (*Driglam-namza*) as well as citizenship qualifications, were carried out in 1988.

Repressive implementation of these policies precipitated violent reactions, conflict and refugees. Ethnic conflict in Southern Bhutan also carries political overtones, where the Nepali resistance, besides demanding protection of their human rights, also claim to be struggling for the establishment of democracy in Bhutan. More than 100,000 refugees have left Bhutan to seek asylum outside as a result of this conflict. Most of them, an estimated 85,000, have gone to eastern Nepal where they are kept in camps supported by the UNHCR. Approximately, 25,000 to 30,000 Nepalese of Bhutan have taken refuge in India's West Bengal and Assam. Whereas India is keeping quiet on this small number, Nepal has been trying through various diplomatic means to persuade Bhutan to take the refugees back.

Bhutan is not responding to Nepal's initiatives and asserts that before the question of repatriating any of these refugees to Bhutan is considered. It is necessary to ensure through proper documents, that they are citizens of Bhutan. The problem of the refugees is that many of them where not given citizenship documents and were pushed out of their dwellings in Bhutan through state repression.

India, Nepal and Maldives are the South Asian states that have not generated major refugee flows to their neighbouring countries as a result of ethnic conflicts.

In case of India, its democratic polity, secular state and federal constitutional structure, notwithstanding their respective limitations and imperfect practices, have given it considerable resilience to deal with ethnic conflicts internally. The examples of Tamil, Assamese, Punjabi and North-Eastern ethnic conflicts may be mentioned. These conflicts have not been fully resolved, but the capacities of the state system and the large size and diversity of India has enabled it to moderate these and keep them localised. The recent years have, however, witnessed signs of serious erosion in India's democratic polity and its secular thrust and the impact of this erosion is clearly evident in the rise of ethnic conflicts, communal tensions and caste conflicts.

For Nepal, the Hindu identity of the state has been far less assertive as compared to the rise of sectarian state in other South Asian countries. The religious and cultural alienation of minorities in Nepal has produced only limited and local ethnic conflicts, partly because there were other cushions available, like the selective co-option of minority representatives by the monarchial state and partly due to the undemocratic character of the Panchayat political order, which did not allow all political nobilisation at the grass-root level or along divisive identities. The establishment of parliamentary democracy under constitutional monarchy, in 1990 has stimulated such mobilisation, including of ethnic regional and religious-minority grievances, which if unattended properly may become major problems in the coming years.

Maldives is a very small island state with considerable sociocultural homogeneity and has, therefore, remained free of ethnic conflicts. Internal political conflict, such as the coup attempt on President Gayoom's regime neither involved the ordinary Maldivian nor forced him to become a refugee.

The incapacity to deal with the challenge of economic development has been a part of the distorted evolution, in the South Asian states. This incapacity has generated economic and environmental migration in the region.

Bangladesh is identified as one of the largest and continuous source of economic migrants, going mostly to India, but also spilling-over into Nepal. Bangladesh's poor economy, fast growing population and pressure on land seem to have encouraged such migration, most of which emanate from the Bangladeshi districts bordering India, such as Mymensingh.

According to the Western estimate, the number of Bangladeshi Hindus and Muslims coming between 1971 and 1981 only to India's Assam state as illegal economic migrants was nearly two million. Indian estimates put the overall number of these migrants at 13 million. The Bangladeshi government has neither formally accepted the fact of economic migration nor that they have any responsibility in the matter. The Indian government continues to resent this but seems unable to do any thing in the matter.

India's inability is also due to the weakness of its own political and administrative system where the border guards let the migrants go for small gratification and the local politicians in Assam and West Bengal have connived at the presence of the migrants for using them as vote banks in the areas that the migrants come and settle. India's attempts to find other means to check this migration like the proposed barbed wire fencing along the border and "Operation Push-back" have hardly been of any avail.

Economic migrants have also frequently crossed the Indo-Nepal border in large numbers, from both the sides. Not only this border is contiguous and long, but it permits free movement of the nationals of one country into the other under the provision of the Treaty of Peace and Friendship of 1950, between them. The Treaty also ensures 'national treatment' on 'reciprocal basis' for Indians and Nepalese in each others' territories. Such provisions have encouraged and facilitated economic migration.

Underdevelopment and deforestation of Nepal's hilly-regions have traditionally forced Nepalese to seek economic opportunities in Nepal's Terai region as also in the vast Indian labour market. A sizable concentration of the Indian nationals of Nepali cultural stock mainly Sikkim, West Bengal and the North-East has many times provided initial contacts and liaison to the Nepali economic migrants to India. There is no reliable account available of these migrants but estimates vary from 5 to 6 millions since India's independence.

The flow of economic migrants from India has been stimulated as a result of modernisation and development in Nepal which has been generating demands for skilled and semiskilled workers since early seventies. Indians have also gone to Nepal for teaching jobs and for sating-up small and medium sized business establishments. Irked by the growing flow of Indians into Nepal, the Nepali government set-up a Task Force in 1992-83 to look into the problem. Though, the recommendations of this Task Force could not be implemented due to political pressures and practical difficulties, but the government has continued to threaten to impose the condition of 'work permits' for the 'foreigners', mainly Indians. In the mid-eighties, the Nepali government also undertook a crude 'push-back' operation to deter Indian economic migration, but could not achieve much. There is an estimated strength of about four million persons of recent Indian origin in Nepal, but many of them have lived long enough to obtain or aspire for Nepali citizenship. The third category of refugee generating factors relate to the developments outside the region and the flow of extra-regional refugees. So far, such refugees have come from Tibet, Afghanistan and Myanmar.

The flow of Tibetan refugees into South Asia has been the result of Communist China's military action in Tibet during the fifties. The Tibetan struggle for autonomy and the Chinese actions to suppress that struggle have continued since then and so also the flow of refugees. The intensity of this flow has varied, depending upon the intensity of conflict in Tibet, which was most serious in 1959, when the Dalai Lama, the religious and political leader of the Tibetans, with thousands of his followers came to India for asylum.

Subsequently, Tibetan refugees have come to South Asia during the second half of the sixties when the cultural revolution in China caused extensive disturbances. Since 1988-89, Tibet's struggle for autonomy has picked up momentum agami, generating more refugees. There is no doubt that the question of Tibetan refugees in South Asia will increasingly come under sharp focus as the issue of Tibetan autonomy gains momentum in view of renewed international support. At the end of 1993, there were nearly 133,000 Tibetan refugees in South Asia, dispersed between India (119,000) and Nepal (14,000). According to Tibetan sources, however the number and dispersal vary.

Tibetan refugees initially came to India, Nepal and Bhutan, mainly because of geographical proximity and Buddhist cultural identity. However, internal political pressures and considerations of China's displeasure has affected the attitude of the host South Asian countries towards these refugees.

In the latter half of the eighties, the Bhutanese government asked all their Tibetan refugees, more than 2000, to leave the Kuwdom. This was the end of simmering suspicion since the beginning of the seventies in Bhutan's ruling circles that the Tibetans were involved in political conspiracies.

In Nepal also the attitude towards Tibetan refugees started changing since 1974, when the Tibetan Khampas were asked to stop their armed operations against the Chinese authorities in Tibet. In recent years, the Nepalese government's attitude towards the Tibetan refugees has hardened, where instances of forcible repatriation of the refugees and forcible prevention of new, incoming genuine refugees have been reported.

In India, Rajiv Gandhi's assurances to the Chinese leaders during his state visit to China in December 1989 that the Dalai Lama and his associates would not be allowed to indulge its political activities against China were resented by the Tibetans. Tibetan demonstrations against the Chinese Premier Li Peng, during his visit to India in December 1991 were treated harshly and there have been instances of clashes between the Tibetan refugees and local inhabitants in 1994 in Himachal Pradesh. The presence of Tibetan refugees in India may continue to be there, but their political fate and prospects of repatriation are closely linked to the changing dynamics of the Tibetan question and the Sino-Indian relations.

Following the Saur revelution of Afganistan in 1978, the Afgan refugee problem started in South Asia.Within a year and a half, the Taraki regime was overthrown by Hafizullah Amin in September 1979, who in turn was removed by the Soviet military intervention in December 1979. Between April 1978 and December 1979, an estimated 193,000 refugees had come to Pakistan to seek asylum.

The flow of refugees became much too large following the Soviet intervention and the Afghan resistance to it. By the beginning of the eighties, there were about 4700 Afghan refugees entering Pakistan every day contributing to a total of 3. 15 million registered refugees at their peak in October 1987. The flow of refugees was linked to the intensity of fighting and economic disruption caused.

Nearly half the total refugees returned to Pakistan following the Soviet withdrawal, completed between 1988 and 1990, but the renewed conflict in Afghanistan has not only slowed down the rate of repatriation, from 910,000, In 1992 to 358,000 in 1993, but brought a new influx, with the result that by the end of 1993, there were still about 1.5' million Afghan refugees in Pakistan.

The conflict resulting from the internal power struggle among the former Mujahideen groups has been further intensified in Afghanistan and since Pakistan continues to play a role in influencing this struggle, it cannot avoid being a host to the Afghan victims of internal war.

Many of the Afghan refugees who have established themselves economically in the Frontier Province and Baluchistan over the past decade may not even be willing to go back to an economically devastated Afghanistan. Pakistan's attempts to encourage a new militant force in the name of *Taliban* to stabilise the political situation in Afghanistan has not yet yielded desired results. Besides Pakistan, some 25,000 Afghan refugees have also been living in India since the early Eighties. These refugees, however, did not belong to the erstwhile Afghan resistance groups, and are therefore, likely to continue to be in India until lasting peace and harmony is established in Afghanistan.

Myanmar has been the third extra-regional source of refugees to South Asia. The flight of the persons of Indian origin from Myanmar during 1948-49, and during the early sixties has already been noted. Myanmar has also sent Rohingya Muslim refugees to Bangladesh. The first flow of such refugees came in 1978, in the wake of the Burmese army's operations in the Arakan region to check illegal migrants and fight insurgency. As many as 200,000 Rohingyas then sought asylum in Bangladesh as they did not have valid citizenship documents and were fearful of the Myanmar army. An agreement was worked out between Bangladesh and Myanmar, with the mediation of UNHCR to repatriate these refugees, many of whom also left for Muslim countries in West Asia.

The recent flow of Rohingyas to Bangladesh started during 1989-90, when in their pursuit to suppress democracy movement and control ethnic insurgences, the Myanmar military regime confronted Rohingyas, cleared them from their villages to establish military bases and forced them to provide 'unpaid labour' to the troops.' The number of Rohingya refugees in Bangladesh peaked at nearly 300,000 by early 1992, when the governments in Rangoon and Dhaka concluded an agreement for the repatriation of these refugees. The continuing fear of army excesses has deterred the Rohingyas from returning voluntarily. By the end of 1993, nearly 200,000 Rohingyas were still living in Bangladesh refugee camps." In 1994, the Myanmar government again assured to create conditions for the smooth return of the refugees with the help of UNHCR and it may be hoped that the problem would be resolved in due course of time.

If we look at the factors generating refugees in South Asia in a comparative context, we find that formation and restructuring of state boundaries as also the explosion of internal ethnic and secessionist wars, where massive military operations are involved affecting ordinary people (emergence of Bangladesh, struggle for a separate Tamil Eelam in Sri Lanka, and Soviet military intervention in Afghanistan), create mass exodus of refugees in the shortest possible span of time. As against this, economic and environmental migration is generally a slow process spread over larger time span, though the total number of people involved may not be small, as India, Nepal and Bangladesh movements suggest.

Two factors that facilitate the movement of refugees are the easy accessibility of the borders to be crossed and the sociocultural identity of asylum seekers with the host population. Both these factors were decisive in the flight of East-Pakistan/Bangladesh, refugees to India in 1971, Afghan refugees to Pakistan in the early eighties and Sri Lankan Tamil refugees to India during 1983-97 period. If the host people and the government support political cause of the refugees, as was evident in all these cases, then the refugees spread out in the host country fast and deep.

Repatriation of refugees has diverse and complex aspects, but what seems to be borne out by the South Asian experience is that sooner the cause of refugee creation is removed, the faster and easier is their repatriation. The dissociation of the host country from the political cause of the refugees also helps in their early repatriation, and some times, international agencies like the UNHCR and NGO's dealing with the refugees may help instill a sense of confidence and security among the returning refugees to facilitate their repatriation.

**Security Implications**

The security implications of the refugee phenomenon, have only inadequately been explored. Refugee movements are peoples movements and in understanding security implications of such movements, particularly in the Third World, a wider and comprehensive framework of security has to be followed, which incorporates riot only the fears and apprehensions of the individuals and groups but also at the levels of states, regions and international forces. Such a framework must also have reference points in political and military dimensions of security, as also in its economic, administrative and identity aspects. The security implications of the refugee movements need to be assessed in relation to the refugee generating *i.e.,* home state, the refugee receiving *i.e.,* host state, and external aspects of the home and the host states' security. The home state, by driving the refugees out, exposes itself to international criticism and embarrassment, pressures, and even intervention, for atrocities on its own people.

The two worst cases where the refugees have contributed to the insecurity of the host state in South Asia were that of East Pakistan in 1971 and Sri Lanka in the early eighties.

The Bengali refugees from Pakistan in 1971 formed the 'Mukti Bahini', fought against the Pakistani armed forces and facilitated the break-up of Pakistan which created the new and independent state of Bangladesh.

The Sri Lankan refugees in India and Western countries activated the Tamil Diaspora outside Sri Lanka which created tremendous international pressure on Sri Lanka not only oil the question of human rights violations in the UN and other fora, but also made it vulnerable to its international donors, demanding an early and peaceful resolution of its ethnic conflict. The Western countries continue to be keen on sending Tamil refugees enjoying asylum in their territories, back to Sri Lanka. Tamil refugees in India included various militant groups which reinforced their separatist struggle in Sri Lanka by exploiting their refugee status. These groups also appealed for and facilitated India's intervention in Sri Lanka in May/June 1987, which forced the Sri Lankan security forces to halt their operations against the Tamil militant groups, and also, consequently accept an agreement with India, which many in Sri Lanka considered as an affront to their sovereignty and national self-respect. In both the cases of Sri Lanka and East Pakistan, the critical factor was of course, the support to, and use of the refugees by the host state *i.e.*, India. In case of Bangladesh, its alleged connivance with the process of illegal migration of its nationals to India brought it considerable embarrassment with Indian responses like raising the barbed wire fence to stop such economic migration.

In case of Afghanistan, the refugees have presented an unusual security threat. Those of the Afghan refugees who were heavily armed and extensively trained to offer resistance to the intervening Soviet forces, have now tom the state and the country apart through their internecine struggle for power.

Security implications of the refugees in the host country are far-reaching and multi-dimensional. These implications are evident both in relation to internal as well as external security.

Regarding internal security, the presence of thousands, rather hundreds of thousands, and even millions of refugees creates conditions for destabillsation and disruption of political, economic and social systems in the host country. The extent and intensity of this internal threat, naturally depend upon tile number of refugees and their demands and expectations on the one hand and the size, nature and capabilities of the host state on the other.

For instance, during their peak phase, the Afghan refugees in Pakistan needed more than US $1 million even at the rate of '30 cents per capita, per day'. Not withstanding the extent of international support available, the host country has to share this burden in one form or the other. Even making provision of essential commodities to a large alien population may excessively burden economic and administrative capabilities. There are different ways in which the refugees strain the law and order conditions in the host country. To begin with, there are conflicts among the refugee groups due to variations in their respective socioeconomic strata, regional and clan loyalties, religious and ethnic identities and political and ideological predilections.

The variations among Afghan refugee group in their wealth and ethnic and regional loyalties, and among the Tamil groups of caste, regional and religious identities were well known. These Afghan and Tamil groups not only have undercurrent of tensions among them, but even indulge in open fights and street wars. The armed militant groups among these refugees also fought with each other to establish their respective dominance and leadership of the struggle back home. Tensions and fights among the Afghan refugee leaders like Hekmatyar, Dostum and Masood, and among the Tamil refugee leaders like Prabhakaran, Uma Maheshwaran and Padmanabha may be recalled.

The tendency of the refugees to indulge in petty crimes and thus become a part of the local underworld and criminal groups in the host country. Trafficking in drugs, arms and women, has been found to be a common feature of the poorer sections of South Asian refugees, including the Burmese Rohingyas in Bangladesh and the Southern Bhutanese in Nepal and India. Compulsion for doing this has come from their pathetic living conditions and inability to meet their basic demands from the assistance and support available in the host country.

Gun running and drug trafficking has been indulged on a large and dangerous scale by those refugee groups which have used the host country as a sanctuary in their struggle back home. Here again, the Afghan and Tamil refugees provide extensive evidence. This gun-running has led to militarization of local populations, the consequences of which have been felt for long time.

As a result of tensions and conflict between the refugees and the local people, destabilising impact of refugees is also felt in the host country. Such conflict emerges from competition for "common property resources" that have to be shared between the refugees and the local citizens in the areas of essential supplies and essential services, health, water, sanitation facilities, power and transport infra-structure and so on. Such facilities cannot be adequately enlarged to meet the demands of thousands and millions of refugees. In addition to this, the refugees compete with the local citizens in the job market, and since they are willing to sell their labour at cheaper rates in desperation, they displace the local citizens from gainful employment. Prosperous sections of refugees even manage to control local business by pushing out the locals. The control of transport network in Peshawar and Sindh by the Afghan refugees in Pakistan is well known.

Resourceful refugee groups get themselves involved in local politics for advancing their political and/or economic objectives. The changing alliances of the Tamil groups with the Tamil Nadu politicians not only intensified the DMK and AIADMK political rivalry, but also contributed to its violent dimensions. The Jamiat-e-Islami and PPP rivalry in Pakistan, with provincial dimensions of politics got involved with the Afghan refugee groups.

Similarly, the Nepali economic immigrants and political refugees, at least up to 1975, were involved in the political struggle of Sikkim's integration with India. They were also trapped in the political rivalries among India's Nepali factional politics in North Bengal and Sikkim areas, adding to the debate and controversy on the relevance and abrogation of the Indo-Nepal Treaty of 1950 which permits and encourages migration across the India-Nepal border.

The presence of ethnic refugees, particularly resulting from ethnic strife in the home country, exacerbates, consolidates and even politicises ethnic groups in the host country. This happens when ethnic identity of the refugees is different from, as also when it is same as that of the local population. The difference in identity makes the local populations conscious of their own ethnic characteristics and their rights and privileges. They also initiate reactive mobilisation in the fear that the presence of an alien ethnic group may result in the loss of their cultural and political control. This leads to the rise of sub-nationalist and 'sons of the soil' movements that, in the long run may threaten peace and stability in the host country.

Where there is a similarity in the identities of the refugees and the host country population, the latter tend to imbibe the sense of discrimination and deprivation, express solidarity with the cause of the refugee groups and in turn, their own sense of alienation from the State is stimulated.

The case of Sri Lankan refugees in Tamil Nadu provides a typical example of this, where the Tamils of Tamil Nadu have not only exercised considerable pressure on the Indian policy towards Sri Lanka on the question of ethnic conflict so as to make it supportive of the Tamil cause, but have also revived and reinforced their own identity and sub-nationalism. This has given rise to concern in India in view of a history of Tamil separatism. The solidarity of the Nepalese towards the refugees from Southern Bhutan in Nepal, and of Bangladeshi Muslims towards the Muslim Rohingyas from Myanmar fall into the same category.

When the conflicts of jobs, economic opportunity, ethnic identity and political approach with the host people become sharper, the refugee groups even turn against the host government and become a source of opposition and embarrassment to the latter. This combined with the resentment of the host population on account of or in relation to, the refugee groups create further difficulties for the host government.

The Zia regime in Pakistan lost its credibility and came under strong internal criticism for the consequences of Afghan refugees. Among the groups of Tamil refugees, the LTTE turned so much against the Rajiv Gandhi regime in India that they are suspected to be behind his assassination. There are allegations that in this assassination, the LTTE had worked in collaboration with the Punjab and Kashmir extremists. There have also been reports of the LTTE's networking and collaboration, including supply of arms, with other extremist and insurgent groups in India.

Refugee movements generate tensions and precipitate conflict between the home and the host states, creating problems of external security. This is particularly so when the refugees actively pursue their armed and/or political struggle against the home state from their sanctuaries and bases in the host country and they include in them, what has been described as the "refugee warrior community".

Continuation of such struggle activises international borders between the home and the host countries, and results in the violation of these borders through armed raids, either by the "refugee warrior community" or by the home state in its endeavour to control such operations through acts of 'hot pursuit', or attacks on the 'rebel' camps and refugee settlements in the neighbouring country. India as a host country has experienced such tensions, of varying degrees and at various times, with almost all of its neighbours. Such tensions between India and Sri Lanka have been complicated due to the fact of unmarked water boundary. Regular irritations between India and Sri Lanka resulting from the latter's naval action against Indian fishermen and fishing boats allegedly carrying arms and cargoes for the Tamil militants, in the Palk, Strait, have been experienced. Pakistan has faced serious violations and threats of the 'hot pursuit' nature from Afghanistan during the Soviet intervention period. Pakistan's borders with India in the Jammu & Kashmir and Punjab sectors have also been militarily activated by India to stop the flow of armed Sikh and Kashmir militants and their couriers.

In South Asia, there are also instances of the host country using force and activising borders militarily to stop the flow of refugees. Bangladesh's action against the Rohingyas in 1978 and 1992-93, and Nepal's action against the Tibetan refugees during 1992-93 may be mentioned here. In India has also used force on its borders with Pakistan, Bangladesh, Sri Lanka and Myanmar, in stopping the flow of refugees, illegal migrants and armed Militants. The border tensions and skirmishes resulting from refugee movements do have a tendency to create conditions for larger international armed conflict. However, refugee movements alone, and the concern for stopping such movements and repatriating refugees have not led to the break-out of full scale war between the home and the host states.

In South Asia, major bilateral conflicts have taken place with broader objectives behind, in which the refugee factor has been a significant, but not a sole and decisive consideration. For instance, in the 1971 War between India and Pakistan, the question of sending back nearly 10 million refugees weighed heavily on India, but, without the strategic considerations of demolishing Pakistan's two-nation theory, eroding Pakistan's military strength, asserting India's pre-eminence and helping Bangladesh to emerge as an independent nation in the larger interest of peace and stability in the subcontinent, India would not have been driven to a full-scale war with Pakistan.

In the case of Sri Lankan refugees, India's approach to repatriate them was dependent upon the resolution of the ethnic conflict in the island which could ensure justice to Tamils. It was to assert India's strategic and political stakes in Sri Lanka's peace, integrity, stability and nonalignment that India had to commit 'relief supplies' intervention in Sri Lanka (May/June 1987), goad Sri Lankan sign the Indo-Sri Lanka Agreement of July 1987, and send a peacekeeping cum peace-enforcing force to fight with the LTTE.

Again, in case of the Afghan refugees in Pakistan, the question of repatriating them was subordinate to the defeat of Soviet military presence. More than Pakistan, it was the US that set the agenda, in the context of the renewed cold war, for Pakistan's role in Afganistan. There were, of course, unrealistic but strong fears and apprehensions, shared by Pakistan that if not pushed back, Soviet Union was likely to Intervene in Pakistan in order to secure a warm water access to the Indian Ocean. It is unfortunate that developments like the withdrawal of the former Soviet Union from Afghanistan and the end of the cold war have not resolved the conflict in Afghanistan.

Generally, the security implications of the refugees movements are a part of wider conflicts at bilateral, regional and global levels. These implications grow in dimensions and complexity when a host state decides to use the refugees as instrument of its policy towards the home state, for political and strategic objectives. Accordingly, the host state not only shares and supports the cause of the refugees, but even provides arms, training and diplomatic support to them as was done by India in case of the East Pakistani and Sri Lankan refugees, and by Pakistan in case of the Afghan refugees. If the political and strategic objectives are strong and compelling, it even goes to war with the home state, along with the 'refugee warrior community'.

A number of security implications, both internal and external, of the refugee movements result from this strategic use of the refugees by the host state, either by itself or in collaboration with third countries. We mentioned the US role in Pakistan on the Afghan question. The US had also trained and armed the Tibetan Khampa refugees in the Mustan region of Nepal bordering China for their raids into the Chinese territory.

Strategic use of refugees result in spread of arms even beyond the targeted refugee groups. The huge quantities of arms supplied to the Afghan 'freedom fighters' not only contributed to the militarization of Pakistani society and its ethnic conflicts, but have also spilled over to fuel insurgency in Kashmir. Arms and training provided by India to the Tamil militants were not only used to have fallen in the hands of Indian insurgent groups.

In the process of using the 'refugee warrior community' the host against the Indian Peace Keeping Force in Sri Lanka, but also seem to have fallen in the hands of Indian insurgent groups. In the process of using the 'refugee warrior community , the host country cannot avoid alienating some of the member groups of this community, who even while receiving moral and material support front the host, may become autonomous in their functioning, This defeats the very purpose for which arms and assistance is provided. The attitude of the LTTE *vis-a-vis* India and of the Afghan Mujahideen groups *vis-a-vis* Pakistan are illustrative case studies in this respect.

The most serious of security implications have emanated from the incapability of the countries of the region to manage refugee influx on the one hand and conscious policies, on the part of both the home and the host states to exploit refugee movements for serving their strategic, political and economic interests. Some of the refugee groups on their part have also not hesitated to abuse the hospitality of the host state and exploit the prevailing tension/conflict between their home, and the host states to further their own objectives. While such policies have led the home and the host states to armed conflicts and even wars, the refugee groups, particularly the large bulk of innocent and politically inactive members, have suffered in various ways.

# 3

# STATELESSNESS IN SRI LANKA

From 1902 until 1948, when Sri Lanka achieved Independence, she was ruled by Britain. From the mid 19th century and more frequently during the 19th century Sri Lanka faced a steady stream of immigrants, mainly from South India linked to the British economic activity that prevailed at the time. In the 1830's British enterprises developed coffee plantations in the hill country of then Ceylon. Later towards the end of the 19th century rubber plantations were also opened in the midlands and the low country areas of the country. All this hectic economic activity necessitated an extensive and cheap labour force which Sri Lanka could not provide at that time. The most practical alternative was to obtain this requirement from nearby South India, which had a surfeit of cheap unskilled labour, ideally suited for the Sri Lankan plantations.

Several factors subscribed to this unprecedented migration. The principal advantage was proximity. Travel facilities were unrestricted, at least until Sri Lanka gained Independence in 1948 and difficulties arose over the preponderance of South Indian Tamils in the majority of the estates. Almost the entire South Indian labour force was Hindu by religion and were part of the joint family system which prevails in several parts of India. These workers left behind part of their families in South India and they were often obliged to send regular remittances to their dependents back home and invariably a substantial part of their savings were repatriated. They even undertook journeys to visit their kith and kin periodically. The short journey involved also suited the British plantation managers as in the event of any depression in the industry some of the estate workers could be asked to return. Conversely in the event of any economic distress in South India due to drought, crop failure or famine the scale of South Indian immigration would substantially increase.

Therefore what emerged at the very inception of South Indian immigrations was that the Indian estate workers lived a life of isolation in separate estate communities, cut off from all contacts with the surrounding Sinhala villages and never participating in their political and social life. It is also important to recognize that the estate workers from South India, who lived mainly in the plantation areas, were very different to the indigenous Tamil community of Sri Lanka who had left India many centuries ago and had become a vital part of the mainstream of Sri Lanka.

The dawn of Independence in both countries in the 1940's and the case of Sri Lanka the decision to reform; the Constitution. The first controversy arose during this reform which was based on the recommendations of the Donoughmore Commission which had proposed that a semi responsible form of Government based on adult franchise be introduced to Sri Lanka and that all existing forms of separate communal representation be abolished. Sinhala leaders had difficulties with the franchise question as it was feared that the introduction of universal adult franchise would lead to the unrestricted enfranchisement of Indian residents in Sri Lanka.

The second critical development was the depression in the early 1930's which seriously affected the plantations and created problems of severe unemployment. Sinhala leaders were firmly convinced that this was mainly due to the practice of free immigration from South India and throughout the 1930's began to exert sustained pressure in the State Council, as the Sri Lankan Parliament was then known, for the curtailment of estate labour immigration. Of course the British planting interests and even British officials circles did not support the view that such restrictions were either desirable or possible.

Therefore when Independence was achieved by both countries, India in 1947 and Sri Lanka the following year in 1948, the stage was set for a major confrontation between the two countries over this contentious issue often involving the Prime Ministers themselves. It is interesting to take note of the series of meetings that took place between the two countries during this period to try to ease this problem. The first was the Indo-Ceylon Relations Exploratory Conference in November 1940 followed by the Indo-Ceylon Conference in September 1941. Then followed an important meeting at the Prime Ministerial level between Pandit Nehru and Prime Minister Senanayake in 1947. This was mainly concerned with two questions. Firstly, who among the 80,000 Indian residents in Sri Lanka should be considered eligible for Sri Lankan citizenship and secondly how they should be admitted to such citizenship and what criteria should be adopted.

The Ceylon Citizenship Act provided for two types of citizenship, by descent and by registration. The provisions relating to citizenship by descent applied mainly to indigenous Sri Lankans and very few Indian residents could claim citizenship by registration with its rigid residence prerequisites. On the other hand, the Indian and Pakistani Residents Act of 1949 laid down somewhat less restrictive conditions for the grant of citizenship to the Indian community. Basically an applicant for registration under this Act had to possess the special residential qualification of continued residence in Sri Lanka before 1st January 1946 of seven years for married persons, ten years for others, occasional absence from the Island for less than one year not being deemed a break in the continuity of residence. In addition he was required to possess an "assured income of a reasonable amount" and prove that no disability rendered it impossible for him to comply with the laws of Sri Lanka. If married, his wife and dependent children should have been resident with him in Sri Lanka during the qualifying period of residence required by the Act.

India's reaction to the Act was very adverse and Pandit Nehru in his correspondence with Prime Minister D. S. Senanayake in 1948 found the Citizenship Act unacceptable. In fact the process of registration and investigation of applications became so slow and tedious that even by 1962 only 134,188 Indians had been granted citizenship under this Act. It was only in the 1950's that the aspect of "Statelessness" crept to this problem. From the very outset Sri Lanka's assumption, as enuniciated at the highest levels, was that those Indians who had failed to qualify for Sri Lankan citizenship were unquestionably Indian Nationals and the Indian Government would regard them as such.

The Government of India was clearly unwilling to accept this position. Although India had not passed a specific citizenship law until 1955 the Indian Constitution had made provision for acquisition of Indian nationality by overseas Indians under Article 5 of the Indian Constitution which stated categorically that only a person born in India, or one of whose parents was born in India or a person who had been ordinarily resident in India for over 5 years prior to the inauguration of the Indian Constitution would be regarded as an Indian citizen. Under Article 8, persons of Indian origin ordinarily resident outside India would be regarded as Indian citizens only if they were registered as such after application to the Diplomatic Representative of India in the country where such persons resided. Therefore conferment of Indian citizenship on overseas Indians was not an automatic process and this was in serious conflict with Sri Lanka's position.

However, behind the scene were some other serious reasons for these attitudes on the part of the two Governments. In Sri Lanka apart from the question of unemployment there were increasing demands, mainly by the members of the Kandan (hill country) community that the Indian workers were depriving them of their legitimate livelihood in the plantations. This was also frequently taken up in Parliament. On the Indian side was the situation that the Indian estate workers mainly hailed from South India and if repatriated would eventually have to be resettled there. This was a problem which the Centre in New Delhi could not unilaterally decide on without consulting the southern states, and centre state relations in India have always been bedevilled by such problems.

Another cogent reasons, which in fact Pandit Nehru explained to Prime Minister SWRD Bandarnaike, was that there were over twelve million Indians overseas in countries such as Malaya, Burma and South Africa and if India accepted the principle of repatriation as advocated by Sri Lanka the same concession would have to be extended to the Indian nationals in these countries.

In this climate of conflict and uncertainty the first realistic appraisal took place at the high level meeting on the Indo-Ceylon Agreement relating to persons of Indian origin in Ceylon attended by Prime Minister Sir John Kotelawala, Mr. Dudley Senanayake and Mr. SWRD Bandaranaike Leader of the Opposition among others which took place in New Delhi in 1954. For the first time at this meeting, illicit immigration between the two countries was taken up by the two Prime Ministers as part of this question. However even this Agreement lent itself to divergent interpretations.

The Sri Lankan Government continued to maintain that only two categories of Indian residents in Sri Lanka would emerge as a result of the Agreement, nationals of Sri Lanka and nationals of India. The Indian Government envisaged a third category of "Stateless persons" in addition to these two whose status would have to be further reviewed by the two Governments. After further debate and disagreement between the two Governments the Prime Minister of India, Mr. Lal Bahadur Shastri and the Sri Lankan Prime Minister Mrs. Sirimavo Bandaranaike, inspired by a mutual desire to explore every possibility of reaching an equitable compromise on this vexatious question of persons of Indian origin in Sri Lanka finally held a historic meeting in New Delhi in October 1964.

The agreement concluded on October 30, 1964 between the Governments of India and Sri Lanka provided that India would agree to accept, within a period of 15 years, as repatriates, 525,000 persons of Indian origin living in Sri Lanka with their natural increase, and that Sri Lanka would agree to grant citizenship to 300,000 persons with their natural increase. The estimated number of such persons was 975,000 on October 30, 1964. This Agreement also provide for a further supplementary agreement to grant citizenship of one or the other country to the balance of 150,000 stateless persons of Indian origin, with their natural increase.

The Objective of the Agreements was to ensure that all stateless persons of Indian origin in Sri Lanka be enabled to become citizens of one country or the other. The period of repatriation was phased over a seventeen year period so that on the one hand Sri Lanka would not be faced with a large exodus of plantation labour if the time frame was shorter and on the other hand India would not be faced with the problem of rehabilitating a large number of repatriates within a short period.

Despite the sincere and intensive effort on the part of both Governments to fulfil the terms of the Agreement there was ultimately an excess in the number of applicants for Sri Lankan citizenship and a shortfall in the number who applied for Indian citizenship. Therefore in the final count, 94,000 persons were reckoned to be in this category, who would have to be deemed stateless. In a spirit of accommodation and in a desire to strengthen bilateral relations Sri Lanka generously accepted this additional commitment of 94,000 persons which meant that Sri Lanka's eventual intake was 469,000 persons. On the other hand India gave an undertaking that they will grant Indian citizenship to all of the 506,000 persons who have applied for citizenship and repatriate them to India. This process is yet underway.

It may be of interest to briefly reflect on how these various changes affected the living conditions of these stateless persons of South Indian origin. As stated earlier, until the beginning of the 19th century, this category which consisted mainly of plantation workers did not encounter too many problems. Mostly illiterate, they lead a life of comparative isolation in their rather frugal estate quarters, with the estates also providing minimum facilities for children's schooling, health care and other needs. However they were content as their basic need of repatriating a part of their saving back to the rest of their families in South India and even periodic visits to their kith and kin were freely permitted.

In later years, with increasing resistance and even some hostility to their continuing presence in the plantations by mainly the Kandyan Sinhala community which was status, undoubtedly made their lives less comfortable. This was the time when there was progressive 'Ceylonisation' not only of employment but also of trade and industry. This was officially described as a process 'to ensure a higher percentage of participation by the nationals of the country in trade, commerce and industrial activities, as regards management, labour and finance'. However this did not materially affect the South Indian community which more or less confined itself to the plantation sector.

However by the 1960 and 70's, when the Indo/Ceylon Agreements of 1964 and 74 had more or less settled the 'Stateless' problem, the situation of the Indians in Sri Lanka, particularly of those who had since been conferred Sri Lankan citizenship, was completely normalised and they were treated not differently to those Sri Lankans who had acquired citizenship by descent.

A brief comment also on the political representation of the Indian community. The Ceylon Indian Congress (CIC) was founded was back in 1939 to protect the interests of the Indian estate workers in Sri Lanka. Incidentally Pandit Nehru visited Sri Lanka in 1939 as a special emissary of the Indian National Congress and he was considered one of the founders of the CIC. Perhaps due to the circumstances of its origin the CIC long retained marked signs of Indian influence.

The successful settlement of what might have been a continuing stateless problem between Sri Lanka and India was indeed a triumph for statesmanship at the highest level. After so many decades of difficult and often acrimonious debate over this question, agreement was finally reached between the two Governments at the highest level in a spirit of compromise that was indeed a good example of how the self interests of two countries, large and small, were made secondary to the larger interest of maintaining and strengthening good relations between two neighbours who had, up to that time, not know any other political problem in the long history of their cordial relationship.

A careful perusal of the statute book of Sri Lanka reveals the total absence of provisions with regard to refugee protection. The laws governing immigration and emigration are silent on this subject. Neither the Controller of the Immigration and Emigration (the Controller) nor any other official possess guidelines or authority to determine, refugee status, to provide protection to asylum applicants and refugees or to enforce the principle of non-refoulement. Only The Extradition Law No: 8 of 1977 marginally provides for this latter aspect by prohibiting the extradition of persons who may be persecuted on the basis of race, religion, nationality or political opinion. The final determination relating to non-extradition is to be made by the courts.

Although Sri Lanka has a relatively satisfactory ratification record with regard of international human rights instruments, it has not ratified either the 1951 Convention or the 1967 Protocol, relating to the status of refugees. As a member of the U.N., Sri Lanka is obliged to respect the protections guaranteed by the Universal Declaration of Human Rights (1948). However, Article 14 of the Universal Declaration merely recognizes the right of individuals to "seek and to enjoy in other countries asylum from persecution". It does not delineate the obligation on the part of states to provide protection to refugees.

The Convention against torture (1984) which was ratified by Sri Lanka in 1994 provides for the non-refoulement of persons to a country where the person would be in danger of being subjected to torture (Art 3). Although the Parliament of Sri Lanka adopted enabling legislation to enforce the Convention, it does not contain provisions to enforce Article 3.

In the absence of a legal framework of refugee protection, there appears to be an informal and *ad hoc* understanding between the Controller and the UNHCR to provide provisional protection to asylum seekers and those stranded. The UNHCR as been informally "permitted" to take care of such persons exclusively at its expense and to make efforts towards their repatriation from Sri Lanka. However, those who seek asylum cannot regularize their stay in Sri Lanka unless they can fulfil other legal recognized conditions for doing so. In the absence of grounds enabling them to do so, their stay in Sri Lanka although protected by UNHCR, is technically illegal.

Under the Immigrants and Emigrants Ordinance of 1948 (Cap. 2458 as amended) an alien (other than those aliens who are exempted by the law) aside from possessing a valid passport has to either obtain a visa or an endorsement by an authorized officer at the port of entry (Article 10,13 &14). Where an airliner is obliged under ICA/IATA rules to take back passengers who are not admitted into the country, then such persons will be sent back, usually to the port of origin, without affording them an interview with the UNHCR at the airport.

If, on other hand, an airline is not obliged to take those who are not admitted to Sri Lanka, the controller permits the UNHCR to interview persons so stranded if they request protection. If not for this informal understanding between the Controller and the UNHCR, all those who are not admitted into the country and who are not accepted back by the airlines will be subjected to detention by the immigration authorities. Sometimes detention can be, prolonged running into years unless UNHCR is informed of their plight and the need for protection.

Generally the UNHCR gets to know about persons needing protection from the airport immigration authorities, the detention centres at the request of the persons seeking protection or embassy staff and UNHCR officials who "discover" such persons at detention centres when checking the cases of others. The UNHCR states that the cooperation extended by the Controller in this regard is "excellent".

When the UNHCR takes over the persons seeking protection, UNHCR certificates are issued. They in effect operate as visas. All the needs of those under its protection have to be borne by the UNHCR. If for some reason a person receiving protection has a visa, and it has to be extended under prevailing laws, UNHCR has to obtain that extension as well, utilizing its resources.

The UNHCR office in Colombo is able in some instances to make arrangements to resettle persons in its care in third countries through the embassies of those countries in Colombo. Example are Canada, Australia and Switzerland. Aside from that process, the UNHCR submits cases to other countries through the resettlement unit of the division of International Protection at UNHCR Headquarters.

However, the available number of settlement places tends to be few given the world wide need. Those who are facing threats to physical safety, are medically at risk, are facing the danger of refoulement or are members of vulnerable groups receive priority in resettlement.

In the absence of a legal framework for the protection of refugees in Sri Lanka, provisional protection is afforded through informal and ad hoc arrangement between the Controller and the UNHCR. The latter has to bear the entire responsibility. This protection is extremely tenuous, as from a legal point of view those who receive UNHCR protection have no legal status in Sri Lanka. When compared with other countries in the sub-continent such as India and Pakistan, the number seeking protection in Sri Lanka is very small. Yet, the need for a legal refuge protection regime is palpable from a human rights and humanitarian perspective. If not for UNHCR intervention those who seek asylum or are stranded in Sri Lanka will be an unknown group of humanity left to wither in detention facing an extremely uncertain future.

The irony is that India and Pakistan have received and continue to provide protection to thousands of asylum seekers, albeit without having legal provisions or, process in place to determine refugee status and to provide for protection.

Given this situation, Sri Lanka should ideally

— ratify the international instruments for the protection of refugees

— at the same time adopt a legal framework to authorize and provide guidelines to a competent authority (i.e. the Controller) to process asylum applications and to make determinations on refugee status in accordance with international standards

— provide for a comprehensive protection framework including health care and schooling for young children entrench the principle of non-refoulement in the legal system provide necessary administrative infrastructure and facilitate coordination among various departments and ministries

— train relevant officials in how to handle refugee protection

In the long run, of course, what is essential is the creation of a social and political environment, through policies and educational activities, which is sympathetic to and respects the needs of refugees.

The high intensity military for the retaking of the Jaffna Peninsula meant that the logistical systems that had been temporarily in place during the period of dual control for the transport and distribution of food and other Supplies were initially disrupted. However by June 1996 the Government succeeded in effecting control over the entire Peninsula and security (subject to isolated insurgent incidents)—transport, health, education and food distribution systems are improving in operation. Both the ports of KKS and Point Pedro are now functional. The implications of this change in the political and economic environment is that the governments obligation of providing relief and rehabilitation to the displaced has become easier and more practicable to fulfil.

Although precise information on numbers and the condition of the displaced in the Peninsula is difficult to come by on account of the prevailing tight censorship on news and movement of media personnel in the North, it can be presumed that as normalcy is restored the condition of the displaced will continue to improve.

The work of UNHCR along with the ICRS, MSF and other International NGOs working in the Northern Province has been considerably disrupted as a result of the conflict in recent months and their services to the displaced have consequently been affected, UNHCRs activities in the fields, particularly after the liberation of Jaffna city by the military in February 1996 have been from Killinochchi but here too there have been restrictions on accounts of the delays in obtaining permission from the government, for high frequency radio transmitting facilities.

Security considerations of the government have taken precedence over considerations of providing facilities to UNHCR and other external agencies which would have had the effect of relieving to some extent, urgent needs of the displaced. Along with this has come an increase including the UNHCR which has proved restraining in terms of the expansion of the role of UNHCR and other agencies. While this may be deemed a natural corollary to the sensitivity that can accompany a long, fluctuating and not wholly successful military campaign against the LTTE, the widespread attitude of not trusting external agencies could have deleterious effects on the ability of, these agencies to continue the support they have been providing in protection and relief services to the internally displaced today and in the future.

An important issue, new in the present phase of the conflict, but one of the major consequences in the past, especially in the period 1984 to 1991, is that of the possible "spill over" of the internally displaced to South India as refugees. Such movement in large numbers has potentially destabilising effects on the bilateral relations between India and Sri Lanka. It has been the cause of friction in the past and can bring a new dimension to interstate relations in the future. According to official reports there apparently still remain in camps in South India about 50,000 refugees from Sri Lanka who went out with the out-break of hostilities in June 1990. Another 50,000 or so, are said to be out of the camps but yet residing in India. These are those who are not included in the repatriation which was conducted with some monitoring by UNHCR in the years 92,93 and 94. In these years the outflow was minimal owing to possibly three reasons; firstly the fact that UNHCR, a neutral party, was present in a practical way in overseeing the return and resettlement of returning refugees, in the overview of conditions at Welfare Centres and had initiated, in 'Uncleared area' the concept of the Open Relief Centres (ORCs); secondly, the fact that the Jaffna Peninsula which was under the virtual control of the LTTE constituted, at least for the Tamil internally displaced, a place of relative security (the Jaffna Govt. Agents Reports indicated that there were about 2,00,000 living in centres in the Peninsula who had moved in from the Islands and from Districts such as Mannar and Mullaitivu to escape the fighting in those areas) and thirdly, the fact that the then Tamil Nadu Government was strongly discouraging the entry of more Sri Lankan refugees and had even threatened to close down the existing refugee camps.

Especially having regard to the important position that the DMK has in the present Indian cabinet and the well known positive attitude of the present DMK Government of Tamil Nadu to the LTTE in the past, the possibility of the Tamil refugee question becoming a "casus belli" for straining Indo-Sri Lanka relations cannot be completely ruled out. Undoubtedly this emerging issues has also several implications for UNHCR's own role both as regards its protection of returning refugees when they are eventually repatriated and for those who remain internally displaced.

**Protection of refugees**

A careful perusal of the statute book of Sri Lanka reveals the total absence of provisions with regard to refugee protection. The laws governing immigration and emigration are silent on this subject. Neither the Controller of the Immigration and Emigration (the Controller) nor any other official possess guidelines or authority to determine, refugee status, to provide protection to asylum applicants and refugees or to enforce the principle of non-refoulement. Only The Extradition Law No:8 of 1977 marginally provides for this latter aspect by prohibiting the extradition of persons who may be persecuted on the basis of race, religion, nationality or political opinion. The final determination relating to non-extradition is to be made by the courts.

Although Sri Lanka has a relatively satisfactory ratification record with regard of international human rights instruments, it has not ratified either the 1951 Convention or the 1967 Protocol, relating to the status of refugees. As a member of the U.N., Sri Lanka is obliged to respect the protections guaranteed by the Universal Declaration of Human Rights (1948). However, Article 14 of the Universal Declaration merely recognizes the right of individuals to "seek and to enjoy in other countries asylum from persecution". It does not delineate the obligation on the part of states to provide protection to refugees.

The Convention against torture (1984) which was ratified by Sri Lanka in 1994 provides for the non-refoulement of persons to a country where the person would be in danger of being subjected to torture (Art 3). Although the Parliament of Sri Lanka adopted enabling legislation to enforce the Convention, it does not contain provisions to enforce Article 3.

In the absence of a legal framework of refugee protection, there appears to be an informal and *ad hoc* understanding between the Controller and the UNHCR to provide provisional protection to asylum seekers and those stranded. The UNHCR as been informally "permitted" to take care of such persons exclusively at its expense and to make efforts towards their repatriation from Sri Lanka. However, those who seek asylum cannot regularize their stay in Sri Lanka unless they can fulfil other legal.recognized conditions for doing so. In the absence of grounds enabling them to do so, their stay in Sri Lanka although protected by UNHCR, is technically illegal.

Under the Immigrants and Emigrants Ordinance of 1948 (Cap. 2458 as amended) an alien (other than those aliens who are exempted by the law) aside from possessing a valid passport has to either obtain a visa or an endorsement by an authorized officer at the port of entry (Article 10, 13 & 14). Where an airliner is obliged under ICA/IATA rules to take back passengers who are not admitted into the country (for lack of documents/ visa,), then such persons will be sent back, usually to the port of origin, without affording them an interview with the UNHCR at the airport.

If, on other hand, an airline is not obliged to take those who are not admitted to Sri Lanka, the controller permits the UNHCR to interview persons so stranded if they request protection. If not for this informal understanding between the Controller and the UNHCR, all those who are not admitted into the country and who are not accepted back by the airlines will be subjected to detention by the immigration authorities.

Generally the UNHCR gets to know about persons needing protection from the airport immigration authorities, the detention centres at the request of the persons seeking protection or embassy staff and UNHCR officials who "discover" such persons at detention centres when checking the cases of others. The UNHCR states that the cooperation extended by the Controller in this regard is "excellent". When the UNHCR takes over the persons seeking protection, UNHCR certificates are issued. They in effect operate as visas. All the needs of those under its protection have to be borne by the UNHCR. If for some reason a person receiving protection has a visa, and it has to be extended under prevailing laws, UNHCR has to obtain that extension as well, utilizing its resources.

The UNHCR office in Colombo is able in some instances to make arrangements to resettle persons in its care in third countries through the embassies of those countries in Colombo. Example are Canada, Australia and Switzerland. Aside from that process, the UNHCR submits cases to other countries through the resettlement unit of the division of International Protection at UNHCR Headquarters.

However, the available number of settlement places tends to be few given the world wide need. Those who are facing threats to physical safety, are medically at risk, are facing the danger of refoulement or are members of vulnerable groups receive priority in resettlement.

In the absence of a legal framework for the protection of refugees in Sri Lanka, provisional protection is afforded through informal and ad hoc arrangement between the Controller and the UNHCR. The latter has to bear the entire responsibility. This protection is extremely tenuous, as from a legal point of view those who receive UNHCR protection have no legal status in Sri Lanka. When compared with other countries in the sub-continent such as India and Pakistan, the number seeking protection in Sri Lanka is very small. Yet, the need for a legal refuge protection regime is palpable from a human rights and humanitarian perspective. If not for UNHCR intervention those who seek asylum or are stranded in Sri Lanka will be an unknown group of humanity left to wither in detention facing an extremely uncertain future.

The irony is that India and Pakistan have received and continue to provide protection to thousands of asylum seekers, albeit without having legal provisions or, process in place to determine refugee status and to provide for protection.

Given this situation, Sri Lanka should ideally

- ratify the international instruments for the protection of refugees
- at the same time adopt a legal framework to authorize and provide guidelines to a competent authority (i.e. the Controller) to process asylum applications and to make determinations on refugee status in accordance with international standards
- provide for a comprehensive protection framework including health care and schooling for young children entrench the principle of non-refoulement in the legal system provide necessary administrative infrastructure and facilitate coordination among various departments and ministries
- train relevant officials in how to handle refugee protection

In the long run, of course, what is essential is the creation of a social and political environment, through policies and educational activities, which is sympathetic to and respects the needs of refugees.

The high intensity military for the retaking of the Jaffna Peninsula meant that the logistical systems that had been temporarily in place during the period of dual control for the transport and distribution of food and other Supplies were initially disrupted. However by June 1996 the Government succeeded in effecting control over the entire Peninsula and security (subject to isolated insurgent incidents)—transport, health, education and food distribution systems are improving in operation. Both the ports of KKS and Point Pedro are now functional. The implications of this change in the political and economic environment is that the governments obligation of providing relief and rehabilitation to the displaced has become easier and more practicable to fulfil.

Although precise information on numbers and the condition of the displaced in the Peninsula is difficult to come by on account of the prevailing tight censorship on news and movement of media personnel in the North, it can be presumed that as normalcy is restored the condition of the displaced will continue to improve. A matter of concern is the reported damaged to housing in Jaffna as a result of the fighting in retaking the city which apparently has affected 80% of the homes Reconstruction work is in hand but transport difficulties, in the absence of a land route to the Peninsula, is a major constraint.

The work of UNHCR along with the ICRS, MSF and other International NGOs working in the Northern Province has been considerably disrupted as a result of the conflict in recent months and their services to the displaced have consequently been affected, UNHCRs activities in the fields, particularly after the liberation of Jaffna city by the military in February 1996 have been from Killinochchi but here too there have been restrictions on accounts of the delays in obtaining permission from the government, for high frequency radio transmitting facilities.

Security considerations of the government have taken precedence over considerations of providing facilities to UNHCR and other external agencies which would have had the effect of relieving to some extent, urgent needs of the displaced. Along with this has come an increase including the UNHCR which has proved restraining in terms of the expansion of the role of UNHCR and other agencies. While this may be deemed a natural corollary to the sensitivity that can accompany a long, fluctuating and not wholly successful military campaign against the LTTE, the widespread attitude of not trusting external agencies could have deleterious effects on the ability of, these agencies to continue the support they have been providing in protection and relief services to the internally displaced today and in the future.

An important issue, new in the present phase of the conflict, but one of the major consequences in the past, especially in the period 1984 to 1991, is that of the possible "spill over" of the internally displaced to South India as refugees. Such movement in large numbers has potentially destabilising effects on the bilateral relations between India and Sri Lanka. It has been the cause of friction in the past and can bring a new dimension to interstate relations in the future. According to official reports there apparently still remain in camps in South India about 50,000 refugees from Sri Lanka who went out with the out-break of hostilities in June 1990. Another 50,000 or so, are said to be out of the camps but yet residing in India. These are those who are not included in the repatriation which was conducted with some monitoring by UNHCR in the years 92,93 and 94. In these years the outflow was minimal owing to possibly three reasons; firstly the fact that UNHCR, a neutral party, was present in a practical way in overseeing the return and resettlement of returning refugees, in the overview of conditions at Welfare Centres and had initiated, in 'Uncleared area' the concept of the Open Relief Centres (ORCs); secondly, the fact that the Jaffna

Peninsula which was under the virtual control of the LTTE constituted, at least for the Tamil internally displaced, a place of relative security (the Jaffna Govt. Agents Reports indicated that there were about 2,00,000 living in centres in the Peninsula who had moved in from the Islands and from Districts such as Mannar and Mullaitivu to escape the fighting in those areas) and thirdly, the fact that the then Tamil Nadu Government was strongly discouraging the entry of more Sri Lankan refugees and had even threatened to close down the existing refugee camps.

Especially having regard to the important position that the DMK has in the present Indian cabinet and the well known positive attitude of the present DMK Government of Tamil Nadu to the LTTE in the past, the possibility of the Tamil refugee question becoming a "casus belli" for straining Indo-Sri Lanka relations cannot be completely ruled out. Undoubtedly this emerging issues has also several implications for UNHCR's own role both as regards its protection of returning refugees when they are eventually repatriated and for those who remain internally displaced.

Government Officials are confident that the movement of refugees across the Pak Straits will subside since food convoys have begun reaching the large groups of displaced civilians now scattered in various parts of the LTTE-controlled Vanni. The strict controls imposed by the South Indian authorities on the intake of refugees may also deter their flight, officials believe.

The movement of refugees by boats to Tamil Nadu has remained a trickle with only a total of 200 reported as landing on the South Indian coast in the past fortnight. A spokesman for the Indian High Commission in Colombo said that although the Indian External Affairs Ministry had issued a brief statement noting the arrival of some refugees, he was not aware of any move by Delhi to raise the matter with the Sri Lankan Government.

According to some Indian newspapers and agency reports, the Tamil Nadu authorities are being very strict in their processing of applications for refugee status by the 200-odd civilian's who have so far landed on the Rameswaram coastline. The authorities were being strict in their investigation of refugee claims because of the need to prevent any infiltration by cadres of the LTTE, these reports indicated. Meanwhile, government officials in Vavuniya said that a further 64 trucks loaded with food and other relief supplies have moved north through Thandikulam. Government officials in the Muilaitivu and Kilinochchi areas have now sent detailed reports to Colombo regarding the conditions of the nearly 250,000 civilians displaced in the, recent intense fighting in the Vanni region.

Details of the food, shelter and health needs of the refugees have been indicated and government and non-government relief agencies are now busy building up the relief operation required to cater to this new refugee problem.

Government has denied permission to NGOs and other relief agencies except ICRC to set up relief camps at places close to Kilinochchi where thousands of civilians are arriving everyday following Operation Sathjaya, a spokesman or an NGO said. It is three weeks since the last food convoys went past the Thandikulam checkpoint. Kilinochchi district has hardly any food or people. Last week, except for the ICRC, all other NGOs were not allowed to set up camps or deploy their officers to assist the fleeing refugees.

# 4

# Human Rights Situation in Nepal

It is difficult to place all the stateless persons in South Asia into neat little compartments, a general classification can be attempted as follows:

— *Rejected peoples*: Governments or dominant ethnic groups may expel from their country ethnic or religious minorities or to put it in a different perspective, make the life of the minorities so intolerable that for real or psychological reasons or both, they are compelled to flee the country for their safety and well being. To be more specific, the flow of Hindus, Muslims, and Sikhs between India and Pakistan after partition of the subcontinent can be mentioned in this category. One should also not forget the plight of the Tamils of Sri Lanka into South India, the flow of the Chakmas from Bangladesh to India, the "return" of the "stranded Pakistanis" from Bangladesh to Pakistan, and the Arakanese Muslims from Burma (Myanmar) to Bangladesh. In each of these cases the rejected people are "thrown" into a neighbouring country with the hope that they would be accepted by the receiving society that shares its ethnic identity.

*Political Flights from repressive regimes*: A classic example would be Tibetans fleeing from Tibet into Nepal and India after the flight of Dalai Lama in 1958-59, due to the Chinese takeover of Tibet. By South Asian standards the number of Tibetans fleeing their motherland was small-only about a hundred thousand. But the duration of the protest movement in Tibet and the insurrection that led the Chinese to crush the rebellion had a long term implication that affected the relation of China with South Asia, in particular, India. Mention can also be made of the Bhutanese refugees into Nepal since 1990, who number 87,303 (as of August 31, 1995), the Bengalis escaping the persecution of Pakistan in 1971 and the Afghans fleeing to Pakistan or Iran after the Soviet campaigns against the insurgents in the 1980s.

— *Unwanted migrants:* This category includes the peasants, labourers, retail businessmen, and the members of the middle class in search of land, employment, trade and investments. Two the largest and most persistent flows across international frontier in South Asia are from Bangladesh (110 million) and Nepal (20 million). Given the population explosion in both the countries this flow far fro ' m subsiding or leveling off, will continue to increase in the coming years. The Nepalis have migrated into the former semi-independent state of Sikkim, Bhutan and North-Eastern India. The Bangladeshis have migrated into the Indian states of Tripura, (where they are in a majority) and Assam.

The unwanted migrants have had social and political consequences in the receiving society and, thus, have disturbed the delicate relationship between the receiving and the sending countries. Thus, migration has created debatable questions of security and stability for the states of South Asia.

— *Internally Displaced Persons (IDPs):* In addition to the twenty million refugees in the world there are millions of IDPs. IDPs, though compelled to leave their homes, due to ethnic and physical - revolt, are living in their own country. Most of them constitute women and children. In South Asia their number is large. In Sri Lanka alone by the end of 1994 there were 128,852 families who were displaced due to ethnic violence. The IDPs do not fall under the jurisdiction of the UNHCR. Since the IDP is a problem common to all countries in South Asia a legal framework for the IDPs has to be devised.

**Stateless persons in the subcontinent and Nepal**

Nepal is not only a refugee receiving country but also a manpower-exporting one. Throughout history Nepal had surplus manpower which she channelized into three directions. First, the export of skilled artisans to build temples, stupas and icons in Tibet, Bhutan and Mongolia as well as China; secondly, the sons of her soil were made available in the Trans-Himalayan trade to serve as merchants (Newars, Thakalis) and porters from the ancient and medieval period to the turn of the century Thirdly, to work as seasonal labourers or semi-permanent and permanent labourers in Sikkim, Bhutan, or North-East India; or as soldiers in the British Indian Army. Nepali experience in the refugee problem can be divided into two categories: Nepalis migrating into north-eastern India, Sikkim and Bhutan and even Myanmar; and Nepali speaking people coming from north-eastern India, Bhutan and Burma.

**Nepalis in North-Eastern India and beyond**

The Nepali migrants (Rais, Limbus, Gurungs, Newars) in North-Eastern India, Sikkim and Bhutan were encouraged by two factors. First, the decline in Trans-

Himalayan trade by the turn of the century compelled the Nepalis, who had earned their living by this trade, to seek their livelihood elsewhere. Second, the Nepali migration in north-eastern India and the neighbouring countries was also encouraged by the British, who were establishing tea-plantations in Darjeeling, which required a labour force that was capable of working on steep slopes. In addition, the British encouraged the Nepali migration in Sikkim for they were convinced that a non Buddhist community in Sikkim could serve as a counter to what the British perceived to be pro-Tibetan British policy in that state designed to "open up" Tibet.

The Nepalis fitted both these criteria admirably well; and became a crucial factor in the rapid expansion of the Nepali community both in Darjeeling and the South-Eastern sector of Sikkim in the late nineteenth century. Thus, by the year 1990. The Nepalis had become the majority community in both the places though not the dominant force politically. It was, however, in 1990 that Kazi Ugyen Doorji was authorized by Tongsa Penlop to recruit the Nepalis as contractual labourers, to be used in clearing vast tracts of tropical forests and building roads. By the 1920s the Southern part of Bhutan had become a Nepali speaking appendage to the dominant Dzongkha speaking Buddhist polity.

Waves of the Nepali migrants also entered into the Southern part of the Brahmaputra valley (Assam). The British encouraged the Nepali migrants to settle in this area but not into the North-eastern section (present Arunachal). This area was prohibited to both Nepalis and the Christian missionaries because of its supposed strategic importance. The Nepali presence was also distinctly visible in the plantation of the Duars areas of the Assam state and the plains of the north Bangladesh that connect Bengal and Assam. From there they went to

Burma.

Both in Sikkim and Bhutan the Nepali community accepted the dominance of the Bhotiya eii-e and the center in exchange for autonomy at the local level. In 1971 the Nepalis in Sikkim engineered a revolt against the Chogyal regime and through the verdict of the referendum decided to join the Indian Union. In Bhutan up to 1980 the relation between the Drukpas and the Nepalis was more or less harmonious. As the Nepalis were important in the economy of Bhutan they were left to run things as they liked in the South. They also did not antagonize the local indigenous elite. Even today a little more than half the present-day population of Nepal proper lives and works in India; and their citizenship remains undefined.

**Return-of Nepali-speaking people from North-East India**

In the 1970s the "Sons of the Soil" movement emerged in most of India particularly in the North-east India, and also Burma. As early as 1948-49 most Indians had left Burma, for few were being granted Burmese citizenship. But the Nepalis remained there as usual. Another exodus of Indians took place from Burma in the mid-sixties, when the government nationalized trade, banking and commerce. At this time the Nepalis in thousands were also compelled to leave Burma. These Nepali-speaking Burmese came to eastern and western Nepal, bought land, built their houses and often clusters of houses which are today identified as "Burmali toles".

The movement known as the "Sons of the Soil" took such a turn in Meghalaya that by the mid-1980s the Nepalis were expelled from the land they had cultivated in the lower hill areas for four decades. Then, by 1985, the Nepalis had been completely forced out of Meghalaya and the other hill states like Manipur and Nagaland. These were the settlements just above the Assam valley and some of the Nepali settlements dated back to the

British Raj. New Delhi did not react to this development in the north states. The Government of India, under the premiership of Nehru, accepted the principle that the north-eastern states belonged to the tribes and that the "outsiders" should be allowed only with their consent. The Government of Nepal on these occasions did not create refugee shelter within the country and the Nepali speaking people who came from Burma and the north-eastern India, merged into the mainstream of Nepali national life.

The diaspora of the types of Nepalis extending from Bangladesh to Burma and the northern part of India with a heavy concentration in the north-east is very large-somewhere between ten to fifteen million. The citizenships rights of this group are very tenuous and controversial. These developments in the tribal hill-states of north-eastern India in the mid 1980s had their impact on the Nepali comnnunity[9] in Bhutan which constituted anywhere between 30 to 50 percent of the national population.

The Drukpa government of Bhutan has prohibited Nepali migrants since 1988. An earlier citizenship law of 1985 confiscates citizenship from the Bhutanese Nepalis by altering the definition of citizenship. It arbitrarily imposes an impossible to discharge burden of proof on one ethnic community (Nepali) while the other ethnic group (Drukpa) are exempted. By 1989 Bhutan had imposed the dress code, made Dzonkha the national language and restricted Nepali language in the southern schools. All this was resented by the Nepali -speaking community of the South. The success of the restoration of democracy in Nepal gave a new impetus to the democracy movement in Bhutan. It was the Bhutan People's Party that launched the pro-Democracy movement in Bhutan.

The government of Bhutan labeled the movement as "anti-national" and began its crackdown on the Nepali community of the South. The result was that Nepali-speaking Bhutanese started to pour out of Bhutan in 1990 and today they number over 100,000. The government of Nepal erected refugee shelters and it is in these camps that 87,303 of them are now living. UNHCR is administering relief to them in these eight camps in the Jhapa and Morang districts of Nepal.

The government of Nepal and Bhutan have entered into a series of dialogues since 1990 to solve the Bhutanese refugee crisis but the stalemate continues. On July 1994 Nepal and Bhutan agreed on four types of categorization of the refugees in the camps; (i) Bonafide Bhutanese, if they have been evicted forcefully; (ii) Bhutanese who emigrated; (iii) Non-Bhutanese people; (iv) Bhutanese who have committed criminal acts. Even if there is a broad agreement over categories I, III, IV, category II presents a formidable problem. Furthermore even if category II is resolved the problem of protection and repatriation of he refugees will still remain. Two other clusters of refugee-like movements in Nepal can be further mentioned.

One includes the flight into Nepal of Indian and Chinese asylum seekers, particularly those who are political dissidents, and regarded as~ national security cases in their country of origin. Another cluster, though not refugee per se, are special category aliens. This includes the immigration of people from India to Nepal for economic reasons. The existence of an open border between India and Nepal makes it almost impossible to control the entry and exit of this type of people. This raises the question of citizenship between Nepal and India.

**Citizenship and immigration**

The relationship between Nepal and India is unique in the sense that they are the only countries having an open border in Asia. This raises the question of citizenship, immigration and border control. Article 7 of the 1950 Treaty of Peace and Friendship between Indian and Nepal stipulates that the two governments "agree to grant on a reciprocal basis to the nationals of one country in the territory of each other the same privileges in matter of residence, ownership of property, participation in trade and commerce, movement and privileges of a similar nature. In the beginning Nepal considered the above provision to be a good thing for the flow of migrants from Nepal was greater than that from India. But as the flow of migrants from India increased Nepal started to impose restrictions in the treaty.

The Land Reform Act of 1964 prohibited the sale and transfer of land to any foreigner prior to the approval of the government. In Nepal, government employment was restricted to Nepali citizenship and the entry of non-citizen Indians in the private sector was also controlled. In 1980 the citizenship act was replaced by a new one which provided citizenship only to those whose fathers were citizens. Then in 1989 Nepal decided to issue work-permits to Indian nationals in the Kathmandu Valley. Even then there were three million Indian origin people living in Nepal; whereas there are more than ten million Nepali-speaking people living and working in India. Since both Nepal and India do not permit double citizenship the reciprocity given by the treaty has created uncertainty about citizenship for millions of people residing in each others' territory.

Even if we disregard the special case of the open border between Nepal and India in South Asia the borders in this region are porous for a variety of reasons.

— There are few natural boundaries that separate one

from another.

— It is impossible for any government to patrol their border effectively.

— On both sides of the border are people who share a common ethnic identity, thus, the individual who crosses the border melts within the local population. Thousands of marriages across the border make this task of assimilation easier.

— Countries of this region have no effective way identifying their citizens. Vital registration is not compulsory.

— The emigrants often have political allies who can prevent the host government from taking repatriation measures.

How Nepal and India will respond to the migratory flows into each other in the coming century will affect the entire spectrum of social, political and cultural relations between the two countries. Here the genius of leadership on both sides will be tested. As regards the solution of the Bhutanese refugee problem the following methodology could be considered.

— parties associated with this issue should take into consideration international norms concerning citizenship and immigration as they move towards a settlement;

— active input from the refugees themselves should be included during the negotiations;

— a third party (India) should be included in the bilateral negotiations between Nepal and Bhutan;

— internal reforms in Bhutan should be included in the package deal so as to provide the safe-return of refugees to Bhutan.

**Instruments to solve the refugee crisis in South Asia**

It is due to the population boom in South Asia that the refugee problem will get worse in the coming century. This will definitely undermine the security and stability of this region. What instiuments can be devised at the regional and international level is a question that deserves serious attention. It must be remembered that refugee situations are notoriously potent sources of international tensions.

The seen nation-states of South Asia have agreed on no regional or international instruments for the solution of the refugee problem. None of them have initiated national legislation or procedures for the management of refugees. True, the signing of the International Convention on Refugees by the South Asian states is an urgent necessity. However, the present mode of inter-state relations in South Asia is rigidly bilateral. The South Asian Association of Regional Cooperation (SAARC) must play a greater role in devising an instrument to check the migratory flows of populations across the international borders and improving conditions in the countries of origin so that refugees can return home and live in honour and dignity.

# 5

# Asylum in South Asia

The U.N. General Assembly urges the grant of asylum and observance of the principle of asylum, and states' constitutions and laws offer the promise of asylum, yet nowhere is the act of states defined". However, do the constitution and laws of South Asian Countries expressly offer such a promise? With the growth of nation states and the corresponding development of notions of territorial jurisdiction and supremacy, the institution of asylum underwent a radical change.

Today, it does not imply just a place of refuge but an equivalent right to give protection to a particular class or category of people viz. the refugee population. It has been observed that the right to grant asylum is to be exercised by the government in the light of its own interest and of its obligations as a representative of social order. Another writer further observed the freedom of each Sovereign State to deal with refugees 'as its domestic policy or its international obligations may seem to dictate.

However, the competence of States to grant asylum was settled upon the 'undisputed rule of international law' that every state has exclusive control over the individuals in its territory, including all matters relating to exclusion, admission, expulsion and protection against the exercise of jurisdiction by other states. "This element, protection granted to a foreign national against the exercise of jurisdiction by another state, lies at the heart of the institution of asylum".

However, the content of that grant of protection is not easy to determine—"whether it encompasses permanent or temporary residence, freedom of movement and integration or confinement in camps, freedom to work and attain self-sufficiency or dependence on national and international charity". However, an important factor is the close relationship existing between the issue of refugee status and the principle of non-refoulement, on, the one hand, and the concept of asylum on the other hand, the three elements being "links in the chain between the refugee's plight and his or her attainment of a durable solution".

Article 2 of the 1967 Declaration on Territorial Asylum, adopted by the General Assembly acknowledges that the plight of refugees remains of concern to the international community, and that where a state finds difficulty in granting or continuing to grant asylum, other states 'shall consider' in a spirit of international solidarity, measures to lighten the burden. However, the principle of non-refoulement has developed to include non-rejection at the frontier, thus promoting admission, but there has been no corresponding development with regard to the concept of asylum, understood in the sense of a duty upon states to accord a lasting solution and to that extent the principle of non-refoulement has become divorced from the notion of asylum. "The political and legal reality is that states generally have not undertaken, and foreseeably will not undertake, an obligation to grant asylum in the sense of a lasting solution". However, summing up the results of consultative meeting on refugees and displaced persons in South East Asia in December, 1978, the High Commissioner acknowledged that there could be no solutions unless Governments granted at least temporary asylum.

The plight of the refugee in search of asylum continues to be a dominant theme while in an era of mass exodus "State practice, however, permits only one conclusion: the individual still has no right to be granted asylum". However, the 1977 EXCOM conclusions [141 in its 28 Session (No.5 XXVIII) on "Asylum" noted with satisfaction the report of the High Commissioner that the States have generally continued to follow " liberal asylum practices". However, the said report also revealed that "cases continue to occur in which asylum-seekers have encountered serious difficulties in finding a country willing to grant them even temporary refuge and that refusal of permanent or temporary asylum has led in a number of cases to serious consequences for the persons concerned".

The Committee has further requested the High Commissioner to draw the attention of Government to the various international instruments existing in the field of asylum and reiterated the fundamental importance of these instruments, from a humanitarian stand point. The Committee has hence appealed to Governments to follow or continue to follow, liberal practices in granting permanent or at least temporary asylum to refugees who have come directly to their territory. Finally, the Executive Committee has called on Governments to co-operate, in a sprit of international solidarity, with the High Commissioner in the performance of his functions-especially with respect to asylum-in accordance with General Assembly Resolution 428(v) of 14 December 1950. After almost two decades of the said EXCOM conclusions on asylum and after four decades since the 1951 Convention relating to the Status of Refugees was adopted, what is the response of South-Asian countries?

The fact remains that not a single country in the sub-continent is a signatory to the said 1951 Convention or its 1967 Protocol. In fact, India had even earlier abstained from voting on the U.N. General Assembly Resolution which set up the UNHCR. Nonetheless, population movements including refugee movements have been taking place within the sub-continent over the years. What has been the approach of South Asian countries to migrants and refugees in the past and what is the present approach? In this connection, it is relevant to note that approximately 35 to 40 million people have moved across national boundaries in India, Pakistan, Bangladesh, Sri Lanka and Nepal since 1947, some as economic migrants and more as refugees.

The largest single bilateral flow in South Asia and perhaps the largest international flow in the world history was the Indo-Pakistan Refugee flow in 1947-48. In the past there has also been exodus of Burmese Indians to India, the exodus of Sri Lankan Indians 'and Sri Lankan Tamils, the issue of "Stranded Pakistanis" (Bihari's) when Bangladesh became independent in 1972, the flight of Burmese Muslims to Bangladesh and the flight of Bangladeshi Chakmas to India. Apart from this, the political flights from repressive regimes include the flight of Bangladeshis to India which numbered nine million in 1971, the flight of Afghans to Pakistan in 1978 and Tibetans to India. Further, East Bengalis began to migrate to Assam in search of land or employment towards the end of the 19 century. Again, the migration that resulted due to open borders as a result of the 1950 Treaty of Peace and Friendship between Nepal and India, and the resentment that ensued are factors to be looked into in examining migration movements. Similarly, in the early 1970's, the Nepali migrants to Bhutan ultimately outnumbered the ethnic Sikhmese.

However, all these past population movements in South Asia highlight one fact, that in the period following independence,' the approach to these migrants and refugees, by host countries, was one of passive acceptance and receptiveness, with a high degree of tolerance as they regarded even the refugee flow as a kind of return migration or an exchange of population associated with the process of state formation. On the contrary, unlike the prior population movements, the present international migration/refugee flows with South Asia are to a great extent not only considered unacceptable by these states but also perceived as a threat to the sovereignty, political stability and security of the host country.

While the causes for these movements are varied, varying from economic reasons to changes of governments and other ethnic conflicts, there are many dimensions to the problem which has global, political, legal, socio-economic and humanitarian implications. These influxes are inevitable and are only bound to increase in the future. In fact, even recently, in 1992, India itself was host to nearly 4000,000 refugees including Sri Lankan Tamils, Tibetans, Bangladesh Chakmas, Nepali refugees from Bhutan and further over 11,000 Afghan refugees assisted by UNHCR in New Delhi. On 24 August 1994, the Government of India stated in the Parliament that a total of 323,182 refugees were then residing in India. These figures do not take into account the refugees assisted by UNHCR.

Hence, the streams of migrations experienced by the South Asian nations continues. However, traditional migratory streams are now arousing the apprehensions of people, promoting them to oppose the influx of migrants into their areas is they pose to a threat to the peace and harmony of a nation, and also anticipating inter-ethnic conflicts. These influxes also have an impact on the maintenance of internal socio-political equation and aggravates ethnic tension. All these instances reveal one factor that none of the countries of South Asia have the capacity to control mass influxes.

The reasons being that they have porous borders, ethnic mix and other historical developments besides lacking the administrative, military or political capacity to enforce rules of entry. These factors lead to massive cross-border population flows which are perceived as a security problem. Cross-border population flows are mostly seen by governments of South Asia as bilateral matters affecting bilateral relations to be resolved within the sovereign jurisdiction of the concerned states and the attitude is to avoid internationalizing such issues. Nonetheless, with the exception possibly of India, where the cross border flows have been very massive, international assistance is required and requested in order to enable the respective receiving governments to cope.

In such situations, UNHCR becomes involved e.g. in Pakistan, Bangladesh and Nepal. With regard to India, the Government itself tackles cross border flows and does not allow UNHCR access to this population. However, with respect to asylum seekers and refugees from outside the sub-continent, the Government of India has permitted UNHCR to continue to deal with these persons but itself handles such persons with the framework of immigration/foreigners laws. Of course, if we took into the record of South Asian countries with respect to responses to mass influx, the-nature of rights extended to the refugee community and the manner in which governments have responded in each significant refugee influx, one would see that the response to asylum was tremendous. For instance in India since the 1950's over 1000,000 Tibetan refugees were granted asylum. In 1971, India gave refuge to 10 million refugees from East Pakistan. As for the treatment rendered to refugees inspite of economic constraints, asylum is provided to large population influxes looking into the general welfare, providing educational facilities, health care etc. However, in the matter of employment opportunities to the 1971 Bangladesh refugees from East Pakistan, the fear expressed was that "such employment will lead to social and economic tensions" with the host country.

> "The reason why the host system imposed such restrictions is easy to discern. It tried to minimize the deleterious impact of an immigrant population of such magnitude on its own system. Struggling to manage its own inner strains, the host system attempts to isolate the new problem rather than allow it to combine with the already existing complex problems. More specially, the evacuees were allowed to remain as a non competitive group in the economy, thus keeping the balance of the labour market undisturbed.

At this point of time, the State of West Bengal which took in 7 million refugees had unemployment to the tune of 2.5 million. This instance is quoted only to highlight the fact that inspite of being very responsive to the refugee problem, probably all countries in South Asia or probably abroad as well, may in similar situations act likewise. However, the same policy was not applicable to all refugee situations because the Tibetan refugees were issued certificates of identity which enabled them to engage in gainful employment and economic activities, probably due to the fact that in their case the possibility of repatriation was non-existent from the very beginning [25]. For various such reasons a like treatment is not meted out to all refugees spread in various parts of the country. In this connection, there is a need to formulate and pursue a policy of equal treatment towards different refugee groups.

The absence of a legal framework in this regard would give an unequal treatment to different refugee groups. In the context of a legal framework, a significant factor to be taken note of is that while the principle of non-refoulement is widely accepted in theory as a non-refutable principle of international law, there is the lack of simultaneous right to asylum. In fact State practice opposes this right as it contravenes state sovereignty. While the principle of non-refoulment is accepted, the absence of right to asylum gives rise to uncertainties in the legal framework for protection of refugees.

Further, though every country may claim to have never initiated a massive refoulement, it has been reported from time to time that means are adopted to either stop refugee flows or deter refugee flows or create within the refugee community a sense of insecurity or a situation compelling them to leave the host country or initiating involuntary repatriation. The entire problem with respect to asylum in South Asia rests with the fact that there is the lack of a legal framework for protection. As mentioned earlier, there is not a single country in the sub-continent which is a signatory to the 1951 Convention or its 1967 Protocol. Further there is no regional instrument relating to refugees, specific to the South Asia refugee situation or a specific refugee rights regime to govern the situation. Nevertheless, the Principles concerning the treatment of refugees have been adopted by the Asian-African Legal Consultative Committee. Probably regional instruments in these lines or modifications if necessary could be attempted. In an era of mass influxes could nations absolve themselves of responsibilities in this regard? To what extent do municipal laws respond to this situation?

In the case of India, Article 51 of the Indian constitution reads :

"The State shall endeavour to

(a) promote international peace and security

(b maintain just and honourable relations between nations

(c) foster respect for international law and treaty obligations in the dealings of organised peoples with one another; and

(d) encourage settlement of international disputes by arbitration.

Besides, the obligations under Article 51, foreigners or aliens also come within the ambit of Article 21 of the Indian Constitution which reads:

> "No person shall be deprived of his life or personal liberty except according to procedure established by law."

This provision which is meant to ensure a life with human dignity is applicable to foreigners as well, but, as observed by the Supreme Court of India.

> "The fundamental right of the foreigners is confined to Article 21 for life and liberty and does not include the right to reside and settle in this country, as mentioned in Article 19(l)(c) which is applicable only to citizens of this country. "

However, India has acceded to the two 1966 Covenant on Civil and Political Rights and Economic, Social and Cultural Rights, which do contain provisions relevant to the rights for refugees, though the said Convenants have not been enacted with the Municipal Law and are therefore not enforceable in a Court of Law, though that does not absolve or relieve India of its international obligations under the Covenant. Similarly, Article 22 of the Convention on the Rights of the Child, 1922, deals with refugee children and India has acceded to this Convention. Further, most of the refugee rights find a place in the category of human rights and concepts of Human Rights has been accepted in principle and is reflected in the establishment of a National Human Rights Commission in India.

The present emphasis on the 'right to remain' advocated by the United Nations High Commissioner for Refugees has its basis in the general human rights law. However India, as other South Asian Countries, has not to date enacted any refugee specific legislation to regulate the 'entry and status of refugees or to spell out the rights or probably even duties of a refugee while in a host country, as a result of which refugees are treated under the law applicable to foreigners or aliens in general. It is to be noted and appreciated that the position of a refugee is to be distinguished from that of other aliens.

The traumatic conditions in which they are while fleeing from their country of origin, the accompanying hardships they face, their vulnerability and insecurity requires a specific treatment - organized and structure and hence a specific legislation also relating to treatment of refugees in clear and precise terms. There is a need to safeguard the rights and interests of refugees instead of giving room for the vagrancies of politics, and in this regard, to enact a refugee specific legislation or a refugee rights regime.

Similarly there are no refugee status determination structures administered by governments within the sub-continent. "Large groups of asylum seekers are granted refuge under policy/ administrative procedures. Those granted refuge have normally originated from countries within the sub-continent or having the same ethnic/religious background as the host country's population and also geopolitical factors have played a vital role in the granting of refuge". While in the case of asylum seekers of other nationalities, usual immigration laws apply and in this regard, the UNHCRs role is emphasized and essential in promoting asylum e.g. in the case of Iranians, Somalians, Iraqis and Afghans.

The historical background with respect to asylum in South Asia, would reveal that in the past refuge was granted at times in the sense of permanent asylum, as in the case of the Hindus from West Pakistan in India and Muslims from India in Pakistan. Besides these movements which were result of historical and political developments, even Tibetans were granted almost a kind of a permanent asylum in India. However, the present trend, attitude and approach towards migratory and refugee movements have changed considerably and more recently only temporary asylum is the practice, if at all granted. Generally, having been granted temporary asylum "fundamental protection" is provided and there is usually no risk of massive refoulement, though "integration based" rights are not accorded.

However, an acceptance of the principle on non-refoulment without an express acceptance of the 'right to asylum' renders the former principle as a meaningless concept of law. Thousand of refugees cramped into camps without the privilege of certain other basic rights rendered the life of a refugee as one of trauma and frustration. These refugees reside in camps awaiting repatriation. Nonetheless de facto situations vary from one country to another in the sub-continent and where the ethnicity of the refugee population is the same as the local population or at least not too dissimilar, a greater potential for local integration exists e.g. Nepali, Bhutanese in Nepal, Pashtoon in Pakistan.

Given that granting of asylum, to large groups with the sub-continent has never been dictated b whether such groups fall within the refugee criteria, the promotion of standards of treatment would not be dependent on whether the group of persons are recognized as refugees but on factors Such as ethnicity and geopolitical considerations as perceived by the host governments concerned. Furthermore to promote "lesser" standards of treatment for non-criteria refugees in the Subcontinent where potential for local integration exists, will seriously jeopardize standards set in the Convention, the accession to which UNHCR is promoting with the sub-continent. The question remains with respect of asylum-seekers of other national groups determined to be refugees under the mandate of UNHCR.

Differential treatment already exists in the way the host government treats individual refugees recognized under the UNHCR mandate and those of mass influxes from neighbouring states. With respect to the former, their non-recognition before the law and uncertain status renders them open to risk of penalization for illegal entry and expulsion whilst there is a greater measure of fundamental protection with respect of the latter. Hence, any regional instrument under which countries of the sub-continent may set common minimal standards of treatment for refugees should highlight the plight of mandate refugees whose status are governed by immigration laws. The question is why are the South Asian countries reluctant to accede to the 1951 Convention? Besides the issue of porous borders and the lack of administrative, military or political capacity to enforce rules of entry, as mentioned earlier in South Asia any refugee influx or population movement is regarded as having an impact on the internal security, political stability and the socio-economic balance of a country, with the indigenous population becoming a minority in their own land. Hence governments in South Asia seem to consider these issues as a matter of bilateral and not multinational relations.

India has further been reluctant to accede to the Convention as they justify the stand that they have in the past and present been accepting and willing to host refugees. They have further permitted UNHCR to open an office in New Delhi. Some of the developing nations, however, perceive the rights incorporated in the 1951 Convention as being unrealistic. However, in such instances, the reservation clause of the Convention could be invoked, as discretionary powers according to international refugee law would still be vested in the State on being a signatory to the Convention.

However, there is a possibility of India reviewing its position in this regard. Nevertheless, India and Bangladesh have taken the initiative to become members of the Executive Committee of the UNHCR. The fact remains that South Asian countries have to reconsider the issue of accession to the 1951 Convention in order to promote humanitarian standards vis-a-vis refugee problems. Further, the South Asian countries could independently or jointly consider the enactment of regional instruments which are refugee specific.

The future direction could be towards a "right to a durable solution" and guidelines could be laid down with respect to temporary protection and/or permanent stay, along with laying down of standards of treatment for refugees considering the fact that the absence of a legal framework for protection would give rise to uncertainties. In situations of large-scale influx the views expressed at the 1981 EXCOM conclusions (at its 32 Session) could be taken as guidelines, considering the fact that such mass influxes are inevitable and bound to occur in south Asian countries, as much at the global level, in the future.

In many instances regional approaches have been an important means of strengthening refugee protection as well as finding solutions to refugee problems, taking into account both the opportunities as well as constraints which exist at the regional level, but which may not be fully appreciated or relevant at the global level. Countries in Africa, Europe and Central America have both acceded to the international instruments and also developed regional treaties or other declarations to meet specific concerns.

The countries of Southeast Asia have, like those in South Asia, largely avoided accession to the 1951 *Refugee Convention* and/or 1967 *Protocol*, but nevertheless took a regional and multilateral approach to resolve the long-standing problem of Indochinese refugees. The most recent effort at adopting a regional approach was undertaken by the Commonwealth of Independent States (CIS) in the context of a conference in 1996 on Refugees, Migrants and Displaced Persons under the auspices of UNHCR.

More specifically, these various approaches can be described as follows.

***(i) Legally binding instruments:***

Legally binding instruments which have adopted a regional approach include the OAU *Convention governing Specific Aspects of the Refugee Problem in Africa (1969)*, and in Europe, the *Schengen* and *Dublin Agreements (1985* and 1990 respectively). Both treaties were sponsored by regional organisations, in one case the OAU and in the other the European Union, and both, were made possible by strong political consensus on the issues. In the case of

Africa, the OAU Convention seeks to broaden the definition of 'refugee' to include those fleeing apartheid, decolonisation and generalised violence. It also emphasises voluntary repatriation as an important solution to refugee problems in Africa.

The Dublin and Schengen Agreements on the other hand were drafted in order to harmonise European practices and procedures relating to asylum seekers so as to ease the removal of internal borders of the European Union. The Central American region chose to take the path of a non-binding declaration because governmental consensus was lacking in the Organisation of American States (OAS) on a regional convention on refugees. Different legal traditions prevail in different parts of the region (Latin America believes in the principle of diplomatic asylum which is not recognised elsewhere). Also the United States, being an immigrant country has a different approach to receiving refugees compared to other OAS members.

The *Cartagena Declaration* was thereby a product primarily of the non-governmental process, yet it recognized the concerns of the region and reflected consensus or practices and policies in the region to such an extent that Governments have tended to follow it as a matter of policy, even though it is not legally binding on them.

Another example of a non-binding instrument is the *1966 Bangkok Principles concerning the Treatment of Refugees* adopted by the Asian-African Legal Consultative Committee which is an inter-governmental body. Because of the advisory nature of the AALCC and the divergence among the member countries of Africa, the Middle East and Asia who comprise the AALCC, the Bangkok Principles have had less of an impact and they remain of value as the only regional refugee document applicable to Asia. However, recently interest in the Bangkok Principles has been revived and currently the text is being examined by the AALCC membership.

### *Operational arrangements*

A third approach has been to develop regional arrangements related to specific refugee problems, such as the Comprehensive Plan of Action for Indo-Chinese Refugees in Southeast Asia (CPA) and the International Conference on Central American Refugees (CIREFCA). Both agreements were reached by the Governments concerned, together with UNHCR, regarding long-standing refugee problems in the region. Their main purpose was to solve the refugee problems in a comprehensive manner, including addressing root causes, providing effective protection to refugees and displaced persons and achieving durable solutions to their plight. Because they related to specific refugee problems they did not necessarily establish a regime for dealing with future refugee problems.

However, they created a precedent for regional co-operation which bodes well for the future. The CIS Conference not only tried to resolve existing problems, but also set out to establish principles, procedures and programmes to manage future population movements. Like the CPA and CIREFCA it is heavily based on co-operation between the international community and countries in the region because the latter realise that they do not have the means to tackle the issues by themselves.

## South Asian approach towards a regional arrangement

South Asian countries have experienced large-scale refugee flows from outside the region as well as from within the region. However, these problems have been handled by the Governments in an ad hoc manner on the basis of administrative policy. None of the countries in the SAARC region have signed the 1951 *Convention relating to the Status of Refugees* or the 1967 *Protocol.* Nor have they adopted national laws or a regional instrument governing refugees.

Generally speaking, there has been little movement to develop a legal framework because accession to human rights instruments and constitutional guarantees, combined with a generous asylum policy and a lenient attitude of the judiciary, have provided some protection to refugees and created a good humanitarian record for the region. However, experience has shown that the protection of refugees has been precarious in the absence of legal principles. Moreover, the failure of the law to distinguish between refugees and other foreigners (especially economic migrants) have also led to in some cases inconsistent treatment among refugee groups and sometimes detention and even deportation and *refoulement* of refugees.

South Asian Governments have preferred to deal with refugees on an *ad hoc* basis because it provides them flexibility without which they could not find solutions to sensitive refugee problems affecting regional stability and national security. Most of the refugees in the region are from neighbouring countries, e.g. refugees moving from Sri Lanka to India, from Bangladesh to India, from Myanmar to Bangladesh, or from Afghanistan to Pakistan. As such, the refugee problem is a major factor in bilateral relations between the host/asylum and home countries. Furthermore, because of the ethnic affinities between the host community and refugees in many cases e.g. Sri Lankan Tamil refugees in Tamil Nadu, Afghan Pashtoons in Pakistan or Bhutanese refugees of Nepali origin in Nepal, the response to the refugee problem has been determined by domestic politics as well as foreign policy.

While an *ad hoc* approach to refugees may have been acceptable in the past for a variety of reasons, a new climate of co-operation among the states in the SAARC region supports consideration of developing an approach on refugees based on commonly accepted principles and practices in the region. Among the factors favouring this approach are the following:

The Indian sub-continent will continue to witness large scale population movements. Socioeconomic factors such as poverty, population growth, environmental degradation, natural disasters, combined with ethno-political conflicts, are uprooting large numbers of people in the region. Because of open borders between India, Nepal and Bhutan, and the difficulty of controlling borders between India and Bangladesh and India and Sri Lanka, large numbers of people are on the move which impacts on the social, cultural and political relations of the countries involved. Such issues may thereby require a longer-term, comprehensive response which by their very nature will build upon co-operation and co-ordination on a regional basis.

Due to the complex mix of refugees, economic migrants, displaced and stateless persons, criteria need to be developed to distinguish the different groups and ensure appropriate responses to different groups. In this regard, national legislation may not be adequate without a common approach among all the countries.

Further, there may be sufficient commonality of problems, policies and practices among the SAARC countries to develop a regional approach. All states in the region are affected by the refugee problem, the problems straddle borders and sometimes affect more than two states. At the same time, South Asia has a rich humanitarian tradition. All countries in the region have received refugees and they have sought to find solutions to the refugee problems, most commonly through voluntary repatriation. Moreover, they share similar legal and administrative systems.

A regional approach may allow South Asia to address its specific concerns on refugee issues. One of the main complaints of South Asian states about the international refugee instruments is that they are inadequate to cope with the particular problems of the region. For instance, due to the complex mix of reasons which underlie population movements in South Asia it is sometimes difficult, if not impossible, to apply the international refugee definition. Again, due in part to the absence of compulsory birth registration in the subcontinent, issues of statelessness have arisen which are peculiar only to this part of the world. These are concerns which could be addressed regionally.

The options available to the states in the SAARC region would include: (a) Accession to the 1951 Convention and/or the Protocol (probably not a good option keeping in mind the developments over a period of time); (b) A domestic legislation to be enacted keeping in mind the specific problems as well as the magnitude of the problem; (c) A regional declaration which is not binding but would give the necessary direction to the state parties; (d) A regional convention based on the rich experiences and the culture of the region; and (e) Any combination of the above. The efforts should be taken to initiate discussion in this direction so that some action or the other would result by the beginning of the next millennium.

A regional approach could improve the prospect for solutions and better co-operation. Some of the initiatives taken at the SAARC for economic co-operation as well as in other fields have shown a positive political will from states in the region. This impetus could be geared towards the refugee issue in order to develop consensus on the principles guiding the search for solutions in the region.

The Informal Consultation on Refugee and Migratory Movements in South Asia has established itself as an important regional forum for discussing refugee issues. The group could consider the following steps:

A. The Consultation could adopt a non-binding declaration on refugees reflecting the practice in the SAARC region along the lines of the *Cartagena Declaration.*

B. Since any regional approach will require the support of governments, the Consultation may wish to consider ways of encouraging interaction between the Consultation and concerned Governments.

C The only governmental regional forum in South Asia is SAARC and the Consultation may wish to consider whether, and if so, how the refugee issue could be put on the SAARC agenda.

D. Greater public awareness and support will be essential to generate interest among the Governments. The Consultation may wish to consider how regional co-operation on refugee issue and could be fostered, for instance, through the media, professional bodies, academic exchange, information sharing, and seminars.

Once any of the above becomes a reality, the national legislation enacted by the states respectively would have greater relevance and provide a meaningful support to the international principles conditioned by regional objectives and necessities.

# 6
# HUMAN RIGHTS SITUATION IN BANGLADESH

**Introduction**

In 1978 about 200,000 refugees crossed into Bangladesh to flee illegal persecution by the Myanmarese army in the Arakan region. Their stay in Bangladesh at that time was short- lived as the problem was resolved through diplomatic initiatives in sixteen months. The situation is somewhat different this time when about a quarter of a million of refugees took-shelter in the Teknaf-Cox's Bazar region. Following the successful completion of the Cambodian operation the Rohingya repatriation constitutes the single largest UNCHR operation in Asia.

In spite of the Bangladesh Government's agreement with the Myanmar authorities and UNHCR's Memorandum of Understanding with both the governments on repatriation, initial steps in the repatriation have been rather slow. Currently the repatriation process has virtually stagnated. The presence of such a large number of refugees, which at one stage appeared to be for an indefinite period, has created tensions in the host communities and impacted adversely the economy and environment of the region. It is in this setting that a study on the Rohingya refugees is being undertaken. The study has three major parts. The first part will attempt to identify the root causes of the refugee problem.

The backwardness and the remoteness of the Rakhine region in Myanmar, the communal tension that exists between the Buddhist and the Muslim populations and the state sponsored repression are some of the obvious reasons that have led to occasional exodus of the Rohingyas from their normal place of habitat. All these will be examined in the context of a complex interaction and cross-migration of the peoples of the Arakan-Cox's Bazar region over the last few centuries. It may be argued that, like a dozen of other sub-national groups in Myanmar, the Rohingyas also failed to be integrated in the mainstream Myanmar nation-building project and continue to be a marginalised community in the remote region of Arakan.

Thus the feeling of alienation of the Rohingyas towards the Myanmarese state and the attitudes and policies of the successive Myanmar governments will constitute important elements of this part. The second part will deal with the question of treatment of refugees by the Bangladesh Government. Although Bangladesh is not a signatory to the 1951 Convention, its acceptance of the Universal Declaration of Human Rights of 1948 and its own experience in the liberation was, when one out of every seven Bengalis was a refugee in India, the nation has a moral responsibility to uphold the basic rights of the refugees.

Ever since the arrival of the Rohingya refugees, the Bangladesh Government has provided relief and shelter to these people. In this effort non-governmental organizations, both national and international, and UNHCR have provided crucial support to the Bangladesh authorities in coping with a crises of such magnitude. In spite of the humanitarian assistance rendered to the refugees, a major policy consideration of the Bangladesh authorities has been their quick and safe return' to Myanmar. This part will evaluate the treatment of the refugees by the Bangladeshi authorities with the aim of suggesting improvements, should there be any recurrence of such phenomena. The third part will deal with the question of repatriation. An important consideration would be the issue of voluntariness. UNHCR has been actively engaged in organizing the repatriation of refugees.

The chapter will identify issues and constraints of the Bangladesh Government-UNHCR-NGO collaboration with respect to the repatriation of those refugees. This will be followed by an examination of change in circumstances with respect to refugees under international law.

*Methodology*

The historical account of the region will be based on secondary sources. For the second and third parts, text of the Bangladesh-Myanmar Agreement on refugee repatriation, texts of the Memoranda of Understanding between UNHCR and Bangladesh, UNHCR and Myanmar, unclassified papers of UNHCR, the Ministry of Foreign Affairs and parliamentary proceedings on the refugee question in Bangladesh, comprise important primary sources. Interviews of the refugee representatives, officials of the various ministries, the UNHCR at Dhaka and field levels in Cox's Bazar and Maungdaw, and NGO's involved in relief and repatriation would provide important insights.

Newspaper reports, journal articles and in-house research reports of aid agencies constitute an important secondary source of information for the study.

***Arakan in historical perspective***

Arakan province is a long stretch of land along Myanmar's coastline in the Bay of Bengal. The northern tip of the region adjoins Bangladesh and there is 176 miles of common border between the two countries. The Naf river separates the two countries. The Arakan Yoma mountain range separates the region from the mainland Myanmar.

Historically, it had more interaction with the west, i.e. the region now comprising Bangladesh. Needless to say over the last thousand years the expanse of land that now covers Chittagong has changed hands a good number of times between the feuding warlords and kings of adjoining regions of Bengal, Tripura and Arakan. Historian Phayre (1884) was of the opinion that Arakan has continued to remain as an independent kingdom until it was annexed by Burma in 1784 AD.

While the Arakanese scholars argue that it was the Aryans from the west who were the first settlers of Arakan the majority opinion of scholars is that the first settlers of Arakan were those of Kanyan tribe of Tibeto-Burman group (Maung, 1989: 2). Of all the kingdoms and dynasties that ruled over parts of Burma the Arakanese have the longest history stretching back to 266 B.C. The Arakanse were basically animists. Over the centuries Brahamanism, Buddhism and Islam shaped and influenced their religious beliefs, as they did over the Burmans. As early as the first century AD the installation of the famous *Image of Mahamuni* in Dinnyawati, the then capital of Arakan, testifies to the influence of Buddhism. Between 788 to 957 AD the adding of suffix of Chandra to the names of the Arakanese kings, and the image of the trident of Shiva on the coins issued by them, suggest dominance of Hinduism and Jainism at that time.

It was Arab merchants through whom first contacts

with the Arakanese were estabished. These merchants on their way to China were, believed to have touched the Rumri port of Arakan. The famous single-domed Bunder Makam mosque of Akyab (Temple, 1925) and historian Harvey's account of Arakanese women in veils (1967:137) are indicative of increased penetration of Islam in Arakani life. Famous historian of Chittagong Mahbubul Alam argues that around 951 Chittagong was annexed by an Arakanese king and the city was named after him.

Between 10 century AD to 1580 the Chittagong, Sandwip and Ramu region was either under the control of the Muslim Sultans of Bengal or under the rule of the Arakanese Kings. For centuries the Maghs of Arakan with the help of the Portugese and the French were engaged in piracy, looting and killing in the coastal regions of Bengal. To sum it up, Bengal's relationship with the Arakan region can be traced to ancient times and there was constant fluctuation in that relation.

When Bengal was powerful, the Arakanes accepted Bengal's tutelage and paid taxes. When the balance of power shifted in favour of Arakan, Bengal was made its vassal state. All this led to increased interaction between the peoples of the region, including traders and regious preachers. There was constant influx of Muslims from as far away as Afghanistan, Persia and Turkey, as well as from north India and the Arabian peninsula. They merged into the existing Muslim society and became the Rohingyas. A distinct dialect emerged as a result of the mixture of Persian, Urdu, Puṣhtu, Arakanese and Bengal. In the 16th century, the Arakanese adopted sailing and war techniques from the Portugese pirate settlers on the coast and began numerous raids in neighbouring Bengal. Capture of slaves was a major purpose of these raids. These slaves and their offspring were used for cultivation work all over Arkan and their presence can be seen in rural Arakan even today. Nicolaus states that these people call themselves Rohingyas, but the Arakanese and the Rohingyas refer to them as Heins, meaning low-caste. Two incidents involving two royal asylum seekers have significantly moulded the history of Arakan. In the 15th century the events relating to royal asylum seeker from Arakan, Narmikheila, significantly boosted Muslim penetration and presence in Arakan. However, in the mid-17th century the events surrounding the Mughal prince Shah Shuja, who sought asylum in Arakan, led to the erosion of the Muslim hold and influence there.

*The narmikheila incident*

Muslim influence in Arakan grew in the 15th century. In 1404, Narmikheila, the king of Arakan, deposed by the Burmans, sought refuge of the lliasshahi ruler of Gaur. Narmikheila was given royal asylum by the then Sultan and lived in Gaur for twenty-four years. It has been claimed that the Buddhist king during this period in exile became well-versed in Islamic history and politics. In 1430 Jalaluddin Shah provided Narmikheila 20,000 soldiers under general Wali Khan and got rid of Burmans from Arakan. But when Wall Khan instead of handing over power to the Arakanese king declared himself the ruler, another 30,000 troops were sent under general Shiddhi Khan to punish him.

Finally, Narmikhella regained power in Arakan with the Gaur ruler's total support and assumed the Muslim name Solaiman Shah. Following him successive rulers of Arakan added a Muslim name to their Buddhist names. Coins issued by them had Arabic inscription on them. In the 17th century one witnesses increased influence of the Bengali language and literature in the Arakan court and assumption of offices of Muslims in the Arakanese administration. It was the contributions of Arakan-based Daulat Kazi, Alaol and Magan Thakur that enriched the Bengali culture of the period. Dr. Ahmed Sharif terms this the golden phase of Bengali culture and literature in Arakan whose tides continued to reach the shores of southern Chittagong till the 18th and the 19th centuries.

Muslims were placed in key positions of the Arakanese administration. One Ashraf Khan was appointed the Defence Minister, while Syed Musa was the other Muslim member of the king's cabinet. In the defence services Muslims dominated the cavalry and archers divisions.

*The Shah Shuja incident*

In the declining phase of the Mughal empire when emperor Aurangzeb assumed power, his brother Shah Shuja, then governor of Bengal, sought refuge in the Arakan kingdom in 1660. Deterioration of relations between the Arakanese king and the Mughal ruler led to the latter's involvement in Arakanese court politics. This in turn led to the preemptive strike by the Arakanese and many Muslims were masscred though Shuja and his family were given a reprieve. In support of Shah Shuja, the Muslims soldiers of the Arkanese king rebelled and were joined by other Muslim residents of the capital. This led to a bloodbath and Shuja and his family were executed. This act of the Arakanese king invited reprisal from the Mughal governor of Bengal. Under Aurangzeb's order Shaista Khan strengthened his navy, captured Sandwip in 1665 and Chittagong and Ramu the following years.

*First Influx of Refugees*

Following the death of King Sri Chandrasudharma in 1684, the political situation in Arakan was unstable. Except for a brief period of rule by king Shandhauza (1710-1731) court intrigue and conspiracies became order of the day. Hall claims that between 1684 and 1784 Arakanese Muslims had a major role in the making and overthrowing of the kings in Arakan. In 1785 the Burman king conquered Arakan and a long guerilla war ensued.

The Burman army committed atrocities on the Arakanese. A good number of men were murdered and women prisoners were sent to Burma. Karim allege that as many as 6,000 Arakanese youth were sent to renovate the Meiktila Lake and none of them returned. In addition, Arakanese forced labour was extracted to built the 500 feet tall pagoda in Mingun in Burma. In 1791, an unsuccessful attempt against the Burman rule in Arakan was followed by massive reprisal from the Burman authorities and one estimate suggests that as many 200,000 Arakanese were murdered.

Another attempt in 1796 ended in failure and resulted in massive influx of Arakan refugees in the Cox's Bazar area. Almost two-thirds of the population of Arakan, most of the Rohingyas and Heins, left Arakan for the Chittagong area. This marked the beginning of the periodic influxes of refugees from Arakan into Bengal. It may, be pertinent to mention here that it was the refugees from Arakan who constituted the bulk of the original settlers between Teknaf and Cox's Bazar. Hiram Cox, after whom Cox's Bazar was named, was appointed by the East India Company as the Superintendent for the rehabilitation of the refugees.

*British rule in arakan and adjoining areas*

The incorporation of Arakan with Burma brought the Burmans in direct contact with British India. The Arakanese refugees under the leadership of their depose king Bering waged a guerilla warfare against the Bhama king. This resulted in the incursion of the Burman army into the British Indian territory and ultimately precipitated the first Anglo-Burmese War. The War (1824-26) resulted in the annexation of Arakan and Tenessarim by the British. The natural resources of Burma led the

British to wage another war, the Second Anglo-Burmese War, which ended in 1853 and ensured British occupation over entire lower Burma, later known as the rice bowl of the British India.

The Third Anglo-Burmese war of 1885 led to British control over all of Burma. With the incorporation of Arakan, and later the rest of Burma, into the British empire, a large section of the refugees returned. Nicolaus argues that together with the refugees new settlers flowed into the depopulated country bringing with them Bengali culture and language (Nicolaus, 1995:3). The British Census figures reveal the level of increase in population:

| | *Year* | |
|---|---|---|
| Area | 1831 | 1911 |
| Maungdaw township | 18,300 | 101,100 |
| Akyab district | 95,100 | 530,000 |
| Pegu district | 95,700 | 293,000 |

The Second World War had a major bearing on the inter-communal relationship between the Rohingya Muslims and the Rakhine Buddhists. The advance of the Japanese army led to the exodus of tens of thousands of Indians from Burma and especially Muslims from Arakan. Communal riots flared up between the communities and some 22,000 Rohingyas were forced to take refuge in adjoining British Indian territories, i.e., Cox's Bazar, Teknaf, Ukhia and Ramu. The Arakanese communities were divided in their loyalities, the Rohingyas were loyal to the British, rendering valuable services in work units, reconnaissance and espionage, while their Buddhist counterparts, the Rakhines, took the side of the Japanese.

***Disillusionment of the Arakanese Muslims***

The end of the war created conditions for the displaced

people to return back to their homes. Although the British promised the Arakanese Muslims autonomy in a Muslim National Area, which would comprise Maungdaw, Buthedaung, and the part of Rathedaung bordering East Bengal, this was not subsequently honoured. After the Buddhist dominated Burmese administration took control over Arakan, the Muslim's sense of alienation and betrayal grew.

The Arkanese Muslims, especially those hailing from the Chhitagong region, took the initiative to form the North Arakan Muslim League in Akyab- They sought the then leader of Pakistan, Mr. Jinnah's support for their plans. That was not forthcoming as Jinnah assured General Aung San that he was not keen on the idea. In 1948 an outbreak of an armed rebellion took place, known to be the *Mujahid* rebellion. The main goal of the *Mujahid* movement was to create an independent Muslim state between the rivers Kaladan and Mayu. The movement created deep schism in the Muslim community of Arakan. The moderates wanted to avoid a confrontation with the government and the Rakhines, while the extremists resorted to firearms. There have been instances where sections within the Rohingya community appealed for arms from the U Nu government to fight the rebels.

### *Impact of muslim militancy*

The end result of the Muslim militancy was that the Muslims were eyed with suspicion in Burma and considered to be disloyal to the Burmese state. The Muslim civil servants, policemen and headmen were replaced by Rakhines and were barred from military service. Arbitrary arrests, extortion of money by law enforcing agencies and member of the civil administration were rampant.

The educational and economic development programmes for the Arakanese Muslims community were neglected. Restrictions were imposed on the movements of Muslims from Maungdaw, Buthidaung and Rathedaung to Akyab. Muslims returnees were not settled in their original place of habitat and some of them were termed as illegal Pakistani immigrants. Property and land of returnees was confiscated.

The *Mujahid's* frustration on ail these accounts made them fiercely committed to their cause and by June 1949, they effectively controlled the whole of northern Arakan. There were reprisals and counter-reprisals of the government army units and the *Mujahids.* Another important element that contributed to the deterioration of relations between the Rakhine and the Muslim communities in Arakan has been the issue of statehood.

The Arakan Muslims vehemently objected to the demands of the Arakan Party for the status of a state for Arakan within the framework of the Union of Burma. They were apprehensive that any such arrangement would ensure the domination of the Rakhine Buddhists over Arakan. Instead the majority of the Muslim organizations demanded autonomy for the region, to be directly governed by the central government in Rangoon without any Arakanese officials or any Arakanese influence whatsoever'. This placed the government of U Nu in a difficult situation because in the general elections of 1960 he promised to confer statehood on Arakan, on par with other states of the Union of Burma. In the face of growing opposition of the Muslim organisations such as the Rohingya Jamiyat al Ulama, the Rohingya Youth and Students' Association, the government in May, 1961, created the Mayu Frontier Administration covering the provinces of Maungdaw, Buthidaung and the western portion of Rathedaung. The Administration was not accorded autonomy and was under the control of Army officers. With the consent of the Muslim leaders when the U Nu government was about to grant statehood to Arakan, excluding the Mayu district, the plan was thwarted by the military coup of General Ne Win in 1962.

The Rohingy militancy was revived following the dissolution of the Mayu Frontier Administration in 1964 by the Military Council and its incorporation into the Arakanese administration. This led to the creation of a new organization, the Rohingya Patriotic Front, and deman for autonomy was back on the political agenda.

***The 1978 operation nagmin and the first exodus of the arkanese muslims***

The Military Council's selective policies towards minority communities was reflected in the policy on naturalisation and citizenship. All ethnic minority communities were granted citizenship except the Indians (among them the Muslims of Arakan) and the Chinese, on the pretext that they were late settlers. This institutionalised state discrimination against these groups and eroded their trust and loyality to the Burmese Union. In 1977 a campaign was launched by the central government to scrutinize individually the population in the state, to designate citizens and foreigners in accordance with the law. This was also meant to take actions against foreigners who have infiltrated the country illegally (Government of Burma statement, 16.11.77).

The operation Nagmin (Dragon King) commenced in the beginning of 1978 in the Kachin and Arakan states. In the State of Kachin it proceeded smoothly, only 45 persons out 15,524 were screened. While in the district of Akyab the number of arrests was much higher. Approximately 1,025 out of total 36,825 were arrested. In an official report on April 29, 1978 the government revealed that it had found, among other irregularities, that there had been an alarming rate of illegal entry into the state of Arakan.

Several thousand prosecutions had been instituted against Chinese and Rohingyas under the Registration of Foreigners Act and other relevant legislation. It is also announced that 19,427 Bengalis had absconded, leaving their 3,723 homes. In another statement the Burmese authorities stated that in Buthidung township alone 108,431 persons were interrogated, 643 prosecuted, 33,596 persons absconded and 6,429 houses abandoned (19.5.78). The government further stated that as many as 101,048 have escaped Buthidaung and Maungdaw to 'escape an immigration check'.

The sharp increase in the number of arrests and harassment of the Arakanese Muslims, often accompanied by use of brute force, resulted in the mass exodus of the Rolingyas into Bangladesh. Faced with a growing number of refugees the Bangladesh government on the one hand began bilateral negotiations with Burma and on the other, appealed to the international community for international assistance for the 150,000 refugees and which was soon expected to reach 200,000. A major international fund raising operation was mounted for the assistance to the growing number of refugees who were kept in 11 camps. The figures on the number of refugees presented by Bangladesh and Burma varied considerably.

The Bangladesh government claimed 252,000 persons sought refuge in Bangladesh, while the Burmese sources stated that 143,900 persons 1 absconded to Bangladesh in order to escape the Nagmin Project'. However, in the negotiations conducted between Bangladesh and Burma during June and - July 1978 an agreement was finally reached on the repatriation of refugees to Burma.

The operation commenced on 31 st August 1978 and ended on 29th December 1979 and involved repatriation of a total of 187,250 refugees to Arakan. In 1991, Bangladesh experienced another influx of Rohingyas refugees in the Teknaf, Ramu, Ukhia and Cox's Bazar region. About 250,000 refugees crossed the Naf river and sought asylum in Bangladesh. In the following section the treatment of refugees by the Bangladesh government and the people will be discussed.

**Treatment of refugees**

Ever since the arrival of the Rohingya refugees the Bangladesh government has provided relief and shelter to these people. In this endeavour the non-governmental organizations, both national and international, and the UNHCR provided crucial support to Bangladesh in coping with a crises of such magnitude. In spite of the humanitarian assistance rendered to the refugees, a major policy consideration of the Bangladesh authorities has been their 'quick and safe return' to Myanmar.

The Bangladesh government's treatment of refugees has been essentially guided by this overriding consideration. This section deals with the question of treatment of refugees of the 1991 influx. It is divided into two parts. This first part deals with the official response to the refugee influx and the second part discusses the people's reaction.

*The influx of 1991*

The Rohingya refugees began moving into Bangladesh following the Myanmar Army's increased activities in the Maungdaw, Buthidaung and Rathedaung townships of Myanmar, region that border Bangladesh. Systematic and massive human rights abuses like, forced labour, rape and confiscation of houses, land and farm animals by the troops of 23rd and 24th regiments of the Myanmar army reportedly triggered off this mass exodus.

The destruction of mosques, ban on religious

activities, harassment of the religious priests and denigration of Islam reflected the intolerance of the authorities of the religious rights of this minority community. Between mid- 1991 through mid- 1992, an estimated 250,000 refugees took shelter Bangladesh.

***Bangladesh government's response***

The Bangladesh government allowed the refugees to enter its territory and provided them shelter and relief. Initially it tried to solve the issue on a Bangladesh/ Myanmar bilateral basis and to manage relief efforts on its own, but increasing number of refugees and strong intervention from donor countries led the GOB to seek international assistance. UNHCR was invited to provide assistance to the refugees in mid-1992.

UNHCRs involvement facilitated the work of international NGO's to complement the work of the national NGO'S. Bangladesh viewed the refugees as a short-term problem. It is on this promise the government signed a Memorandum of Understanding with Myanmar on 28 April, 1992 under which Myanmar agreed to the return of those refugees who could established their bona fide residency in Myanmar prior to their departure for Bangladesh. (in depth assessment of the MOU is presented in detail in Part Three on Repatriation). In spite of the initial hospitability and cordiality extended to the refugees the mood of the Bangladesh government changed following the signing of the joint Statement with Myanmar.

During 1992 and 1993 human rights groups and UNHCR raised concerns over coercion and forceful repatriation of refugees by the Bangladesh authorities. Certain international NGOs confirmed that such allegations were well founded. Following UNHCR/ NGO's protests about alleged forcible repatriation and their demand for a halt to such process the Bangladesh government blocked their access to the camps, irrespective of the agreement signed between the government and the UNHCR on 8 October 1992, which allow the latter a role in verifying the voluntary nature of the return movement. As a result UNHCR withdrew from the repatriation programme on 22 December 1992.

***The people's response***

Like the Bangladesh-government the people of the affected regions, Teknaf, Ramu and Cox's Bazar, had been very sympathetic to the refugees when they first came. But gradually increased pressure of the refugee's on the local society, economy and environment eroded that sympathy and dissatisfaction against the refugees became more and more pronounced.

A major factor contributing to the changed perception of the refugees had been the violence in camps. Such violence mainly took place when refugees protested their forceful repatriation. The media took an unsympathetic view of the refugee presence in Bangladesh, portraying them to be an aggressive and disorderly bunch of people. This can be illustrated by a series of newspaper articles published during that period, which articulated that the refugee presence has caused great damage to the local flora and fauna, deforestation which has caused major burden on the local environment.

Perhaps the most immediate impact of refugee presence was felt in the increased prices of essential commodities in and around refugee areas which is one of the most undeveloped regions of Bangladesh, where the purchasing power of the vast majority of people was already very low. In July 1992, there were public meeting in Ukhia demanding a stoppage on work intended to set up new camps (Jummarapara camp). The local people's opposition to the refugees resulted in the forming of two committees, the Refugee Repatriation Action Committee and the Refugee Repatriation Coordination Council, which voiced concern over the continued presence of the refugees and accused international NGOs and UNHCR of a 'hidden agenda' for prolonging the repatriation process. In order to assuage growing dissatisfaction of local people UNHCR organised the Affected Villages Rehabilitation Programme where infrastructural projects were taken up to soothe the peoples sentiments. The involvement of the local people in designating and prioritising, and most important, in implementing these projects, yielded effective results for UNHCR. The criticisms gradually waned.

**Repatriation**

This section looks into the issue of repatriation in details. It commences with the Bangladesh government's policy on repatriation and its signing of an agreement with the Myanmar government. This is followed by an appraisal of the changing relationship between the host government and the UNHCR, an organization which was invited by the former to help the relief and repatriation of about 250,000 refugees. Shifts in the UNHCR policy from individual interview to mass registration, and the policy from information dissemination to promotional activities will also be examined.

The activities of the non-governmental organizations, though mostly involved in relief efforts, on the question of repatriation will be examined. In particular, their concern about what they see as 'involuntary nature' of repatriation and their claim of 'lack of awareness' of the refugees during mass registration. The chapter will also deal with the prospect of reintegration of the returnees and discuss the efforts mounted by the UNHCR and the WFP on the operational area in the Arakan state. It will also present the refugees' own perception of repatriation based on the findings at the field.

***Bangladesh government's policy on repatriation***

When the refugees first began to arrive from Myanmar the people and the government of Bangladesh received them with great degree of sympathy and provided them with all forms of support. The Government of Bangladesh took effective steps in providing relief to the refugees and provided them temporary shelters, food, medicare and health and sanitation facilities.

A large number of officials were mobilised to share the relief efforts. Later international agencies (the UNHCR and the WFP) and the NGOs (both local and international) were involved in the relief activities. However, an important consideration of the policy-makers in Dhaka all along had been that the duration of the' refugees' stay in Bangladesh be short and they were to return to Myanmar as soon as the situation permitted them to do so. It is in this context that one sees Bangladesh's eagerness to negotiate the return of the Myanmar authorities.

The GOB held that the country did not have the capacity and resources to host the refugees over an uncertain period of time. Added to this perhaps there was a degree of self-confidence in the Ministry of Foreign Affairs, Dhaka (which later proved to be misguided), that solution to the problem could be worked out through normal bilateral diplomatic channels, as was done during the 1978 influx. Bangladesh continued to view the refugee as a short-term problem and repeatedly demanded the immediate repatriation of all Rohingyas refugees. In April 1992 the Bangladesh Foreign Minister Mostafizur Rahman stated that the repatriation of refugees would be completed in six months. It is out of that sense of urgency that Bangladesh signed a joint

Statement with the State Law and Order Restoration Council (SLORC) of Myanmar on April 28, 1992. 3.2 Bangladesh Myanmar Memorandum of Understanding (MOU) According to the joint Statement Myanmar agreed to take measures that would halt the outflow of Myanmar residents to Bangladesh and to accept after scrutiny all 'those carrying Myanmar identity cards', 'those able to present other documents issued by relevant Myanmar authorities' the Memorandum is the role of the UNHCR.

While it was agreed that the GOB would fully involve the representatives of the UNHCR to assist the process of safety and voluntary repatriation, the Government of Myanmar (GOM) agreed that 'the services of the UNHCR could be drawn upon as needed at an appropriate time' (Author's emphasis). Thus, the MOU failed to assign any role to UNHCR in Myanmar. Another important limitation of the Memorandum was that it failed to specify—that all refugees, without exception, would be taken back. An important coincidence was that Bangladesh signed the Memorandum at a time when there were efforts by the UN to get access to Myanmar by the Mission of Under-Secretary General of the United Nations, Mr. Eliasson. It has been reported that in later negotiations with Bangladesh, SLORC's position, at least for some time, was that the involvement of UN agencies has become obsolete, since both countries agreed on the terms of solution and repatriation.

Another important omission for Bangladesh was her failure to point out that most of the Rohingya refugees were stripped of their Myanmar documents prior to their crossing to Bangladesh and many of them were not in possession of any identity papers in the first place. It is difficult to assess the reasons for Bangladesh's rush to sign the Memorandum without mounting a concerted pressure of the international community on Myanmar and particularly at a time when refugees were still arriving "at the rate of about 1,500 per day".

***The first phase of repatriation***

The Bangladesh government's attitude towards the refugees underwent a significant change following the signing of the Memorandum. On 22 September, 1992 the first repatriation took place on a very limited scale without UNHCR involvement. It has been suggested that the UN agency was notified after the repatriation had taken place (US Committee for Refugees, 1995:5).

UNHCR believes that "this movement was accompanied by considerable pressure coercion from the Bangladesh authorities, who insisted that they could not give the refugees long-term asylum. This has been further corroborated by nongovernmental organizations who reported that in September, 1992 cases of forced transfer to transit camps by taking away family books, coercion in the form of physical abuse, had increased significantly; In addition, it was alleged that camp officials -were given quotas to come up with a number of 'volunteers' per month. That the first phase for repatriation was not voluntary is evident from the increased outbreaks of violence that had occurred - in camps, often resulting in death of the refugees (officially stated to be 15). Protest demonstrations in camps were held in all camps against the repatriation demanding a total halt to al I repatriation.

***UNHCR and GOB relations***

On 8th October 1992 an agreement was reached between the UNHCR and GOB which allowed the UN agency a role in verifying the voluntary nature of repatriation. Following signing of the agreement two batches of repatriation took place on 12th and 31 st October which, according to UNHCR, were voluntary. But following this several rounds of repatriation took place without UNHCR's involvement.

A UNHCR Situation Report states that 84 percent (4,814 refugees) of the total number of repatriations held in months of November and December 1992 took place without UNHCR supervision. The Bangladesh/ government's intransigence to accord the UNHCR its due role in the verification of the voluntary process of repatriation as agreed upon early October 1992, and to continue to coerce refugees to repatriate, ultimately led the agency to withdraw from the repatriation programme on December 22, 1992.

An additional 11, 216 persons were repatriated after the withdrawal of the UNHCR which has been deemed by some as 'involuntary' (USCR, 1995:6; MSF Holland and France press release). This form of repatriation also came under criticism from the US Department of State which viewed it as "coerced repatriations". Following these criticisms the GOB suspended its unilateral repatriation in late January 1993 and announced its plans to discuss the issue with the UNHCR. Negotiations for a MOU between the two began soon after. After several rounds of negotiations and exchange of letters the two sides finally signed a Memorandum of Understanding on 12 May 1993.

The Memorandum provided GOB to allow "free access to officials of the UNHCR to independent interview of refugees in transit camps... to determine the voluntary character of their decision to return" (1/a) and "for conducting independent interviews with prospective returnees for certifying the voluntary nature of the repatriation" (1/b). It further commits the Bangladesh government that "no refugees... will be coerced into leaving against his/her will"(4/f). In addition the

Memorandum provided UNHCR free access to and a presence in all refugees camps during the day time (5). An important provision of the Memorandum is that the UNHCR undertook to carry "promotional activities to motivate the refugees to return home once international presence for observing reasonable conditions of safety for the returnee is established in Myanmar in line with the Agreement of 28th April 19 92 between the GOB and the Myanmar"(6/c).

Two most important concerns of the UNHCR were taken care of by the Memorandum, (a) protection of refugees in the camps and (b) voluntary repatriation, guaranteed by private interviewing of refugees by UNHCR- For the Bangladesh government the tying of the Memorandum to that of Bangladesh-Myanmar Agreement (April 1992) was an important achievement. A grave limitation of the Memorandum was that it did not clearly spell out that repatriation would be promoted only when an appreciable improvement in the conditions had occurred and the safety of the refugees could be assured. This issue became a major bone of contention between the aid agencies and human/refugee rights groups and the UNHCR and on the one hand, and Bangladesh government, on the other, in the later phases of repatriation.

Discussion with aid agency officials as well as with the refugees suggest that even after the MOU was signed there was significant degree of coercion in the camps to make refugees 'volunteer' for repatriation. USCR Report cities a high ranking official who reckoned that as many as fifty percent of the repatritions that occurred prior to August 1994 "were effected either through overt force or other coercive, methods" (1995:7). Threat, intimidation and liberal use of broad powers of arrest by the camp officials had been resorted to promote repatriation. In spite of all these problems repatriation process continued and another 50,000 people were repatriated.

***Preparation for mass repatriation***

The signing of MOU with Myanmar by the UNHCR completed the triad that was felt to be necessary to mount a major repatriation initiative. Accordingly on 19th December 1993 an Operational Plan for mass repatriation was presented by the UNHCR. The objective of the plan was to facilitate voluntary repatriation of approximately 190,000 refugees at the rate of 15-18,000 refugees per month (1,500 every other day). The Operation Plan (henceforth the Plan) had taken into account UNHCR's presence in Arakan to assist return and reintegration and the sufficient improvement of the situation in Myanmar.

It was further assumed that all refugees would decide to return and GOM would accept them all. As part of the Operational Plan it was decided to promote confidence among refugees, governments and the NGOS. Although preparations were being made principally on the GOM-UNHCR MOU, there was no convincing evidence about the situation of the 50,000 refugees who had by then returned to Myanmar prior to the beginning of mass repatriation. In addition, very little could be gathered from independent sources about the situation actually then prevailing in the operation area in Arakan.

The NGOs felt that very little information was made available to them and that they were not involved/ consulted in the planning process of mass repatriation. It was generally believed by the non-governmental community that the refugees were not being provided information that they needed to make an informed choice. In addition, the staffing position, particularly at the Arakan side, was too low to handle and monitor such a major operation. In early January 1994, the UNHCR

Head of Desk, Regional Bureau for Asia and Oceania, made a visit to Dhaka following his trip to Yangon, Sittwe, Maungdaw and the 5 reception centres on the Myanmarese side. In his briefing in Dhaka he expressed his confidence of the goodwill of the Myanmarese authorities and expressed his feeling that they 'had the commitment'. In reply to a question if forced labour was still practiced he said 'No'. It is interesting to note that the senior official of UNHCR was making-optimistic statements though he did not speak to any returnee and was not allowed to enter Bangladesh over the Gundum bridge (as was originally planned) by the Myanmarese authorities. Till then UNHCR lacked any effective physical presence in the Arakan state (Myanmar) to provide integration assistance and to ensure monitoring of the well being of the returnees. This made the refugees reluctant to repatriate.

Thus far in an hostile environment of uncertainty and fear, the camp-inmates gradually began to trust the UNHCR as 'promoter of their interests and protectors. This the UNHCR earned through its strong stand against the involuntary repatriation that Bangladesh was pursuing at the initial stages. However, the distinction between the GOB and the UNHCR began to fade When UNHCR began the information campaign using the public address system of the camp in charge which so far had aired very few things that the refugees could really trust. NGOs claimed that this perhaps was the beginning of an erosion of trust of the refugees in the UNHCR.

By March 1994 the situation showed an upward trend in repatriation. However, there were fresh instances of new refugees and some double-backers and UNHCR was not ready to receive refugees on the Myanmarese side. The dissemination of information could not satisfy the refugees. They were particularly, concerned with the citizenship rights and freedom of movement. In April 1994, Myanmar announced the partial completion of the reception facilities. It was in this month that, repatriation was organised with the cooperation of UNHCR.

The first group of refugees crossed the border on 30 April 1994, accompanied by the UNHCR Representative in Bangladesh 'to establish confidence of the refugees'. The efforts however were disrupted by the 2nd May cyclone. The impasse was further compounded by the Bangladesh Foreign Secretary's accusation that UNHCR was obstructing the repatriation process.

The Foreign Secretary also threatened not to renew the MOU that was to expire in May. He demanded that interviewing should be stopped and that all refugees should leave Bangladesh before the end of 1994. The repatriation process was dealt a severe blow by a cyclone on 2nd May 1994 that destroyed all camps, departure and reception points. The total numbers of returnees since January 1994 was 3,278. It was only in July 1994 following the mass repatriation registrations that repatriation figures gradually picked up with the monthly figure being 3,592. There were positive developments following the arrival of the new Relief Commissioner.

The UNHCR was given permission for the first time to begin interviewing in all non-transit camps. It should be noted that prior to July 1994, UNHCR was authorised to interview refugees only in transit camps, to ascertain voluntariness of the refugees to repatriate. Kutupalong was the first camp where 25 percent of the interviewed stated that they wanted to return. During this exercise there was a shift in UNHCR's policy from information to promotion of repatriations. The new message was that it was time for the refugees to return to their home country as UNHCR was present there and the situation there was 'conducive'. According to UNHCR, the final result revealed that 90 percent of those interviewed said "yes" to repatriation. On July 18 the first group of returnees went over to Myanmar over the Tumbru bridge, the second departure point.

*Assessment of UNHCR repatriation procedures*

A careful assessment of the repatriation operation of UNHCR would indicate two different stages. In the first stage the UNHCR followed the standard repatriation procedures in line with its Guidelines on Voluntary Repatriation. During this stage individual refugees were interviewed and were provided with information about developments in the country of origin. The return of refugees must be on the basis of an individually and freely expressed wish. This stage lasted until July 1994. Since then UNHCR adopted new procedures in the repatriation operation, whereby refugees were encouraged to repatriate, and individual interviews were replaced by mass registration sessions.

However, refugees who had genuine reasons for not returning would have the possibility of expressing their opinion, and UNHCR would* not register them for repatriation. Their cases would be discussed at the end of the operation. These procedures were also followed in recent operations in Sri Lanka (1987), Iraq (1991), Guatemala (1993) and Rwanda (1994). That new procedures raise a number of important issues which are tantamount to a change of policy on repatriation, has finally been acknowledged by the High Commissioner in her statement to the ExCom meeting during the 46th session. Referring to some recent experiences she stated that "in none of these instances is return likely to be under ideal conditions. In many, it will be dogged by political insecurity and economic uncertainty". Pointing' to returnees from exile requiring continued protection and monitoring, the High Commissioner said, that this creates a "new dimension to our protection responsibilities and has led us to Interpret our mandate for solutions in a protection-oriented and proactive' manner.. we can no longer passively wait for conditions to change so that refugees can volunteer. Instead, we must work actively to create the conditions conducive to their safe return" (emphasis added).

The new procedure contrasts with the UNHCR Guideline on voluntary repatriation and ExCom Conclusion Nos. 18 and 40. Under the new procedure onus of repatriation shifted from individual refugees to UNHCR. UNHCR's policy of promoting voluntary repatriation has become one of the contentious issues. In its recent operations mentioned above UNHCR has actively promoted voluntary repatriation before a substantive change of circumstances in the country of origin had taken place. Here the question arises about stances in which UNHCR can get itself engaged in active promotion of repatriation.

The 1951 Convention, the 1967 Protocol and the ExCom Conclusions did not specify under what circumstances can UNHCR promote repatriation. The basic foundation of refugee protection is that individuals fleeing the country of origin as a result of risk to life and freedom (persecution and/or fear of persecution) due to political, religious belief, and and/or membership of social groups (Art 1), should be given asylum. Thus, under no circumstance such individuals should be returned to their country of origin against their wishes. However, Article I.C. 5 clearly indicates that UNHCR can apply cessation clause to withdraw refugee status if there is fundamental change of circumstances whereby there no longer exists risk to life and/or freedom of those who fled. In other words, Art I.C. 5 says that the continuation and/ or absence of risk to life is the main criteria for granting asylum and/or withdrawing it. By applying this analogy one could safely argue that UNHCR can promote voluntary repatriation if risk to life and freedom no longer exists in the country of origin for those who have fled it. To say the contrary would mean that UNHCR can promote return when risk to life and freedom exist, something which is totally against the basic foundation of asylum law. Therefore, one can only conclude that UNHCR, in principle, can promote voluntary repatriation if and when it believes that risk to life and/or freedom no longer exists.

Thus one can say that if there is a partial change and/or improvement of circumstances in the country of origin, refugees should not be encouraged to return on a group basis. This is important considering the subjective and objective elements of persecution as defined in UNHCR Handbook on Procedures and Criteria for Determining Refugee Status. As against this background and considering the high degree of illiteracy of the Rohingya refugees, on the one hand, and on the other, lack of credible information about the situation prevailing in the country of origin, absence of cross-border visits and reports of human rights violations in Myanmar, one may wonder whether High Commissioner Ogata's statement that "we can no-longer passively wait for conditions to change so that refugees can volunteer. Instead, we must work actively to create the conditions conducive to their safe return" is in consonance with the principle of voluntary repatriation. With respect to UNHCR`s promotional activities in Rohingya repatriation four points may be raised; (a) the refugees were not well informed about their right to refuse repatriation, (b) they did not have access to full and proper information on the situation in their place of origin, i.e., the Rakhine state and (c) various reports indicate that there has not been any fundamental change of circumstance in Myanmar, and (d) UNHCR's monitoring ability in Myanmar remains of great Questions are being asked by concerned academics, NGO/human rights/refugee activists in Bangladesh as well as overseas: are the recent operations including the Rohingya repatriation case indicative of the policies to develop in the future? Has there been a significant departure here from the practices and procedures followed in other operations? Is the sudden shift in policy symptomatic of things to come under the amended mandate of the organization? It would be conjectural to seek answers to these questions given our dearth of knowledge about the actual dynamics of the UN system, particularly that of UNHCR. However, one may dwell on the rationale of this sudden shift in policy within the framework of the operation itself.

The shift in policy of UNHCR was announced in July 1994, from information sessions to promotion sessions and from private interviewing in transit camps to massive registrations in all camps. This has been officially attributed to the situation in Myanmar being "conducive" and .refugees had shown to be interested to return to Myanmar as evidenced by the large scale interviews conducted in Kutupalong recently". As a part of the new strategy, "UNHCR will conduct promotion sessions in the camps in which UNHCR will provide the refugees with:

— information about UNHCR's role in Myanmar, arrangements for their repatriation, guarantees of safety, and plans for their reintegration, and
— an assessment that the situation in Myanmar is conducive to their return and will advise them that they should return. " (Emphasis added)

This change in policy may have major ramifications over the very concept of voluntariness of repatriation. As one of the leading aid workers stated, private interviewing fought for in the past in order to prevent (further) forced repatriation, what guarantee would massive registration provide as far as voluntariness is concerned?"In the discussions with aid workers, UNHCR staff members suggested the fact that coercion incidents have significantly dropped in the preceding three months showed the goodwill of the Bangladesh government. At a separate meeting with MSF/H, a representative of UNHCR stated that if this new system would lead to coercion, again UNHCR would go back to the system of interviewing.

As stated earlier it is difficult to attribute the real motive behind this sudden change in policy, particularly at a time when the previous system was beginning to work and reaping results. There might have been a convergence of many factors. In July 1994, with the change in the Relief Commissioner, the GOB had a shift in policy to authorise UNHCR to organise promotion sessions and interviews in all camps instead of only in transit camps.

The second factor could be rethinking in UNHCR on new means of being proactive in the preparation of repatriation. This might have been prompted by the completion of the preparation for repatriation in the Rakhine state where UNHCR has a presence with WFP and initiated an integration assistance programme. The third factor could lie on the draft MOU submitted by GOB to UNHCR. In the draft MOU the Bangladesh government demanded "that the level of voluntariness in repatriation of Rohingya refugees should be determined on the basis of the present attitude of the Myanmar government to the refugees".

The MOU stated Myanmar has already recognised 135,000 of the total refugees as its citizens, so these Rohingya people should not be treated as refugees anymore and they should be sent back to Rakhine state as soon as possible. The draft claimed that this proposal was very compatible with the 1951 Geneva Convention and 1967 Protocol. (Holiday, 29 July 1994). The draft however was never finalized. The newspaper cites a highly placed Bangladesh government source that the UNHCR officials have agreed to stop individual interrogation of the refugees and instead they would go for mass registration of the refugees.

The fourth factor could be that the refugees decided to return in view of the living conditions in the camps where they stayed too long and where there is no education for their children or economic life for themselves and which might be less comfortable than in their village of origin. The NGOs were particularly concerned about the promotional activities of the UNHCR. They were of the opinion that the repatriation process was not voluntary. The NGOs alleged that refugees were not well informed on their right of saying 'no' to repatriation and access to full and proper information on the human rights situation in their place of origin was limited. They further argued that the situation in Arakan had not changed fundamentally.

The NGOS, particularly MSF/H and MSF/F claimed that at the promotion sessions refugees were confused and did not know what the registration meant for them. They suggested that UNHCR to improve its information dissemination and counselling of the refugees. UNHCR accepted the suggestion to improve the information session and to organise verification sessions through private interviews with refugees to ascertain that they still wish to repatriate or would have any problem for their repatriation.

The verification session is a Meeting between a refugee and a UNHCR staff member whereby the latter communicates to the refugee the decision of Myanmar authorities on his/her clearance. During this meeting., the refugee concerned could still withdraw his/her name or give justification to defer his/her return. The NGOs also requested an independent survey on the level of information available to refugees. While this was not forthcoming, the NGOs decided to organise their own survey "to convince ourselves whether we were right in stating that the repatriation was involuntary".

The survey conducted on 15 March 1995 reported that 65 percent of and 61 percent stated having concerns regarding repatriation. On the question of concern expressed by refugees, UNHCR statistics (March 1995) also showed that, of the camp population of 55,000 19,000 were on hold by UNHCR, this does not differ much from the firglire indicated by MSF. UNHCR analysed the reasons for these 19,000 persons who chose not to return. It was found that family reunification, medical care, change of mind etc. were the principal factors. At this stage UNHCR also geared its information dissemination programme towards the female population of the camps.

***Situation in myanmar***

This constitutes one of the most important areas of concern of the refugees themselves and the human rights and NGO community about the on-going process of repatriation of the Rohingya refugees. Discussions on this issue may be divided in two sub-heads; situation prevailing in Myanmar and presence of UNHCR in Arakan.

*Situation prevailing in myanmar:* The situation in Myanmar has basically continued to remain unchanged while there can be no doubt that a modest degree of change has been reflected in the Myanmar government's willingness to take back the refugees.

The SLORC regime is still in power in the country and has so far failed to legitimise its rule by holding election or referendum. It may be recalled that the military regime refused to hand-over power to the elected assembly of 1990 and no election has been called since. An important landmark in the on route to democracy there has been the release of Aung San Suu Kyi in August 1995 after a long period of incarceration. The SLORC regime's human rights records continue to fall far short of recognised international human rights standard.

The Myanmar government human rights record came under careful scrutiny by the United Nations. In December 1994 the General Assembly passed an unanimous resolution which expressed grave concerns "at the continued violations of human rights in Myanmar, as reported by the Special Rapporteur, in particular, summary and arbitrary arrests, torture, forced labour and forced relocations, abuse of women, politically motivated arrests and detention, restriction on fundamental freedom, including freedom of expression and assembly and the imposition of oppressive measures, directed in particular at ethnic and religious minorities". In addition to this depressing situation an aspect that continues to work against the return of the refugees is the persistence of discriminatory citizenship law of Myanmar. The UN Special Rapporteur specially urged the Myanmar authorities to consider reviewing the 1982 citizenship law and to abolish the 11 burdensome requirements for citizenship" and "discriminatory effects on racial or ethnic minorities, particularly Rakhine Muslims". The US Department of State in its 1994 Report on Status of Human Rights in Myanmar suggests that the Myanmar authorities "took only limited steps to correct long standing serious human rights violations".

The Report confirmed the continued practice of forced labour along with a policy of forced resettlement of civilians by the regime, which are gross infringements of human rights. Likewise an US official termed the Yangon regime "one of the world's worst violators of human rights". In its 1994 report entitled 'Myanmar: Human Rights Still Denied' the Amnesty International stated that so far "SLORC has failed to make any real progress or sincere attempts to address the issues... and to ensure that its citizens are able to peacefully exercise their rights of freedom of expression and association".

UNHCR, however, insists that there is no relation between the situation in Myanmar in general, including human right issues and the arrangements for repatriation of refugees. UNHCR argues that it concluded a MOU with Myanmar on 3 November 1993 to facilitate the repatriation process, and up until now, Myanmar has complied with the implementation of the MOU fully. Any issue raised by UNHCR has been addressed to by the authorities' in the most positive manner. To illustrate the point, UNHCR raised the issue of forced labour which was one of the main reasons stated by refugees for their flight to Bangladesh. In June 1995, a SLORC decree was passed regarding forced labour. Though it did not discontinue compulsory labour as a matter of policy, it restricted the practice to tasks of portering and sanitation work. UNHCR also raised the issues of relocation of population and land distribution programme, which was unfair to some groups of people including the returnees.

The two programmes have been discontinued. On the Protection issue, where officials abused returnees, they were arrested and charged at UNHCR's intervention.

*Presence of UNHCR in Arakan:* An important consideration behind the policy shift of UNHCR has been its new presence in Myanmar and particularly in Arakan from the first quarter of 1994. Such presence has been argued as a key to ensure protection to returnees. The protection of the returnees has been the most important question that has been faced by the UNHCR. Given the fact that very little substantive progress has been made in terms of the political and human rights situation in Myanmar and the SLORC regime is in effective control, and the military dominated IMPD over Arakan, any possibility for an improvement or a deterioration in the situation rests squarely on the wishes and policies of those in authority. In the absence of any move towards a democratic, accountable and transparent institutionalization of the administrative processes in Myanmar, the regime's claim to respect its commitments would always remain suspect. Concern has been expressed a some quarters about the unclear nature of the UNHCRs legal mandate to intervene on behalf of the returnees in their country of origin and vis-a-vis the national (sovereign) authority of that country. In addition, a major limitation for UNHCR operations in Arakan has been the difficult terrain and the poor infrastructural facilities.

The region is very undeveloped. Only Maungdaw and Buthdaung are connected by a metalled road. UNHCR field officers may have to spend one to two days to follow-up a case which generally involves travel on foot, bikes and boat. Considering the vast nature of the area of operation and the absence of any other human right monitoring groups, it would not be improper to suggest that with a strength of only 9 field officers (other 4 of the total 13 expatriates being technical consultants) the capacity of the HCR to effectively monitor protection issues, along with their other routine tasks, is insufficient. Added to this is unreliability of the local staff, who can either be lined with the intelligence agencies, or can be quite susceptible to their pressures, protection issues in such a regimented structure have to be a major area of concern. However, on this issues UNHCR maintains its position stated above.

*Economic factors:* 'The main concern", according to a senior UNHCR official in Myanmar, "is not the human rights situation in Arakan, which can be vastly improved. (It is neither a paradise, nor a hell.) It Is the economic anchoring of the people that would prove to be crucial". A proper anchoring of the people to diffuse future exodus situations will require significant improvement in their economic conditions, i.e., development of infrastructure (wells, roads, bridges, schools, water pumps) and more importantly, human resource development.

Emphasis should be laid on developing income generating projects so that there is a positive move towards poverty alleviation. Two important elements for such a development initiative is this economically depressed region are, (a) commitment of the government and its interest in the region to mobilise resources both internally and from outside; and (b) interest of the donor community. Given past experience one may reasonably predict that none of these would be forthcoming at least in the near future. UNHCR is neither mandated nor has the expertise to be involved in development projects and the UNDP is yet to make its mark in Arakan. In spite of its understanding with the UNHCR the Myanmar authorities have not taken any decision about allowing a major NGO involvement in the region. None of the two NGOs that operate in Arakan are involved in reintegration.

The ACF is involved with water supplies in reception camps and hydrological survey of the area and the Japanese Bridge. Asia mainly repairs 'transport' of UNHCR. The World Food Programme is the only other UN body engaged in the returnee areas. Although there had been talks of Myanmar Red Cross becoming involved, particularly in health and community development sectors, not much progress has been made since. Thus we find that the situation prevailing on the Myanmar side is faced with a number of problems. Apart from the general lack of progress in the political and human rights realms, the protection umbrella of the UNHCR seems to be limited. Absence of independent monitoring groups further compounds the problem. It is said that the failure of the Myanmar authorities to take steps for economic rejuvenation of the region and their continued discouragement of the NGOs have cast major shadow on the future of anchoring programme which the UNHCR technical consultants are striving to develop.

A very pertinent' arena for discussions is the questions of change in circumstances and the voluntary nature of repatriation. It has been demonstrated in the previous section that a number of international agencies, both private-independent, and inter-governmental, feel that there has not been any major change in the situation in Myanmar, the country of origin of the Rohingya refugees which warrants promotion of repatriation of refugees. For this they argue that the continuation of the SLORC regime, its human rights practices which include forced labour, relocation of villages, restriction of religious practices, mainly of minorities, such as Muslims, restriction of freedom of movements and the issue of citizenship represent a serious breach of basic human rights of members of minority groups and are the reflections of the poor state of human rights in Myanmar. An important issue for discussion with the refugees during field visits has been the question of developments in Myanmar and their decision to go back. While almost all refugees met and interviewed claimed that the would eventually go, none indicated their willingness to go then. When asked about the reason for such a decision there was a degree of similarity in responses.

The refugees stated that the military regime which drove them out was still in full control of Myanmar and they were still pursuing their policies of forced labour and religious persecution. They further suggested that there had not been any positive feedback from the returnees who had gone back to Myanmar. They claimed that hardly anyone had got back their land and homes and they were yet to be provided with any concrete evidence about the normality of the situation in Arakan, that some of the agencies and the Bangladesh government had been claiming.

*The legalistic interpretation:* In this part it will be argued that the marginal improvement in the situation in the country of origin should not necessarily be construed as a change in circumstance as both the Bangladesh government and the UNHCR seem to be doing.

Article I/C (5) of the 1951 Convention says that the Convention will cease to apply to any person if "(H)e can no longer, because the circumstances in connection with which he has been recognized as a refugee have ceased to exist, continue to refuse to avail himself of the protection of the country of his nationality". It is this principle of change of circumstance which has been dealt with by a corpus of literature in international law. James Hathaway identifies three distinct elements in this regard. First, the "change must be of substantial political significance, in the sense that the power structure under which persecution was deemed a real possibility no longer exists" (1991: 200). This, among others, may be reflected in the collapse of the persecuting government, coupled with holding of genuinely free and fair democratic elections and coming to power of a government committed to human rights.

The second element that Hathaway stresses is that "there must be reason to believe that substantial political change is truly effective". As the dissenting opinion in Ruiz Angel Jesus Gonsaivez notes "there is often a long distance between pledging and the doing"; and "good intentions may have existed, but I refuse to believe that there were no chance mishaps". Here explicitly citing the Peruvian situation of 1980-81 Hathaway categorically states that cessation is not warranted where " de-facto executive authority remains in the hands of the former oppressors" ... "nor can it be said that here has truly been a fundamental change of circumstances where the police and military establishments have yet fully to comply with dictates of democracy and respect for human rights".

The transitory shift in the political landscape must not be the guiding principle of decision concerning cessation of refugee status, but rather 'should be reserved for situations in which there is reason to believe that positive conversion of the power structure is likely to last". The UNHCR in its promotional campaign highlighted the improvements of situation in Arakan. The Bangladesh government, in its turn, strongly believes that the level of voluntariness in repatriation of Rohingya refugees should be determined on the basis of attitude of the Myanmar government to the refugees. On this premise, in the revised MOU of the Bangladesh government argued that refugees who have been accepted by Myanmar should not be treated as refugees and they should be sent back in Rakhine state in Myanmar as soon as possible. Thus a minimum degree of familiarity with refugee laws concerning cessation helps us understand upon the "attitude" of the home government towards the refugees and a slight degree of Improvement on the surface of political 'landscape.

The Extreme Liberal Interpretation: One may, however, invoke an extremely liberal interpretation of the question of voluntariness vis-a-vis the legalistic position discussed above. Such liberal Interpretation can be based on the premise that the Rohingya operation is somewhat unique among UNHCR operations and therefore the question of voluntariness merits flexible application.

The gradual return of Myanmar to the international community by opening up its economy and the release of long detained opposition leader Aung San Su Kyi are small but significant indications of incremental changes that are taking place in that country. The very recent SLORC decisions to discontinue forced labour, payment for communal labour and suspension of relocation of villages may be considered as major steps forward in human rights practice of the regime. All these would have an important bearing for the Rohingya refugees and indicate the liberlizing trend of the Myanmar authorities. The improved on-ground cooperation between UNHCR and Myanmar authorities in the Arakan region and recent UNHCR reports that returnees have not been subjected to any form of harassment as evident from the figure that only 61 of the 193,000 so far repatriated have been arrested on various charges provide evidence of some changes since 1991.

The UNHCR further argues that there are adequate safety nets for the refugees to opt out of repatriation, even at the last minute before crossing the border. All these combined together, the liberals hold, ensured the voluntary nature of repatriation and had been in the best interest of the refugees. In addition to these, if one takes the following issues into consideration then one may be inclined to go beyond the strictly legalistic position presented earlier.

The peculiar history of the Rohingyas within the Myanmar Union, the unresolved question of their citizenship and associated discrimination as a national minority over the hundreds of years, the Myanmar government's perception of them as 'illegal migrants' and a possible concomitant implicit national agenda of driving them out to their 'home country' i.e., Bangladesh, make it a compelling case that any opportunity to send them back to Myanmar by ensuring their personal safety is to be availed.

Delay in their repatriation would only weaken these people's right to live there and would further complicate their claims to land and homes. In addition, the stand taken by the host country, that the refugees must go and Bangladesh cannot provide them with any permanent home, further augments the case for repatriation. The denial of Bangladesh authorities to open schools and income generating activities in camps only reflects their firm determination to accept the refugees as a temporary-phenomenon. The policy makers in Bangladesh realise any effort of integration of the refugees would only invite more refugees from across the border, whom the Myanmar authorities would be only too willing to see go. Added to this the question of donor fatigue could be very well be in UNHCR's policy -makers mind. With the number of refugees worldwide touching the 23m figure, UNHCR could find it legitimate to assess specific situation more pragmatically and apply its principles and policies more creatively.

# 7
# Economic and Social Rights in India

Besides political and allied rights, there is need for economic and social rights. In fact, economic rights are most important in developing states, where people suffer from poverty, hunger, illiteracy, and malnutrition. It is, therefore, necessary to examine how far Indians have these economic and social rights. These rights may be categorised as the rights to property, work, education, medical care, the rights of a child and senior citizens, the right to culture and the right to a decent cremation or burial.

**Right to property**

Right to property has become the most controversial right in the Indian society. But, that is not the fault of Indian thinking alone. The right to property has always been controversial. In the ideal ancient society there was no family, no private property and no government. Slowly but surely, these began to creep in. These are institutions which have developed with the growth of society in a State. During the middle ages, even the Church was not in favour of private property. St. Augustine, famous ecclesiastical legal philosopher, was against the institution of private property. In his opinion, private property was an evil. However, there was some change in the views of the Church when St. Thomas Acquinnas said that there was no harm in the institution of private property if it was utilised for the common welfare of people. This aspect of private property has however been forgotten.

There has been fair emphasis on the right to private property. It is said that it develops man's personality and is the fountain of all rights. The industrial revolution towards the end of the eighteenth century added a new dimension to the concept of private property. Locke championed the rights of life, liberty and property for a citizen, This process continued until the first quarter of the present century. There was a thinking that government has to protect life, liberty and property of its citizens, chief amongst them being property. Since then, the State has changed its role from that of maintaining law and order to that of an agency for the social welfare of its people. It is realised that private property cannot be used as an instrument of oppression. These vicissitudes in thinking on the concept of private property are clear even in international documents.

Article 17 of the U.D.H.R. in 1948, guaranteed the right to private and corporate property and the prohibition against arbitrary deprivation of property. The International Covenant on Economic and Social Rights which was adopted by the U.N. General Assembly eighteen years later, in 1966, omitted this clause. The omission is very conspicuous in view of the fact that most of other rights in the Covenant have been borrowed from the U.D.H.R. This shows the shift of emphasis on the other rights. Perhaps, international elites thought it desirable to leave it to the discretion of each individual State to decide upon the right to private property.

In India, there has been dual thinking, on the concept of private property. In 1947 when India became independent, while the ruling Congress Party was in favour of land reforms, it was not against the institution of private property. It advocated land reforms because it wanted to stop exploitation of the tillers of land by absentee land holders. For this, while Article 19(1-f) of the Constitution guaranteed the right to acquire, hold and dispose of property, it legalised the various land reforms as enacted by the State Governments by bringing in Article 31B, thus, amending the original Article which provided that no "person shall be deprived of his property, save, by authority of law."

An extra Article, 31 (a) was also introduced by the First Constitutional Amendment in 1951 which enabled the acquisition, takeover, amalgamation of two or more companies, extinguishment or modification of rights of managing agencies or agreements relating to minerals or oil by State, notwithstanding Articles 13, 14, 19 and 31 of the Constitution.

The right of property is the fountain of all other rights. The freedom of expression and the press cannot be enjoyed without owning a press. Freedom of trade unions will be thwarted if they are not allowed to own property.' Free movement throughout India would be meaningless if the people were to have no property or money and were not allowed to acquire property in places of their choice.

As stated, Article 19(1-f) of the Constitution gave the right to an Indian citizen to acquire, hold and dispose of property. The word "property" was interpreted by the Indian Supreme Court as extending to all types of interests which have the insignia or characteristics of property rights.' Earlier, the Supreme Court had held that the word "property" included concrete as well as abstract rights.3 It held in that case that the word should be given a wide connotation. In that light, an office of a *mahant* of a math (priest and manager of a particular church) was held to be property. All rights which can be evaluated in terms of money should be considered as constituting property.'

**Right of Eminent Domain**

In law, there is a doctrine of eminent domain. It represents the inherent power of a sovereign State to acquire private property for public purposes. The power was well explained by Justice Mahajan, in the case of State of Bihar vs. Kameshwar Singh. According to him, there is an inherent power in the State to acquire property for public purposes.'

The power of compulsory acquisition has been described by the term "eminent domain". This term seems to have originated in 1625 by Hugo Grotius who wrote of the power in his work, *De Jure Belli ac Pacis*. He stated that the property of subjects is under the eminent domain of the State which may use it, alienate or destroy it not only in case of extreme necessity but for ends of public utility. Private interests must give way to public interests.

The power has been exercised in the United States. As early as in 1883, Justice Field considered the exercise of this power as inherent in every sovereign State.6

The right of eminent domain can be exercised only for public purposes. It cannot be used for individual benefit. This was observed by Justice Mahajan in the case of State of Bihar vs. Kameshwar Singh in following words:

> As between individuals, no necessity however great, no exigency however imminent, no improvement, however valuable, no refusal however unneighbourly, no obstinacy, however unreasonable, no

> offers of compensation, however extravagant, can compel or require any man to part with, an inch of his estate.7

Eminent domain, therefore, can only be exercised for public purpose. But while the exercise of this right by a sovereign State is unchallengeable, there is controversy whether the same can be exercised without just compensation. The controversy remains alive even though Article 31(2), which dealt with compulsory acquisition or requisition of private property for public purpose has been deleted by the Forty-Fourth Amendment of 1978.

The original Article of the Constitution, as it appeared in 1950, contemplated that adequacy of compensation shall be justiciable. This was consistent with Section 299(2) of the Government of India Act 1935. The Fifth Amendment to the U.S. Constitution provides that no private property can be taken for public purpose without just compensation. The Indian Courts had also held that there must be fair and just compensation.

However, the Fourth Amendment to the Indian Constitution in 1955 barred the jurisdiction of the Court as to the adequacy of the compensation. Nevertheless, the Indian Supreme Court held in various cases that, while the court cannot go into the adequacy of the compensation, it can intervene if the compensation offered were to be a sham or illusory. This was held in the cases of Union of India vs. Metal Corporation of India, and R.C. Cooper vs. Union of India, popularly known as the Bank Nationalisation case.'

Perturbed at these trends of decisions by the Supreme Court, which struck off the legislation if the compensation was sham or illusory, the Twenty-Fifth Amendment to the Constitution was passed in 1972 which replaced the word "compensation" with "amount". The purpose of the amendment was to bar the court's jurisdiction with regard to the amount fixed by law for acquiring property without treating it as compensation.

The amendment was challenged in the Supreme Court. As. Palkhiwala argued that if the amount and principles are entirely at the whim of the State, there would be no meaning in keeping Article 31(2) as a fundamental right and making payment as an essential feature of that right. According to him, the State may fix such an amount for acquisition of property as may not restrict or abrogate any of the other fundamental rights. He, therefore, exhorted upon the court to declare the 'Twenty-Fifth Amendment as void on the ground that it damaged or destroyed the core or essence of the right to property and of several other fundamental rights. However, the court did not agree with Palkhiwala and upheld the Twenty-Fifth Amendment.

Although, it may be desirable and argued that there should be proper compensation for acquisition of any property, the socio-economic conditions as are operating in India cannot be lost sight of. There is appalling poverty on the one hand and appalling plenty on the other hand. This contradiction has to be so managed that poverty is eliminated as far as possible.

Article 39 (b & c) of the Constitution says:

b) Ownership and control of the material sources are so distributed as best to subserve the common good;

c) Operation of the economic system does not result in the concentration of wealth and means of production to the common detriment.

These two clauses of Article 39 dwell upon the principles -which govern State policy and aim at ameliorating the lot of common people by opposition to the development of monopoly houses and concentration of wealth in the hands of a few individuals. This may result in the acquisition or diversification of some industries relating to material sources. Besides, the Government has to keep a watch on some industrial houses so that there is no concentration of wealth.

The individual's right to property, therefore, has to be balanced with the socio-economic regulation of right to property. The capitalist concepts of compensation may be of little relevance in India. The nearest principle that can be applicable in Indian conditions in the matter of compensation for property acquired in public interest would be the Norwegian doctrine of socially justifiable compensation.

In view of the above conditions, the Forty-Fourth Amendment deleted the clauses relating to property from Fundamental Rights. Articles 19(1-f) and 31(2) have thus disappeared. Instead, Article 300(A) has been added. It reiterates that no person shall be deprived of his property, save by the authority of law. It became effective with effect from June 20, 1979.

What is the effect of the Forty-Fourth Amendment which omits the right to property as a fundamental right from Article 19, brings Article 31(1) to new Article 300(A) outside the chapter on Fundamental Right and repeals Article 31(2) which dealt with compulsory acquisition of property with compensation? Can property be acquired without adequate compensation by the State Agency?

There are two views on the point. Tripathi thinks that although property has ceased to be fundamental right, it cannot be acquired without compensation under Article 300(A)9 which has its parallel in Article 299 of the Government of India Act 1935. However, another view is that in view of property having ceased to remain as a fundamental right and Article 31(2) having been repealed, there is no scope for the right of compensation for acquired property.' However, it must be admitted that no person can be deprived of his property without authority of law. And law must be fair, reasonable and just. Otherwise, there was no use to introduce a new Article in 300(A). No law will be construed as fair, just and reasonable if it does not give adequate compensation for the property acquired by the Government for any public purpose or in furtherance of its social welfare programmes. It may not be the prevailing market price but it cannot be just a sham. It must be fair and appropriate as envisaged under the Charter of Economic Rights and Duties of States, 1974.

**Right to work**

Article 6 of the International Covenant on Economic and Social Rights recognises the right to work. This was earlier recognised by Article 23 of the U.D.H.R. However, while there is clamour for such a right to be included into fundamental rights of an Indian citizen, it has not yet materialised. But, he has been given the right to choose his profession under Article 19(1-g) of the Indian Constitution. Article 39(a) which deals with the Directive Principles of State Policy states that citizens have the right to an adequate means of livelihood. Under Article 41, the State promises to make effective provision for securing the right to work.

The right to practice any profession is circumscribed by clause 6 of Article 19 which provides that the State may make laws relating to:

i) Professional and technical qualifications necessary for practising any profession or carrying on any occupation, trade or business,

ii) carrying on business partially or exclusively by State or, State controlled or managed corporations;

iii) imposition of reasonable restrictions in the interests of general public.

These restrictions are for the overall common good of the people. No freedom is unlimited. Restrictions on choice of profession are to control development of spurious professions. For example, no person can practice medicine without being qualified in the study of medicine. Similarly, no one can practice at the bar without having the appropriate qualification. The State could also decide whether a given business can be in the private or public sector or in both. Thus, banking or insurance halve been nationalised in public interest. The State has made some Central Acts which go to ameliorate the lot of workers. The Minimum Wages Act, 1948, fixes minimum wages for a worker so that he is not exploited because of his poverty. Men and women are to be given equal pay for equal work. This is regulated by the Equal Remuneration Act of 1976. This is one of the Directive Principles of State Policy given in Article 39 clause 6 of the Constitution. The two Acts, Minimum Wages and Equal Pay, have been recommended by Article 7-a(i) of the Covenant on Economic Rights. Article 43 of the Constitution ensures living wages. Living wage has been aptly interpreted by judge Higgins of Australia as wage which fulfils the normal needs of an average employee, regarded as a human being and living in a civilised society. The Committee on Fair Wages in its Report in 1949 said that minimum wage must provide not merely for the bare sustenance of life, but for the preservation of the efficiency of the, worker. For this purpose, minimum wage must provide for some measure of education of children, medical requirement and amenities.

There is Article 24 of the Constitution which prohibits employment of children below the age of 14 years in a factory, mine or for hazardous work. There is also the Employment of Children Act, 1938 which regulates employment of children. Section 3 of this Act prohibits employment, of children in some hazardous vocations as required under Article 24 of the Constitution. Recently, the Supreme Court advised that children below 14 years of age should not be employed in constructional work in accordance with Convention 59 of the International Labour Organisation which has been ratified by India. Article 10(3) of the Covenant prohibits employment of children in harmful work.

Article 23(1) of the U.D.H.R. promises just and favourable conditions of work. Article 7(b) of the Covenant ensures safe and healthy working conditions. The above international provisions are reflected in Articles 39, 42 and 43 of the Constitution. Article 39(e) states that health and strength of workers are not abused. Article 42 expects the State to make provisions for securing just and human conditions of work. Article 43 seeks to secure conditions of work which ensure a decent standard of life. The Inter-State Migrant Workers (Regulation of Employment and Conditions of Service) Act, 1979 takes care of the working Conditions of the labour in various vocations and seeks to ameliorate the working conditions of labour and ensure decent living with basic human dignity.

Working conditions are also governed by the Contract Labour (Regulation and Abolition) Act of 1970. The Act entitles workers to proper living conditions as well as medical and other facilities. Some prosecutions have been made for violation of these Acts.

Workers in India have the right to join trade unions under Article 19(1-c) of the Constitution. Besides, they have right to join trade unions of their choice under other relevant Acts.

Article 9 of the Covenant on Economic Rights recognises the right to social security. Article 23 of the U.D.H.R. promises protection against unemployment.

This right, unfortunately, is wanting in India, although the State would wish to provide public assistance in case of unemployment under Article 41 of the Constitution. This lack of right is consequential because there is no right to work. The right to work gives right to social security. Perhaps, it may be difficult for the State to secure work or social security for millions of people. The State of Maharashtra has some sort of unemployment allowance scheme on a limited scale. The Central and State Governments are aware of the high rate of unemployment. This has motivated the Govern-ments to introduce schemes of self-employment and disbursement of soft loans for those who want to open their own industries. Unemployed graduates are encouraged to open their own business for which they are given necessary facilities. There is also a proposal in some States to give an unemployment allowance to degree holders of any University but the same has not materialised.

**Right to education**

Literacy means enlightenment and awareness. More so in a developing country which has a low rate of literacy. People have the right to know about their country and the world that they live in. They should also know as to what are their rights and social duties. This cannot be done without education. Education develops human personality, understanding, tolerance and comradeship. The right to education, therefore, is essential. Article 26 of the U.D.H.R. states that everyone has a right to education. Article 13 of the Covenant on Economic Rights recognises the right to education.

In India, there is no fundamental right to education. But its importance has been recognised in Article 41 of the Directive Principles of State Policy. It promises that the State shall make effective efforts to secure to its citizens the right to education. The State is further obliged to endeavour to provide free and compulsory education to children up to the age of 14 years. While most of the States have introduced free primary education, it has not been possible to make it compulsory, perhaps due to financial compulsions. Nor have all the States succeeding in making education free up to 14 years. Financial stringency and rising population have been the main factors for this shortcoming. There are concerted efforts however, to popularise adult education and make it purposeful, although, it is on a voluntary basis. Some States have provided free mid-day meals for students in primary schools.

At the High School and University levels, States have strived to make education less expensive. Despite rapid increase in cost of living and continued hike in remunerations of academic and administrative staff, tuition fees have remained static. Governments have also introduced freeships and loan scholarships for deserving students. Members of Scheduled Castes and Tribes have, in many cases, been exempted from payment of regular fees. Student amenities and hostel facilities have been provided in all universities. Although these cannot be considered adequate, number of such facilities is increasing steadily.

**Right to medical care**

Article 12 of the Covenant emphasises on medicare of persons by the State. It assures physical, mental health and medical attention. Article 41 of the Constitution enjoins upon the State—to strive to give public assistance to sick and disabled persons within the limits of its economic capacity. Article 47 enjoins upon the State to raise the level of nutrition and improve public health.

States have tried to give medical aid by opening hospitals and other public health clinics, where free medical assistance is given to the people. In some cases, only a nominal fee is charged from the patient in respect of medical assistance rendered and in relation to the individual's gross income.

While medical attention is normally assured to people in the metropolitan cities of the country, the same type of medical attention and expertise is not available in small towns. In State capitals, one gets comparably good medical service; next coming in order of priority are Divisional towns, Districts, Sub-divisions, and Blocks. The medical facilities available need to be considerably enhanced and improved.

**Rights of child**

A child is a country's future. Everywhere in the world, the child is well taken care of because the future of a country depends on the healthy growth of its children. Article 24 of the civil Covenant seeks protection measures for the welfare of the child and assured nationality.

Article 39 (f) of the Indian Constitution seeks to protect the child against exploitation and moral and material abandonment. A child is to be encouraged and facilitated to grow in a healthy manner under conditions of freedom and dignity. Article 23 prohibits traffic in human beings, including children and as already stated, Article 24 prohibits engagement of children below 14 in hazardous jobs. Article 39(e) seeks to protect the child against engagement in jobs unsuited to his age and strength. Article 45 promises to make education free and compulsory for children under 14 years of age. The year 1980 was designated as the Year of Child by the United Nations. There has been a Declaration of the Rights of Child.

The rights of a child have not been well protected.

In developing countries, including India, more than fifty per cent children suffer from hunger, malnutrition and disease. There is a high rate of infant mortality. The Government's provision for primary education of child is inadequate. Parents seek to employ their very young children to add to their paltry incomes. People seek to exploit poverty by employing children in all sorts of jobs. Children are mostly exploited by *dhabas* (wayside eating houses) where they develop all sorts of vices which become incurable in due course of time.

**Rights of senior citizens**

Old persons should be treated as senior citizens and given respect due for their age, experience and expertise. Article 41 requires the State to give public assistance to persons of old age. It is heartening to know that most of the States have made some provision for old-age pensions for indigent persons, although it must be admitted that all have not been covered. Limited resources have probably dampened the government efforts to extend old-age pension schemes to a larger section of people.

Pensioners must be treated humanely. There should be no discrimination amongst them. In a recent case, the Supreme Court aptly remarked that "with the expanding horizons of socio-economic justice, the socialist republic and welfare state which we endeavour to set up and largely influenced by the fact that the old men who retired when emoluments were comparatively less and are exposed to the vagaries of continuously rising prices, the falling value of the rupee consequently upon inflationary input, it would be unfair to deny liberalised pension rules to those who retired before 1979." The Supreme Court, therefore, ordered application of liberalised rules of pensions to all pensioners, irrespective of when they retired

Some States have opened old-age homes for old and homeless people. But the practice is not common. States should be urged to open more such homes for the aged not only in capital cities but at least in divisional towns as well.

Some facilities should be extended to old people in the form of discounted fares in transport, subsidised food or discount rates in canteens and other utility services as is being done in other countries. They could also be admitted to cinema houses and other places of entertainment on concessional rates. The Government should pay more attention to security arrangements in respect of premises, occupied by aged people who often become easy prey to anti-social elements.

Similar facilities should be extended to the disabled, handicapped and terminally sick persons.

**Right to cultural life**

Article 15 of the Covenant and Article 27 of the U.D.H.R. give the right to cultural life to every person. Article 29(1) of the Constitution gives the right to conserve the cultural life by any section of citizens.

While no individual person may have separate culture, sections of society may have some separate cultural traits and qualities. These sections must have the right to maintain and conserve their culture without any government or outside interference.

Culture is part of man's living. Disassociate culture and man becomes barren. It is the culture which boosts the man's spirits. It is, therefore, necessary to preserve culture.

It is on this account that different sections in the Indian society exhibit their folk dances, songs and their local sartorial habits, dialects, festivals and other cultural peculiarities at national and other important occasions.

**Right to decent cremation or burial**

The State should ensure decent cremation or burial, as the case may be, of indigent and unclaimed bodies, although there is no such constitutional right in India. There is, however, provision in the administration manual where a District Collector is, authorised to defray expenses for cremation or burial from Government imprest money which is left at the disposal of the district administration in respect of unclaimed bodies.

# 8

# Refugees from Bangladesh

Around 10 million Bangalees took refuge in India during the liberation war of Bangladesh (March 1971- December 1971). Similar to the partition of India in 1947, the forced movement of 10 million people during 1971 constituted Bangladesh. These people left East Pakistan for shelter in the neighbouring Indian states of, mostly, West Bengal and Assam to escape massacre for their political religious beliefs. The violence perpetuated against the people was clearly reflected as a constituting cause for the declaration of Independence of Bangladesh. The Proclamation of Independence stated:

Whereas in the conduct of ruthless and savage war the Pakistani authorities committed and are still continuously committing numerous acts of genocide and unprecedented tortures, among other, on the civilian and unarmed people of Bangladesh... In 1971, the Indian Government granted refugee status to these millions of people who left the territory then known as East Pakistan. The international community and organisations as well as the Indian Government undertook massive measures to assist the refugees. There are no precise numbers available, but generally it is believed during April-November, 1971 as many as 10 million people may have crossed the international boundary between the then East Pakistan and India. After the independence of Bangladesh, most of these refugees were able to return to their home within a few short months. Again massive international help made the repatriation of such huge numbers possible.

It is generally assumed that most of Hindus from East Pakistan and Bangladesh during 1961-1991 have been forced to move to India, owing to, primarily, discriminatory practices against them and, secondarily, fear of persecution both by the state and the majority religious community of Bangladesh.

On a more technical-legal count, two legislation—Defence of Pakistan Ordinance 1965 (Ordinance No 23 of 1965) including Defence of Pakistan Rules, 1965 framed under that Ordinance; and The Bangladesh Abandoned Property (Control, Management and Disposal) Order, 1972 (President's Order No 16 of 1972) can be generally construed as having created situations of 'fear' and 'insecurity' for the Hindu minority community, compelling them to steadily leave Bangladesh for India. The study quoted above indicates the possible quantitative magnitude of this forced migration. The first of these laws, popularly known as 'Enemy Property Act' was enacted in 1965, during the 17-day India-Pakistan War to prevent the use of properties of 6 enemy' against the war-efforts of Pakistan. The second was purportedly enacted to take care of the properties of those who left the newly independent Bangladesh for Pakistan (i.e., Biharis).

Both the enactments, arguably, were meant to be temporary measures for temporary exigencies. However, these enactment's came to be abused and virtually became legal tools for denying the minority Hindu community of their rights to immovable properties and forcing them to sell off their properties. Over the last three decades there had been an unending stream of litigations under these two laws, most often in the nature of attempts by the members of the minority communities to restore the ownership of their lands which had allegedly been declared 'to be "enemy" or "abandoned" and, "vested" with the government. Such "vesting" is often done fraudulently and the abuse of these two enactments are at the core of the feeling of insecurity of the minority communities.

It has been estimated that about 1 million acres of land belonging to the minority community, out of a total arable land 21 million of the country, has been subjected to transfer from the owners belonging to the minority community to those of the majority community. And about one-third of all the minority households of the country had been adversely affected by these laws.

The impact of these laws and consequent litigations has been manifested in the dramatic reduction in the Hindu population of the country—their migration to neighbouring India. Partially, such migration can be laid at the steps of 'search for better opportunities'. However, the inequitable and often illegal denial of such opportunities in Bangladesh is an important approximate cause.

The movement of people into and from the territory comprising Bangladesh is not only a historical phenomenon but a continuous process. In present times, movements of people from Bangladesh to more affluent lands have been an important economic factor for the country as remittance by these people constitute a large share of the foreign exchange earnings of Bangladesh. This present movement of people is, however, replete with contradictory and dichotomous images of plenitude and hardship.

The Government of Bangladesh has taken certain steps, including setting up of the Bureau of Manpower Employment and Training and authorised certain manpower employment agencies, to channel temporary migration of people abroad for employment purposes. However, as the figures above indicate, the process has broken down, partially, if not completely.

More alarmingly, there does not seem to be any agency or body responsible for looking after the welfare of these hundreds of thousands of Bangladeshis employees abroad, except skeleton structures at the embassies. Given the importance of these temporary migrants to the national exchequer and the limited prospect for employment generation within the country, it is conceivable that the figure of Bangladeshis working in various countries will reach five million in the foreseeable future. Such numbers, both in the humanitarian and financial contexts, certainly call for turning the issues and concerns of the Bangladeshis abroad into one of the most important concerns of the Government. Few paltry efforts at training the manpower and inadequate regulations of the 'manpower agencies' are hardly enough.

The current legal system do not take into account the requirements of this vast number of people working abroad, nor are the government agencies in a position to take any effective measures to provide ' support to such people abroad. Consequently, the current legal and administrative systems dealing with migration issues need to be re-evaluated and forward looking arrangements undertaken. Particularly, undertaking a comprehensive study of the situations of Bangladeshis abroad, both legally and illegally; assessing their needs and requirements; devising and undertaking measures and steps to protect their interests (legal and financial); assisting them to legalise their status in foreign lands;

and ensuring proper and easy remittance of their earning are some of the propositions which need careful response. Besides, there is no support group to advise these people. Hence, interventions of the NGOs into this arena also needs to be considered.

Those whose legal status has been of the longest standing controversy in Bangladesh are certainly the Biharis or Stranded Pakistanis. Biharis are the people of the Indian state of Bihar. In 1947, the population of Bihar numbered around 30,000,000 of whom about 4,000,000 were Muslims. Partition gave Bihar to India, with its 4 million Muslims. A year before partition, in October of 1946, some 30,000 Bihari Muslims were killed by Bihari Hindus in alleged retaliation for killings of Hindus in Noakhali. These killings precipitated the movement of Muslim Biharis into Pakistan, about 700,000 chose to settle in East Pakistan and the rest in West Pakistan.

The ethnic gap between the recently arrived Urdu-speaking Biharis and the Bengali-speaking Muslims of East Pakistan, for several political and economic reasons, never bridged. Biharis continued to live as a separate community and their role in support of the Pakistani Army during the war of liberation precipitated retaliation against them, both during the liberation war and after the liberation.

Many Biharis left for West Pakistan during 1971, and after Liberation War in 1971, 462,000 Biharis were left stranded in Bangladesh. These Biharis demanded to be repatriated to Pakistan. The Pakistani Government initially agreed to take 83.000 Biharis but later took some others. By 1974, 108,000 Biharis had been transferred to Pakistan, mainly by air. Further negotiations led to the transfer of a total of about 163,000 Biharis. As a result, between 250,000 and 300,000 Biharis were left in camps in Bangladesh.

The pertinent issue concerning the legal status of the Biharis revolves around their stated desire to migrate to Pakistan on the one hand, and the reluctance of both Pakistan and Bangladesh to grant them citizenship, on the other hand. It seems that according to the laws of Citizenship of Bangladesh 27 the Biharis, who were in the territory of Bangladesh, are eligible to become citizens. Article 3(d) of the Bangladesh Citizenship Act, 1951 provides the following criterion:

Who before the commencement of this Act migrated to the territories now includes in Bangladesh from any territory in the Indo-Pakistan sub-continent outside those territories with intention of residing permanently in those territories.

Furthermore, article 2 of the Bangladesh Citizenship (Temporary Provisions Order, 1972 (President's Order 149 of 1972) provides:

i) who or whose father or grandfather was born in the territories now comprised in Bangladesh and who was permanent resident of the territories now comprised in Bangladesh on the 25th March, 1971, and continues to be so resident; or

ii) who was a permanent resident of the territories now comprised in Bangladesh on the 25th day of March, 1971, and continues to be so resident and is not otherwise disqualified for being a citizen by or under any law, for the time being in force:

As most of the Biharis came to the territories comprising Bangladesh from the India-Pakistan subcontinent with the intention of residing permanently and virtually all of them were permanent residents before 25 March, 1971, a plain reading of these two sections would confirm their entitlement to citizenship of Bangladesh.

However, article 2B of the Bangladesh Citizenship

(Temporary Provisions) Amendment Ordinance 1978 (Ordinance No VII of 1978) added that a person shall not qualify to be a citizen of Bangladesh if he:

> 2(B) (1) (i) owes, affirm or acknowledges, expressly or by conduct, allegiance to a foreign state, or....

This rule may ostensibly seem to strip those Biharis who have applied for or expressed their desire to become citizens of Pakistan, the right to be citizens of Bangladesh. However, such a reading is fraught with contradictions. First, a literal application of this rule may deprive those citizens of Bangladesh who holds dual status, with, for example, the United Kingdom. Their status in the United Kingdom obviously implies their allegiance to a foreign state, yet they are citizens of Bangladesh. Secondly, thousands of Bangladeshis have applied for OP-1 and/or DB-1 'visa' of the United States, indicating their intention to migrate and owe allegiance to that country, if chosen.

There is hardly any likelihood that such applications by the citizens would be construed as expression of allegiance to a foreign country, as has purportedly been done in case of the Biharis vis-a-vis their intention to migrate to Pakistan. Moreover, this proviso introduced by the amendment is a restrictive one. Hence, such a restrictive qualification introduced in 1978 is not likely to be deemed effective retrospectively from 15th December, 1972, i.e., the day The Bangladesh Citizenship (Temporary Provisions) Order, 1972 came into force; though it was given effect from 26 March 1971. In the Appellate Division judgement referred to above, it was pointed out:

> Article 2 conferred citizenship on a body of persons by a legal fiction, not by the Government or any other executive authority, but by the legislature...

More importantly:

> There is no power under article 3 denuding a person of his citizenship for the offence of collaboration with the Pakistan Occupation Army. Indeed there is nothing in President's Order No. 149 of 1972 which authorised the Government on the date of the impugned notification to disqualify a citizen on the ground of collaboration with the Pakistan Occupation Army. President's Order No. 149 of 1972 was never intended to punish an alleged collaborator of the said Army by stripping him of his citizenship.

More generally, in this very important judgment on citizenship the Appellate Division also held that:

> It is not a power in the hands of the Government to 'cancel' a person's citizenship to make a 'declaration' of any sort or to disqualify any person from citizenship or to review one's citizenship under article 2.

More pertinently, the same judgement also held that:

> One cannot continue to be a citizen of Pakistan merely by his choice or stay in Pakistan unless State of Pakistan accepted him as such.

This principle of law can be traced back to a judgment of the Dhaka High Court of 1969:

> There is no principle recognized in international law which would enable a person by his volition and by his own act regardless of the will of a State to acquire or terminate a nationality merely by his own choice. A nationality can neither be acquired nor retained except with will of the State. Other nuances of the citizenship provisions vis-a-vis the Biharis, such as the status of their children born after 1971 etc., need not be dealt with here in detail. General provisions of the relevant law seem to support the claim for citizenship of the Biharis who have been residents on or before 25th March, 1971.

It would seem that the present situation of the Biharis vis-a-vis their citizenship status in Bangladesh, if they or any of them so wishes, may be resolved through the courts and probably expeditiously by invoking the writ jurisdiction of the High Court Division of the Supreme court of Bangladesh. A political decision, however, in favour of granting them citizenship rights and status is unlikely, due to their perceived participation in acts against the liberation forces during 1971.

After almost a quarter of a century, the Biharis still continue to live in 'refugee camps'; in conditions of alienation, deprivation, and unemployment without any prospect of improvement of their lot in the short run. Conventional wisdom suggests that such a hopeless situation for a large group of alienated people is the breeding grounds for lawlessness, at the best, and violence and terrorism, at the worst. Moreover, the children born in these camps, many of whom are already in their late teens if not older, are paying the price for wrongs, if any, committed by their forefathers. Theirs is a plight which needs to be resolved not within the narrow confines of refugee and citizenship laws, but by invoking human rights and humanitarian principles of human kind.

Secondly, general principles of issues of nationality in consequence of state succession suggest negotiations between the predecessor and successor states. Such negotiations between Pakistan and Bangladesh did result in the transfer of 163,000 Biharis to Pakistan during the first decade after succession. The negotiations regarding the rest seem to have come to a halt. The situation has become further complicated by the linkage of the issue of the Biharis with that of the allegedly illegal movements of hundreds of thousands of Bangladeshis to Pakistan. Consequently, Bangladesh may not be in a position to demand unilateral repatriation of these Biharis without invoking a counter-demand from the side of Pakistan vis-a-vis the Bangladeshis in Pakistan.

However, irrespective of the bargaining and negotiating stances, claims and counter-claims of the sides involved, the states are obliged to prevent statelessness, particularly when such statelessness is consequent upon state succession. Given the long standing residence of the Biharis in Bangladesh and their legal entitlement under the citizenship laws of the country, there does not seem to be much justification in denying the Biharis their citizenship status, if any or some of them so desires.

Furthermore, though Bangladesh has not acceded to the Convention on the Reduction of Statelessness 1961, yet it is important to note the desirability of reducing statelessness, as expressed by the Convention and the continued denial of nationality to Biharis is contrary to this Convention as well as Article 15 of the Universal Declaration of Human Rights to which Bangladesh is a signatory.

Thousands of Rohingyas from Burma came to Bangladesh in 1978 and again in 1991 as refugees. They were refugees because their condition coincided with the relevant criteria laid down by the 1951 Convention Relating to the Status of Refugees and the 1967 Protocol Relating to the Status of Refugees. Although Bangladesh is not a signatory to the Convention and the Protocol, Memorandums of Understanding were signed by the UNHCR with both the Governments of Bangladesh and Burma and on the basis of these 'understanding' UNHCR has taken over the situation concerning these Rohingya refugees.

In 1978 some 200,000 Rohingyas crossed the border into Bangladesh. At that time the Bangladeshi Government claimed that there were as many as 252,000 Rohingya refugees while Burma acknowledged a number of 143,900 who, according to the Burmese authorities, absconded to Bangladesh in order to escape the Nagmin Project. Following the negotiations between the two governments in June-July, 1978, an agreement was reached on the repatriation of the refugees to Burma. The repatriation operation commenced on 1st August, 1978 and ended on 29th December, 1978 and involved repatriation of a total of 187,250 refugees.

Both the Chittagong region of the southeastern Bangladesh and the neighbouring Arakan region of Burma came in contact with Muslim Arab merchants in the first millennium. Large numbers of inhabitants of both the regions subsequently became Muslims. An Arakanese king occupied the Chittagong region in 951 and named it after him. In 1430, the Mughal Governor of Bengal, Jalal al-Din Muhammad Shah helped Narmikhila (the deposed king of Arakan) install himself on the throne of Arakan with the consequent increase of the influence of the Mughals in Arakanese affairs. In 1785 the Burman king annexed Arakan into his kingdom and the Muslims of Arakan came to fare badly under the Burmese kings.

The incorporation of Arakan with Burma brought the Burmans in direct contact with British India. The Arakanese refugees in Chittagong area organised raids against the Burmese rule and, in pursuit, the Burman army led incursions into the British Indian territory. This led to the first Anglo-Burmese War (1824-26), resulting in the annexation of Arakan and Tesessarim by the British. British colonial expansion subsequently led to the second (1853) and third (1885) Anglo-Burmese wars, resulting in British control over entire Burma.

The advance of the Japanese army during the

Second World War led to the exodus of tens of thousands of Indians (who had earlier moved into Burma from India) from Burma and especially Muslims from Arakan. Riots flared up between the communities and some 22,000 Rohingyas (i.e., Arakanese Muslims) took refuge adjoining British territory of southern Chittagong. The Arakanese communities were divided in their loyalties, the Rohingyas were loyal to the British, rendering valuable services in work units, reconnaissance and espionage, while their Buddhist counterparts, the Rakhinese, sides with the Japanese.

Although the British had promised, after the end of the war, to settle the Araknanese Muslim in an autonomous Muslim National Area, this was not subsequently honoured. After the Buddhist dominated Burmese administration took control over Arakan, the Muslim's sense of alienation grew and this was translated into armed resistance against the Burmese authorities, further aggravating the relation between the communities.

Gradually, over the last few decades, the Arakanese Muslims (Rohingyas) came to be distrusted and prosecuted by the ruling powers of Burma. Sporadic demands for autonomy, armed clashes and continued discriminatory steps escalated the situation, leading to the exodus of 1978.

Faced with a growing number of refugees crossing the border in 1978, the Bangladesh Government, on the one hand, began bilateral negotiations with Burma and, on the other hand, appealed to the international community for international assistance. A major international fund raising campaign was mounted for the assistance to the refugees and they were kept in 11 camps in the Chittagong region, bordering Arakan. These refugees were repatriated by the end of December, 1978.

In 1991, Bangladesh witnessed another influx of Rohingya refugees into the bordering region. The figure soon escalated to 250,000. Similar to the attempts in 1978, the Bangladesh Government soon began bilateral negotiations with the Myanmar Government regarding repatriation of these new refugees and signed a Joint Statement with the State Law and Order Restoration Council (SLORC) of Myanmar on April 28, 1992. Later UNHCR was invited by the Bangladesh Government to render assistance to the refugees, from mid-1992. UNHCR's involvement facilitated the work of international NGOs to complement the work of national NGOs.

Under the Memorandum of 28 April, 1992, Myanmar agreed to the repatriation of those who could establish their bona fide residency prior to their departure for Bangladesh. The initial cordial treatment of the refugees were, however, not sustained neither by the Bangladesh Government nor by the local people who increasingly began to feel the pressure of the presence of such a large number of people in their midst. Bangladesh soon attempted to repatriate refugees, involving use of force. In view of the subsequent protests by the UNHCR and other relevant bodies, the repatriation procedure was changed and made more transparent.

The first repatriation of these 1991 refugees took place on 22 September, 1992, without the intervention of the UNHCR. UNHCR believes that this repatriation was "accompanied by considerable pressure (coercion) from the Bangladeshi authorities", who insisted that they could not give the refugees long-term asylum. In the wake of international criticism of the 'forced repatriation', albeit on a limited scale, the Bangladesh Government agreed to allow free access to the UNHCR in May, 1993 to ensure the voluntary nature of further repatriation.

In November 1993, the UNHCR signed a Memorandum of Understanding with Myanmar. The Government of Myanmar assured that returnees will be allowed to return to their respective places of origin from the UNHCR-assisted camps in Bangladesh and enjoy civic rights of Myanmar citizens. Thus the signing of Memorandums of Understanding between the UNHCR and both the Governments concerned paved the way for voluntary repatriation of the refugees; at the rate of 15 - 18,000 per month. Under these new arrangements, the first refugees returned to Myanmar in April 1994, accompanied by the UNHCR Representative in Bangladesh "To establish confidence of the refugees". After some dislocation caused by the cyclone in the area in May, 1994, the repatriation process continued. According to available figures, a total of 204,000 Rohingya refugees were repatriated by the end of August, 1996.44 However, in recent months there were reports of fresh influx, though on a much smaller scale (7,000 by July, 1996) of Rohingyas coming back into Bangladesh. During this period of 1991-1996, despite mounting evidence to the contrary, the Bangladesh Government seemed to have acted on the assumption that the Rohingya refugees were in Bangladesh for a very short period of time.

Consequently, adequate measures were not taken to provide basic facilities to the refugees during their stay in Bangladesh. Particularly, their movement was restricted, arrangements for education of the young refugees were virtually non-existent and similar other required facilities were not offered, inspite of assurances of financial support for these measures. After initial warmth, the growing hostilities of the local Bangladeshis and negative reporting in the national newspaper, particularly regarding deforestation caused by the refugees and violence within and amongst the refugees were constraining factors. For a country virtually born out of displacement of millions of refugees, the moral obligation vis-a-vis refugees forced to move into this country, thus remained unfulfilled.

The plight of the indigenous and 'tribal' people of the Chittagong Hill Tracts has been and continues to remain the darkest episode in the national integration process of Bangladesh. The indigenous people of the Chittagong Hills Tracts (CHT) are the only significant group of people of Bangladesh who are ethnically different from the majority community. Their number, in the context of 110 million people of Bangladesh, is relatively small indeed; less than 800,000.

The compartmentalisation of the tribal people, as 'Other', is best reflected in their treatment in isolation, i.e., without any contemplation of the interaction between them and the majority community. This hill area of the southeastern Bangladesh is known as Chittagong Hill Tracts, subdivided into three administrative districts. It forms part of a mountain range which stretches north for some 1800 km from western Myanmar to the points where it meets the eastern Himalayas in China. Apart from the narrowstrip (roughly 280 by 60 km) as part of Bangladesh, this mountain range is almost equally divided between India and Burma.

This strip of mountainous land is inhabited by a large range of people, speaking variety of languages, adhering to various creeds and organised socially in different ways. The British annexed this region in 1860, administered it through the local kings and chiefs and later under the Chittagong Hill Tracts Regulation, 1900 (Act 1 of 1990). During the Partition of 1947, the Hill Tracts were awarded to Pakistan and subsequently became a part of the new country (Bangladesh) when it succeeded in 1971.

The inhabitants of the Chittagong Hill Tracts are primarily agriculturist and depend upon subsistence farming. Theirs are shifting cultivation, locally known as 'jhum'. This area, comprising roughly 10% of the total area of Bangladesh is rich in forest and forest resources. Before the influx of large number of Bengalis, beginning in the late 70's, the indigenous people constituted less than 1% of the total population of the country. Now, in the mid-90s, the number of the Bengali settlers are becoming equal to the number of indigenous people.

The indigenous people of the CHT are sub-divided into 13 ethnic groups, the Chakmas being the numerically largest, constituting about one-fifth of all the indigenous people of Bangladesh. Other ethnic groups are: Marma, Tripura, Murong, Tangichamgya, Bown, Pankhoo, Khumi, Mro, Khyara, Chak, Lushai and Riang. Kabriaul Khaleque, deriving from some sample surveys and inconsistencies in various parts of the Census 1991, suggests that the actual figure "might be more than the figure given in the Census Report. The Bengali settlers started to come into the Chittagong Hill Tracts in the wake of construction of the Kaptai Dam and Karnaphully Paper Mills in the mid-60s. Their number, however, started to swell from the late 70's.

During the Pakistan period the huge hydroelectric project, Kaptai Dam, was built, displacing 100,000 tribal inhabitants of the area. 40% of the arable land of the region was submerged and estimated 40,000 people left for India. Most of them live in the Arunachal Pradesh of India today. Government officials freely acknowledge today that there were little compensation or rehabilitation, though it had been promised. By most counts, the hydroelectric project and the subsequent neglect of the affected people left a deep legacy of bitterness and distrust and may have triggered the current dilemma. For example, one survey conducted among the Chakmas reported that 69% felt that the Dam created food and financial problems for them, 89% had to change their residence due to inundation, 69% complained of inadequate government help for resettlement and 93% felt that the economic condition of the tribal people had been better before the Kaptae Dam.

The Kaptai Dam and subsequent 'development' of the CHT region both during the Pakistan and Bangladesh period proceeded from the racialist assumption that the indigenous people were incapable of 'development' without the intervention of the more advanced sections of the country, i.e., people from the plains and hence restrictions regarding access and settlement of non-indigenous people into the region was removed in the late 60s.

From the standpoint of the Bengalis, similar to their allegation regarding the Biharis, the tribal people of the Hill Tracts are seen to have collaborated with the Pakistani army during the liberation war, as well as have hoisted Indian flag in 1972, indicating a preference for India, then.

In 1972, a high powered delegation of the people of the Hill Tracts met the President of Bangladesh and placed their demand for autonomy for the region, including (i) its own legislation, (ii) retention of the 1890 Regulation, (iii) continuation of three chiefs' officers and (iv) a ban on the influx of non-hill peoples. The demands were rejected outright. The Bangladesh constitution had no provision for any autonomous region in the country.

From the mid-70s steady stream of Bengali settlers poured into the region. Some of it were part of 'normal' movements of people within the country. Later, successive governments encouraged migration into the region which gradually led to increased tension between the Bengali settlers and the indigenous people. During the same period the government tried to resettle the indigenous people into newly created and concentrated village, further aggravating the sense of alienation. Meanwhile a number of skirmishes between the new Bengali settlers and the indigenous people turned into riots.

The government moved in army reinforcements, beginning a process which culminated into continuous posting of, by many counts, almost one fourth of the total Bangladesh army into the region. The Shanti Bahini, the military wing of the indigenous people, began their armed attacks on government outpost. The pattern was captured in a report in the Far Eastern Economic Review in June 1986.

A reorganised Shanti Bahini force carried out its biggest coordinated attack on 29 April [1986] as it simultaneously raided several Bangladeshi army camps and the outposts of paramilitary Bangladesh Rifles and followed it up with swoops on new settlements of immigrant Bengali Muslims. In turn, the Muslim settlers and government forces carried out reprisals on tribal villages forcing the tribes-people to flee to India on 30 April. By 1987, refugee camps in India began to provide shelters to the tribal people of the Hill Tracts who were forced to flee their homeland. Earlier, in September 1986, Amnesty International issued their major report on the situation in CHT, entitled "Unlawful Killings and Torture in the Chittagong Hill Tracts".

Negotiations were initiated in 1988 between the representatives of the government and the Jana Samhati Samiti (JSS)—the People's United Party. The stance of the JSS in this negotiation were similar to demands put forward as far back as 1972; removal of non-tribal settlers from the CHT, withdrawal of all Bangladeshi armed forces, retention of the 1900 Regulation and autonomy for the CHT with its own legislature. The last few years has not witnessed any dramatic improvement in the relationship between the settlers and the tribal people on the one hand and the government and the JSS on the other.

# 9

# CONCEPT OF HUMAN RIGHTS

The concept of human rights is necessarily evolving in nature apace with the evolution of human civilization in the context of a changing social, political, economic and cultural milieu. It is, therefore, a daunting task for anyone to assess the state of implementation of human rights in a society. The arrogance of sitting in judgment over the human rights performance of the society apart, it is a function often tainted by a preferred perception and prioritization of human rights inter se and an eclectic identification and impressionistic evaluation of human rights situations.

The exercise usually ends up in a fault-finding judgement, without taking into account the intrinsic correlationship of the development of the individual with the development of the society, and without addressing the question of social and economic costs of conditioning the correlationship between the individual and societal development. For these reasons, the present study does not claim to be a comprehensive and holistic assessment of the human rights situation in India or an elaborate prescription of preventive and remedial measures. Its aim is rather modest: to present a general overview of the human rights situation in India, as the nation celebrates the Golden Jubilee of its independence. The ethos and problems of a developing ancient oriental society like the India must first be understood before an acceptable standard of rights performance assessment is evolved. Indeed, the non-derogable rights to life and dignity do provide a universal bottom line. Yet, to look at a society purely through that looking glass is to ignore the ground realities in the midst of which the human rights culture has to nurture.

**The vision of the makers of modern India**

The Indian culture perceives the individual, the society and the universe an organic whole: Everyone is a child of God, and all fellow-beings are related to one another, belonging to a universal family. Religious prayers would ask of God to make all peoples of the world happy. The same cultural ethos rang in when Mahatma Gandhi said:

> I do not want to think in terms of the whole world. My patriotism includes the good of mankind in general. Therefore, my service to India includes the services of humanity'.

While the ancient texts tend to emphasize the principle of equality between individuals, there is no doubt that there was always a gap between he ideal and the ground reality. Humans in any society have never been equal inter se and there have always been dominant groups/ classes seeking to monopolize social and material benefits unto themselves and deprive others from access to them. Stratification is the bane of all societies. In India, for instance, the caste system arose from the principle of division of labour as a method of social organization.

However, over a period of time, those castes which could gain power and wealth, such as the Brahmins and the Kshatriyas, exploited the society and its institutions. The chasm between the religious, scriptural norms and practice grew wide. The historical responses came from Buddhism and Jainism, both of which emphasized the principles of equality, non-violence and denial of materialistic pleasures. The religious reformers like Sankara then took upon themselves the task of purification of the Indian society, through a process of synthesis of new thoughts. Subsequently, the advent of the Muslim rulers from the north brought with them the teachings of Islam. This historical process of synthesis, aided by enlightened reformers, and great kings like Ashoka and Akbar, now forms the foundation of the amazing phenomenon called the Indian culture. On it stands the coexistence of and mutual respect for diverse religious and philosophical beliefs and subcultures. While the dubious credit for the unification of India must largely go to the British rule, the British achieved it with systematic destruction of the traditional social, political and economic institutions, and exploitation of the social and religious weaknesses of the Indian masses in furtherance of the cause of British imperialism.

The British stood to gain by sharpening the caste and religious differences in the society in pursuit of their divide and rule policy. In the Indian cultural history, the British colonial period shall remain the Indian equivalent of the "Dark Ages". The renaissance came about thanks chiefly to the rise of nationalism and religious and social reformers. The leaders of Indian nationalism have, however, been a new breed of men and women of vision synthesizing the traditional cultural values with newly imbibed ideas of the American and the French revolutions. Mahatma Gandhi was the foremost among them. His test of freedom has always been what benefit it would accrue to the poorest of the land.

The ultimate welfare of the poorest of the Indians was Gandhiji's fundamental yardstick. He dreamt of an India "in which the poorest shall feel that it is their country, in whose making they have an effective voice, an India in which there shall be no high class and low class of people, an India in which all communities shall live in perfect harmony. There can be no room in such an India for the curse of untouchability or the curse of intoxicating drinks and drugs. . . . Women will enjoy the same right as men".

Addressing the nation on the threshold of independence, Jawaharlal Nehru declared in the same vein:

> We shall look to the common and forgotten man of India and seek to bring him relief and raise his standard of living. We shall continue our fight against the curse of untouchability and other forms of enforced inequality, and shall especial] ', try to help those who are economically or otherwise backward. Today millions lack food and clothing and houses, and many are on the verge of starvation.'

Thus the leaders of India's independence struggle had already set a clear "Indian" human rights agenda for action even as the nation was emerging independent. Small wonder, the new legal and political norms and institutions reflected this agenda, although it was left to these institutions and ultimately to the people of India to evolve and redefine these norms through the ever changing national political and social processes.

**Institutional Framework of Human Rights**

The Preamble to the Constitution pledges to secure to all the citizens of India Justice-social, economic and political, liberty-of thought, expression, belief, faith and worship, Equality--of status and of opportunity; and Fraternity assuring the dignity of the individual and the unity and integrity of the nation. Two parts of the Constitution embody most human rights, distinguishing between judicially enforceable fundamental rights and rights not so enforceable, namely Part III and Part IV. The judicially enforceable fundamental rights, which encompass all seminal civil and political rights and some of the rights of minorities, are enshrined in Part III of the Constitution (Articles 12 to 35). These include the right to equality, the right to freedom, the right against exploitation, the right to freedom, of religion, cultural and educational rights, and the right to constitutional remedies. Judicially non-enforceable rights in Part IV of the Constitution are chiefly those of economic and social character. However, as Article 37 makes it clear, their non-justiciability does not weaken the duty of the state to apply them in making laws, since they are "nevertheless fundamental in the governance of the country".

Additionally, the innovative jurisprudence of the Supreme Court has now read into Article 21 (the right to life and personal liberty); many of these principles and made them enforceable. In the scheme of the Constitution, there exists a separation of powers among the legislature, the executive and the judiciary, with the judiciary being fiercely independent of the other two, charged with the task of enforcing (lie constitutional norms, including human rights, and adjudicating upon all interindividual, interinstitutional disputes. In order to monitor implementation of the constitutional objectives for the welfare of the weaker sections of the nation, the central government has appointed a National Commission for Minorities, a National Commission for Scheduled Castes and Scheduled Tribes and a National Commission for Women. The appointment of a National Commission for Backward Classes is now on the anvil. The National Human Rights Commission (NHRC) came into being in 1993 by virtue of the Human Rights Protection Act, 1993. The freedom of the Press is monitored chiefly by the Press Council of India since 1979.

A network of laws, too wide to be portrayed in *extenso*-in this essay, exists to give effect to the broad range of human rights recognized in the Constitution. It must be noted, however, that the human rights enumerated in the various multilateral treaties to which India is a party, and also found in the Indian Constitution and laws have not been defined in identical terms in the latter, nor are all the rights mentioned in the treaties specifically recognised in the Constitution and the laws in extension.

However, the innovative jurisprudence of the Supreme Court seeks to update and harmonise the Indian law with the emerging international norms, and application of these norms taking into account the special conditions obtaining in India. It would seem, therefore, that the guarantee of life and personal liberty in Article 21 of the Constitution is adequately all-pervasive of all human rights, both present and evolving.

**Implementation of Human Rights**

Article 28 of the Universal Declaration of Human Rights, 1949 recognizes that "Everyone is entitled to a social and international order in which the rights and freedoms set forth in this Declaration can be fully realised". Closely following this, Article 38 of the Indian Constitution requires the state to "strive to promote the welfare of the people by securing and protecting as effectively as it may a social order in which justice-social, economic and political-shall inform all the institutions of the national life". This indeed is the ultimate objective of the whole Part IV of the Constitution. The right to development has now come to be recognized as "an inalienable human right... in which all human rights and fundamental freedoms can be fully realized". It is also recognized that "The human person is the central subject of development . . . The right to development in India is grossly impeded by the stupendous nature of the developmental problems which India faces. At the root of these problems are poverty, illiteracy and overpopulation which form a vicious circle each contributing to the other. While the British could be blamed for the conditions in which the country found itself in 1947, the succeeding governments have not done enough for the eradication of poverty and illiteracy and reverse the process of population explosion. At independence India's population was around 360 million, it is now touching 950 million.

In 1970 some 16 per cent of the population was below the poverty line, now it has risen to 37 per cent of the current population. These problems have a multiplier effect on all other social and economic problems. In 1992, the top 20 per cent of the population accounted for more than two-fifths of the total consumption expenditure, while the bottom 20 per cent had a share of a mere 8.5 per cent of the total consumption. The top 10 per cent spent eight times as much as the bottom 10 per cent. There are parts of India, such as the tribal belts of the Districts of Kalahandi and Bolangir in the state of Orissa, exposed to "the scourge of poverty, malnutrition and even starvation" attributed to repeated crop failures, inhuman exploitation of the tribals and politicization of human calamities, with the administration "woefully unequal to the task". Evidently, the poverty eradication programmes started with a new zeal since the seventies have failed to mitigate, let alone prevent, such human tragedies. The Government of India has announced plans of setting up a nationwide public distribution system whereby availability of 10 kilograms of foodgrains per head per month at cheapest rates is ensured for each family below the poverty line.

The ninth five year plan (1997-2002) is likely to have a special thrust for rural development "with poverty alleviation programmes as its major component". These would encompass programmes for reduction of rural unemployment land reforms, improved access to water resources, drought prone area programme and desert development programme. The Chief Ministers Conference of January 1997 had identified "seven basic minimum services", namely safe drink water, primary health services, universal primary education, public housing assistance to the shelterless poor, better nutrition for children, road linkages with all villages and habitations, and public distribution system for the poor.

The Prime Minister of India has recently admitted that over 400 million Indians are Illiterate, despite the fact that the first fifty years of expansion of educational facilities have credited India with one of the largest educational infrastructure in the world. The shelter shortage of by 1997 was estimated to be 7.57 million dwelling units. The process of globalization and liberalization, now afoot in India, has not found favour in certain quarters and the fear that it is harmful for the uplift of the poor is often expressed. It is contended that trade liberalization has led to decline in foodgrain production and consumption. It would hit hard the landless rural communities due to the loss of traditional markets, and deprive them of food entitlements and purchasing power.

The International Labour Organisation, in its World Employment Report for 1996-97, cautioned against economic liberalisation on all fronts at one go as it would lead to sharp increases in unemployment under-employment and poverty. While economic reforms are essential, they should be pursued in a phased manner, accompanied by programmes to strengthen the productive capacity of the poor, development of rural infrastructure, credit schemes and improved access to education and health services.

India has registered a discernible level of development for the last Fifty years on many fronts. It has also mastered some of the most modem technologies such as those in the fields of communications, space and nuclear energy. However, the magnitude of the problems engendered by poverty, illiteracy and population explosion has apparently dwarfed these achievements and demand greater and more sustained efforts. In the meantime, the Indian society will continue to be bedevilled by the maladies of inequality and exploitation, unless the governmental efforts are equally complemented by committed non-government ones.

**Rights of women**

Two principal facets of rights of women in India are highlighted here, namely the problem of equality with men, and trafficking and other undesirable practices and atrocities against women. Underlying these are the age old attitudes and customs of an ancient male dominated society. While violations of women's rights are not unknown in other societies, including the developed ones, what aggravate them in the context of the Indian society are poverty, illiteracy and some of the rationally and morally untenable social customs, such as dowry, sati, etc. The right to equality in the context of women has many aspects-equal pay for equal work, equality of opportunity, equality before law, political equality, equality of status and so on.

A number of laws exist in the statute book. However, implementation of these laws has left much to be desired. Parliament enacted the Indecent Representation of Women (Prohibition) Act in 1986 to expand the law of obscenity contained in the Indian Penal Code, 1860 and to counter a growing tendency of indecent representation of or references to women in publications such as advertisements, which is derogatory of women. However, the implementation of this Act has not been effective. Despite the Suppression of Immortal Traffic in Women and Girls Act, 1956, poverty has pushed a number of women into one of the oldest Professions in the world. Coordinated action is called for not only to retrieve and rehabilitate them, but to prevent their exploitation. There has been a significant increase in reported crimes against women atleast in certain metropolitan cities like Delhi.

Parliament is currently considering a law to reserve 33 per cent of the seats in the Lok Sabha (the Lower House of Parliament) and the state legislative assemblies. This follows the 73rd Constitution (Amendment) Act, 1986 which reserved 30 per cent of seats in councils at village, block and district levels. However, the male dominated political parties have so far stalled all attempts at getting the measure adopted into law. In order to address the problems of implementation of women's rights, Parliament enacted the National Commission of Women Act, 1990. While the Act empowers the Commission to investigate, examine and review all matters relating to the safeguards provided for women under the Constitution and other relevant laws, the Commission feels that its powers are not equal to its tasks, and that it should have power to prosecute/summarily decide on cases of violation of gender justice. Also, there should be commissions for women at state and district levels as well. Given the traditional male domination in the Indian society, the Commission has a most unenviable task.

**Freedom from Bonded or Forced Labour**

Despite the constitutional interdiction, poverty and illiteracy continue to be the breeding grounds for exploitation of humans keeping them often in perpetual bondage. The Bonded Labour (Abolition) Act adopted in 1976 has been an attempt to implement Article 23 of the Constitution. However, the indigent circumstances keep people in bondage and their exploiters reaping profits from their cheap or free labour. The Supreme Court's decision in the *Bandhua Mukti Morcha* case injected a fresh momentum in efforts to eradicate forced labour. It led to a 1985 amendment to the Act of 1976 to broaden the application of the law. It also led to further Court judgements declaring that labour on payment of unreasonably low wages amounts to forced labour prohibited under the law. Pledging one's labour or the labour of one's children for little or no wages in repayment of a debt has been the bane of India's problem of rural indebtedness. Clearly, no effective answer to it is in sight except long term economic development. In the meantime, there will continue to be reports of forced or bonded labour.

**Rights of the Child**

India became a party in 1992 to the International Convention on the Rights of the Child, 1989, following popular demand. There is no doubt that all human rights (save perhaps the political rights) must apply to the child, as they are essential for the development of the human beings.

While the rights of the child call for a comprehensive treatment, we shall confine to its two aspects in the context of the Indian society which have lately highlighted the need for urgent affirmative action. They are the incidence of violence against children, including violence by the criminal justice system, and the practice of child labour.

*Violence against Children*

Trafficking in children is prohibited under the Suppression of Immoral Traffic in Women and Girls Act, 1956 (strengthened by an amendment of 1986). Yet the Act is not wellimplemented. The National Crime Records Bureau's report on "Crime in India" has reported a rise in crime against children in recent years. There are also reports of growing violence against street children in many urban areas. Parliament enacted the Juvenile Justice Act, 1986 principally for "the care, protection, treatment, development and rehabilitation of neglected or delinquent juveniles.

The Act improves on and replaces the Children Act, 1960 and other various state enactments on the subject. It creates the following new offences: cruelty to juvenile, employment of juveniles for begging, giving a juvenile intoxicating liquor or narcotic drug or psychotropic substance, and exploitation of juvenile employees. It provides for juvenile homes for neglected children and special homes and observation homes for delinquent juveniles.

However, for lack of resources the number of such juvenile homes so far established has been limited. Also, some of those few which exist are not properly run, even a brutal murder of an inmate by another took place in a Delhi Observation Home. The National Crime Records Bureau's data indicate that juvenile delinquency continues to show a declining trend. In 1994 it recorded a 17.2 per cent drop over 1993. A total of 5,962 cases were registered against juveniles in 1994, and 38.4 per cent of juvenile in custody were awaiting trial. A disturbing trend, however, has been the introduction of juveniles to serious crimes.

*Child Labour*

Large scale exploitation of children for a free or cheap labour has been a bane of independent India. Them is no reliable data on the exact number of children being exploited at work. In India the estimates range from 20 million to 100 million. Children are engaged in a variety of industries or vocations-making of matches and fireworks, carpet making, glass bangle-making, brasswares, plastic and rope weaving, salt extraction, incense stick production, diamond cutting and polishing, biscuit-making, steel rolling and chips recycling, domestic work, prostitution, construction industry, etc. This painful reality exists despite the Employment of Children Act, 1938 (amended 1985), the Child Labour (Prohibition and Regulation) Act, 1986 (which prohibits employment of children in hazardous occupations and regulates it in others), and other laws like the Factories Act, 1,948. Indeed, child labour exists more in unorganized sector than in organized, which makes its detection difficult, although some of the NGOs seem to be doing extremely effective work in this regard. The Prime Minister of India in his Independence Day address to the nation on 15th August, 1994 pledged elimination of child labour from all hazardous industries by the year 2000.

The government's hands are now being forced by a revolutionary Supreme Court judgement of 10th December, 1996. The Government has been given a period of one you to implement this decision. One hopes that the Supreme Court's initiative will operate as the much-awaited shot in the arm. It would appear that there is also scope for private initiative. The rights of the girl child have received a special emphasis the world over recently. India is notorious for its neglect of the girl child.

The problem is multifaceted, it encompasses foeticide, female illiteracy, social discrimination, child marriage and so on. There is a need for changing social attitudes through a process of social mobilization. There is also a need for concerted administrative, legal and social action to eliminate inequality of the girl child, female foeticides and female infanticides.

### Rights of the Scheduled Castes and Scheduled Tribes

As seen already, for historical and socially wrong reasons, the Indian society perpetrated a system of exploitation and dehumanization of some of the socially and economically most backward classes. These classes, as identified in a Schedule to the Constitution, are known as the Scheduled Castes and Scheduled Tribes. Majority of them are below the poverty line. The legal and political system provides for a range of measures of affirmative discrimination in their favour, such as reservation of seats in legislatures, reservation of jobs, reservation of seats in educational institutions, special scholarships, etc. Yet much of their lot is yet to cross the Rubicon of inequality, and still subjected to indignities, humiliation and harassment by some of the members of more advanced classes in society.

The rationale behind the Scheduled Castes and the Scheduled Tribes (Prevention of Atrocities) Act, 1989 has been to stem the atrocities against them and to strengthen the constitutional interdiction. Also, in 1990 the Constitution was amended to establish a seven-member highlevel National Commission for the Scheduled Castes and the Scheduled Tribes to investigate and monitor all matters relating to the safeguards provided for Scheduled Castes and Scheduled Tribes, to examine specific complaints of violation of rights and safeguards, and to make recommendations to the government for effective implementation of these rights and safeguards. Despite these legislative measures, atrocities against the Scheduled Castes and Scheduled Tribes are being reported whether as part of custodial violence, bonded labour, violence against women or other human rights violations.

The Commission on Scheduled Castes and Scheduled Tribes has expressed concern over the rise in the number of such atrocities. Protection of land rights has become a crucial issue. The answer to the economic backwardness of these classes appears to lie in spread of education, not necessarily in reservations or measures of affirmative discrimination. The reservations or affirmative discrimination has a knack of benefiting more advanced segments of these classes, and in the process, other less fortunate ones remain left in the lurch. Problems of tribals too cannot be solved within the framework of reservations alone. The recent Indian politics have thrown up another issue-Protection of other Backward Classes (OBCs). It is true that the Indian society is highly segmented and that there are other backward classes other than the Scheduled Castes and the Scheduled Tribes, which need special attention.

However, the approach to meet the problem of bringing social justice to these sections of people adopted by the government appears to be two-pronged-one, creation of a system of reservations, and two, determination of OBCs based on caste rather than economic criteria. Both tend to be populist measures aimed at "vote-grabbing through causing social divisions". There is much truth in the statement: "Today backwardness is neither a social stigma nor a handicap. It is the politician's chartered vehicle to power and pelf".

**Minority Rights**

Article 30 of the Constitution speaks of all minorities, whether based on religion or language". While it does not deny the existence of minorities identified on criteria other than religion or language, the current political vocabulary accepts only religious and linguistic minorities. The founding fathers of the Constitution were indeed more keen to ensure the protection of religious minorities as part of the transition of India into independence.

The partition of India into two countries resulted from the false apprehensions that the majority community In India would not ensure the rights of a minority community. Yet India has had a tradition of tolerance and social synthesis of diverse religions, a tradition lately marred by the rise of groups and political parties advocating religious fanaticism. The politics of religion have to do with this more than anything else. Such groups were responsible for the pre-planned destruction of the Babri Masjid in December, 1992 which fomented considerable ill-feelings leading to several riots aimed more at one community than the other. Happily, the religious fanaticism is confined to small groups and the Indian electorate has time and again endorsed secularism and forced many of these groups even to moderate on their policies. The National Commission for Minorities Act was enacted in 1992 aimed at protection of religious minorities such as Muslims, Sikhs, Buddhists, and Parsis.

While the legislation and the Commission need strengthening, much more can be done by the Commission than what it has been able to achieve so far, Spread of secular education will go a long way in providing a firm foundation for development of minorities in India, There is enough law to protect various religions, or to prevent misuse of religious institutions for purposes other than religious.

**The Rights of the Disabled**

The rights of the disabled came to be formally recognized in India only recently, although they are readily read into Article 21 of the Constitution. According to one estimate, there are about 60 million disabled persons in the country belonging to various categories of disability. These categories include, the blind, the deaf, the dumb, physically handicapped, the mentally retarded and the mentally ill.

In the context of the Indian society, the disabled suffer from social stigma of various degrees, and this, more than other factors, stands in the way of their claims to equality and social justice. Thanks to the pressure exerted by the NGOs, Parliament adopted the Persons with Disabilities (Equal Opportunities, Protection of Rights and Full Participation) Act in 1995. However, the NGOs feel that there is considerable tardiness on the part of the government in the implementation of the law. The 1995 law awaits formulation of rules and regulations, and appointment of the Central and state coordination committees as well as the executive committee and the Chief Commissioner of the Disabled Persons. While there are reservations of seats in the universities, no such provision exists for the school level education yet. Therefore, the legislation largely remains merely on paper, despite its coming into force on 7th February, 1996. Regardless of any legislation, the Indian society has done precious little for a "barrier-free environment" for the handicapped.

The public buildings, public transport system, public places, all unfortunately remind one of this. Similarly, the Mental Health Act, 1993, which replaced the archaic Lunancy Act, 1912, has not come into force in all states, despite the requirement that it be implemented by 1st April, 1993. A number of judgements of the Supreme Court have revealed the shabby management of some of the 37 mental hospitals in the country. It is, however, gratifying to note that the social awareness about the need for protection of the rights of the disabled and also the awareness on the part of the disabled themselves of their rights, has been gradually growing.41

**Catalysts of Rights Implementation**

The state has the unenviable, yet complex, duty to protect and promote individual and group rights as well as to umpire the conflicting claims to rights, against the overall requirements of the development of the society. The Indian polity has, over time, and particularly in the post-Emergency era, evolved four principal catalysts of human rights implementation, which have developed new, often effective, strategies to catalyse rights implementation. They are the judiciary, the NHRC the NGOs and the communication/information media.

*The judiciary*

The Supreme Court of India has in fact declared that it has a special responsibility "to enlarge the range and meaning of the fundamental rights and to advance the human rights jurisprudence." We have already seen that the Supreme Court of India and the State High Courts have broad powers under the Constitution in respect of enforcement of fundamental rights and that they have liberally interpreted these powers. The major contributions of judiciary to the human rights jurisprudence have been twofold: one, the substantive expansion of the concept of human rights under Article 21 of the Constitution, and the other, the procedural innovation of public interest litigation. Since the role of judiciary in promotion of human rights has received more than adequate coverage in a number of legal journals and the media, no attempt is made here to elaborate the above points.

*The National Human Rights Commission*

India enacted the Protection of the Human Rights Act in 1993 more in response to considerable international pressure than the domestic pressure, chiefly to ward off the criticisms it encountered on human rights violations in the terrorism or insurgency affected areas. Be that as it may, this was a piece of beneficent legislation in that it established a new national human rights institution, namely, the National Human Rights Commission (NHRC). NHRC's functions are extremely broad, pursuant to section 12 of the Act—to inquire, either *suo motu* or on a petition, into human rights violations, intervene in court proceedings, visit jails or other places of custody, review human rights safeguards and make recommendations, review factors, including terrorism, inhibiting the enjoyment of human rights, study international instruments on human rights, undertake and promote research, spread human rights literacy and awareness of safeguards among the masses, encourage NGOs, and institutions working in the field of human rights, and perform any other functions that NHRC may deem necessary for promotion of human rights. NHRC has so far given priority to civil liberties—custodial deaths, state violence against civilians, torture and other cruel, inhuman or degrading treatment, custodial rape, disappearance from custody, atrocities against vulnerable sections of the society such as women, children and the disabled (including dowry deaths, bonded and child labour), and promotion of human rights education and training. Indeed in its very first year of existence, NHRC proposed to the government that its role be restricted, by defining "human rights" under section 2(1) (d) to mean the rights relating to life, liberty, equality and dignity of the individual. In 1996, the Commission has also included in its priorities the issues of prison reforms and undertrials.

NHRC has pledged that it would strictly observe the principles of autonomy and transparency. Its reports and the Human Rights Newsletter seek to fulfil both, by reporting the activities of the Commission. NHRC earned considerable prestige and reputation by its suo motu action in the case of the *Bijbehara* incident (in Jammu and Kashmir) in which there were press reports of death of about 60 civilians as a result of firing by security forces. Upon investigation, it recommended disciplinary proceedings against 14 members of the security force, prosecution after a magisterial inquiry, payment of compensation, and a review of circumstances and conditions of deployment of security forces. NHRC's Annual Reports and the Newsletter regularly cover the various investigations by the Commission.

The Commission also took a lead in building up public opinion which forced the government to terminate the TADA. A recent development is the use of NHRC by the Supreme Court as an investigative arm of the Court."

On a public interest relating to cremation by the Punjab Police of several dead bodies as 'unclaimed' during the past few years, the Supreme Court described the issue as a "flagrant violation of human rights on a mass scale", in asked the Commission to launch a thorough probe and "determine all the issues raised by the petitioner," including the question of payment of compensation. So far the states of West Bengal, Himachal Pradesh, Madhya Pradesh and Assam have established State Human Rights Commissions.

The State of Jammu and Kashmir has announced its decision to set up a Commission in that state. The Chairperson of at least one State Commission, viz., Himachal Pradesh, seems to wear more than one hat, other than the charge of the Commission, not necessarily conducive to the effectiveness of the Commission. An overview of the year 1996 shows that the main strength of NHRC is its access to the media to build up a climate of human rights. It was in the news rather intermittently. There are complaints from some NGOs that NHRC has not lived up to the principle of transparency, as it does not give NGOs full access to its activities.

A criticism one could offer is that NHRC is increasingly becoming bureaucratized in its internal structure-with its personnel chiefly drawn from government. One may also fault NHRC's bureaucratic approach to evolving human rights syllabii for teaching purposes. The Commission should, but does not seem to, offer assistance in the effective functioning of other national institutions like the National Commission on Minorities, on Women, and on the Scheduled Castes and Scheduled Tribes. Indeed, part of the blame on this count should rest with the Chairpersons of these Commissions themselves who are ex *officio* members of NHRC. Further, the Government, on its part, has at times failed to respect the independence of the Commission, as is illustrated by the appointment of two of the Commissioners as state governors. In sum, however, NHRC is doing landable work in the field of human rights implementation, its main contribution being its role in the spread of human rights awareness and education, particularly among the security Forces of the state.

*Non-Governmental organizations*

There are a number of NGOs, both national as well as international, performing useful work in the monitoring and implementation of human rights. Indeed, there are NGOs with political or other motives and those wedded to selfless service. At times, it is difficult to discern one category from the other. In the face of allegation of misappropriation by certain NGOs of funds received from the Union Welfare Ministry, the Ministry decided to constitute a 15-member committee to study the working of NGOs attached to the Ministry. Among the foreign or 'international' NGOs, the Amnesty International (AI), the Human Rights Watch/Asia (HRWA) and the International Commission of Jurists (ICJ) are prominent in the field of civil and political rights. AI and ICJ were highly rated in India for their reports on human rights violations in India during the emergency (1975-77).

However, the recent situations of terrorism in Jammu and Kashmir and in Punjab have led to highly exaggerated reports of rights violations by these bodies, and non-notice of government responses to the specific cases raised with it. Until recently, these foreign NGOs ignored the heinous human rights violations perpetrated by terrorists and militants. They also fail to focus on the role of Pakistan in terrorism in India. The recent revelation of a bloomer in AI reports seem to have led to explanations from AI which in turn revealed that certain terrorist organisations, active in India earlier, had access to At. Despite a record number of killings and other violations of human rights to its credit, a terrorist organisation was reported to be an "international member" of AI. If the newspaper reports are to be believed, at least so far as India is concerned, AI's credibility can only be retrieved if it launches a full scale and open (transparency?) inquiry into the genuineness of its India-related members. Them are a number of Indian NGOs which perform useful work in various fields of human rights-social welfare, old age care, health and community medicine, assistance to depressed classes, women's welfare, child welfare, rehabilitation of bonded labour, rehabilitation of people uprooted by economic development projects, welfare of the disabled, consumer rights and so on.

The chief problem with these NGOs is that there is a lack of coordination of their activities in terms of their fields of activity, territorial area, and target groups of their activities. Indeed, at times, they reveal a sense of rivalry. At least among the Indian NGOs in the field of civil liberties, there is a complaint that the government is too readily responsive to foreign NGOs, but does not treat the Indian NGOs at par with them. By and large, NGOs have arrived on the Indian human rights scene and have begun to play an important role not only in monitoring human right violations, but equally in rehabilitation of victims and promotion of implementation of rights.

*The Media*

The information media is an important arm of any modem democratic polity through which the people enjoy their freedom of information. The freedom of information, the democratic right to know, is crucial in making all other human rights effective and providing an Important safeguard for the enjoyment of all those rights. Traditionally, the vehicle of public information has been the press and now thanks to modem technology, the media. The 'Fourth Estate' plays a crucial role in a large democracy like India. India has about 1,500 newspapers. The period of national emergency saw, for the first time, gagging of the free Press. Many depended on BBC for 'impartial' news about India. Small wonder, the freedom of the press or media became a watchword for human rights after emergency. Under the Indian Constitution, the freedom of information is implicitly covered by Article 19 (freedom of speech and expression, freedom of trade) and Article 21 of the Constitution.

Since the 1970's the Indian media has played an extremely important role in sensitizing people with information about governance, development, science and technology, foreign relations and so on. However, lately it has also come in for criticism, as highlighted by the above Supreme Court decision. There is a decline in journalistic credibility, as noted by the Chairman of the Press Council of India as well as President K.R. Narayanan. Recently, due to the media preoccupation with the trivia, personality cult, one-sidedness, and instant news as against in-depth investigation, senior journalists feel that the media shies away from important people's issues such as tribal issues, that it is losing social content and becoming a consumer product with a manager overshadowing the editor.

The Press has also come in for rough treatment by terrorists/ insurgents, and some individual politicians. The media has a tendency to launch "trials by the media", even sentencing by the media, while a Court proceeding is underway. Taking the totality of impact of the media for the past two decades, despite the above pitfalls, one must recognize that the contribution of the media, in revealing and highlighting human rights causes, has been most impressive. A colonial law relating to official secrecy, the Official Secrets Act, 1923, remains an impediment in the effective exercise of the freedom of information.

# 10

# RIGHT OF SUSPECTS

The police often starts with a presumption that the suspect is the culprit. in the ab sence of sophisticated modern techniques of investigations, third degree methods are adopted to force a confession of guilt. To the suspect, often false coDfession of guilt appears to be a lesser evil inerely to avoid further torture. In this context illite racy and poverty are a great curse. Because of illiteracy, a person is often unable to understand and comprehend the gravity of being a suspect in a criminal case. He also remains unaware of his legal rights. Because of poverty, it becomes almost impossible to defend himself or to seek the services of competent legal counsel. In desperate situation of poverty the food, shelter and clothing promised in a jail becomes an attrac tive proposition. People in general exhibit lack of sympathy and compassion for poor suspects. The law provides an umbrella to suspects to protect themselves against police atrocities and uncooperative people. All these rights are discussed in detail here.

**Right against arrest**

Article 21 of the Indian Constitution Provides that no one

shall be deprived of his personal liberty except accordin g to procedure established by law. Here procedure has been interpreted by the Supreme Court to mean that it should be fair, reasonable and just. Law which seeks physical restraint of a person must be fair, just and reasonable. Article 22 of the Constitution envisages that a person who has been arrested must be supplied with grounds for his arrest, allowed to consult a lawyer of his choice, be produced before magistrate within twenty-four hours from the time of his arrest who alone can authorise any further detention.

In the case of State of Bombay vs. Atma Ram, the Supreme Court has held that if requirements of Article 22 are not complied with, the detention will be declared as illegal although the initial arrest was in accordance with law In Khatri vs. State of Bihar, the Supreme Court expressed unhappiness over the nonproduction of suspects before a magistrate within twenty-four hours of arrest. It ordered the State Governments that such irregularity should not occur again. In the case of Madhya Pradesh vs. Shobharam, the Suprerne Court held that the right of services of a counsel becomes vested in the person as soon as he is arrested, irrespective of the fact that he was later released on bail. The right of being produced before a magistrate within twenty-four hours, apart from journey time, is protection against arrest on the behest of executive authorities. There is similar provision under Criminal Procedure Code.

The statutory provision has been reinforced by constitutional guarantee. The magistrate before whom the detenue has been produced has to apply his judicial mind to the case of arrest and determine whether detention should continue. A detenue cannot be produced before the magistrate responsible for his arrest. He is an interested party and, therefore, cannot be objective. In Ram Manoliar

Lohia vs. Superintendent, Central Jail, the detenue was produced before the city magistrate who was all an executive magistratc. That was not proper. He should have been produced before some other magistrate.

**Communication of charges**

Article 9 of the Covenant says that a person shall be informed of reasons of his arrest when he is arrested. Besides, Article 14(3-a) of the Covenant provides that a person must be informed promptly and in detail in a language which he can understand of the nature and cause of charges against him. Article 22(l) of the Constitution fulfils this requirement when it says that a person who is arrested must be informed of the grounds of his arrest as soon as may be possible.

In Madhu Limaye's case the Supreme Court has held that non-supp'y of reasons as required under Article 220) of the Constitution would vitiate the arrest and the detenue would be released. Supply of grounds of arrest are part of any criminal jurisprudence. It is essential that grounds be supplied to the detenue to enable him to consult his lawyer, to prepare his defence and move the court for *habeas corpus,* as may be necessary. In the absence of supply of grounds of his arrest, the detenue cannot do anything. It is unreasonable to keep the detenue in the dark in respect of the charges against him which have motivated his arrest. Grounds must be specific and not vague. He cannot be told that he has been arrested on a charge of murder unless he is also told as to whose murder.

The requirement of supply of ground cannot be ignored on the plea that the person has been released on bail." The phrase 'as soon as may be' should mean within reasonable time. Of course, no fixed period can be considered as reasonable. It is for the court to determine whether the grounds have been supplied within a reasonable period in a given case. If the court holds that grounds were not supplied within a reasonable time, the detention is vitiated and the detenue must be released.

**Protection against torture**

Suspects are subjected to interrogation during, the initial stages of their arrest. It has been noticed that in the process of inter. rogation, suspects are subjected to acts of torture and inhumane, cruel and degrading treatment. Some are permanently disabled. In extreme cases the detenues succumb to their injuries. Amnesty International has reported a number of cases of police brutalities and torture? By virtue of being suspects they do not cease to be persons. They continue to be human persons despite charges against them.

The Supreme Court has ordered the Bihar Government for rehabilitation of persons connected with the Bhagalpur blindings. It is also gratifying to note that some of the perpetrators of the Bhagalpur blindings were prosecuted and have been punished. But this has been done only after Supreme Court intervention. It would have been better if they had been prosecuted before Supreme Court intervened. It is essential that the Indian police should abandon outmoded techniques of investigations through interrogation. These methods are crude and cruel.

**Right against self-incrimination**

Article 20(3) of the Constitution provides that no person "accused of any offence shall be compelled to be a witness against himself." This is a basic right guaranteed to a suspect. Article 14(3-g) of the Covenant also provides that suspect cannot be compelled to testify against himself or to confess guilt. This is a very important safeguard given to the suspect. Instances would not be lacking where stage-managed prosecutions and convictions are made on the basis of forced confess]oils, which could also be false.

Such practices are reminiscent of Star Chamber Courts which still operate in some countries. These countries should perhaps be called police states. Fortunately, India can claim that barring a few cases of police-inspired self-involvement by suspects, criminal trials are free from such practices. Nevertheless, courts may be advised to exercise great caution in cases of confession by detenues. No convictions should ordinarily be based entirely on the confession of an accused. Some independent evidence should be mandatory to warrant conviction of a suspect, apart from a confession which could be a result of fear or falsely motivated. Indian law requires independent evidence for conviction of a suspect.

**Free Legal Aid**

A suspect is in need of legal advice as soon as he is apprehended. He must prepare his defence. All persons are not capable of preparing their own defence. He must have the services of a competent lawyer of his choice. But he may not be able to afford to have one. It has, therefore, been held that the right to free legal services is an essential ingredient of the reasonable, fair and just procedure of law which can be instrumental in depriving a person of his life and personal liberty. It has been held by the Supreme Court that free legal services must be provided when the accused is first produced before the magistrate." Therefore, "State is under a constitutional obligation to provide free legal services to an indigent accused, not only at the stage of trial but also at the stage when he is first produced before the magistrate as also when he is remanded from time to time.

Perhaps, it may be fair to say that an indigent accused is entitled to free legal aid from the time he is arrested because he would soon be interrogated. Naturally, he would need competent legal advice to prepare his statement which may implicate Jilin if no expert legal advice is given to him. Article 14 ofthe Constitution guarantees equality before law. Equality requires that both parties should be equally placed. The State has competent legal advice. An accused should also have the sarne quality of services. legal aid is essential for the indigent accused when he prepares his statement before police, while he is arrested, seeks bail pending trial and prepares his defence during trial.

Justice Bhagwati extended the legal aid services by ordering that all rnagistrates and session judges must inform an indigent accused who appears before them without legal counsel that because of his/or her poverty and indigence he or she is entitled to free legal aid. This is a very healthy interpretation of legal aid which is mostly denied to detenues because of their ignorance and goveinment's plea of financial constraints. Both these bottlenecks have been removed by the Supreme Court by liberal interpretation of the provisions for fundamental rights for the weaker sections of society.

**Right to be released on bail**

Suspects must be released on bail, soon after their arrest. They cannot be condemned before they are convicted. Technically, there are two categories of offences in India, bailable and non-bailable. In case of bailable offences, release of suspects on bail is comparatively easier. In case of nonbailable offences, release on bail is time-consuming and cumber-some.

Release on bail has a number of advantages. It enables the suspect to prepare for his defence, continue to earn his bread be with his family and be free from psychological and physica; deprivations of jail life. From the State point of view, it saves some money which it would normally spend on suspect's maintenance during his detention.

Release during trial is often opposed by the police for two main reasons. The accused may tamper with evidence or he may liump bail and abscond. The third valid reason is that be may continue to commit offences while be is released on bail. While it is understandable to prevent release of suspects who are habitual or professional criminals, it is unfair to withhold release of suspects and keep them in prisons on the suspicion that they may have committed crime. Suspects are bailed out only against sureties of large amounts of money. As a result poor and indigent suspects never get free unless by providence they get acquitted after long trials. In some cases, destitute suspects lose track of their families and friends. In India, money is the only means for securing bail. This is indeed unfortunate.

The problem was prevalent in the United States of America until the jail reforms were effected in 1966. At the signing ceremony, President Johnson aptly remarked: "The defendant with means can afford to pay bail. He can afford to buy his freedom. But a poor defendant cannot pay the price. He languishes in prison for weeks, months and perhaps even years before his trial. He stays in prison for one reason only because, he is poor. Equating money with the release of a suspect on bail is a misconception. It was wrongly believed, that the monetary security will prevent the flight of a fugitive and ensure his attendance at trial. It is in total contradiction with the concept that every suspect is considered to be dishonest and a potential evader. Statistics, however, indicate that there is a very small percentage of such people who abuse release on bail."

There is, therefore, emphasis today on release of suspects on personal recognisance. This was recommended by the Gujarat Legal Aid Committee Report in 1971 when it said: "If a magistrate is satisfied after making an inquiry into the condition and background of the accused that the accused has his roots in the community and is not likely to abscond he can safely release the accused on order to appear or on his own recognisance. Social justice requires release of suspects on their own bond with or without sureties depending on each individual case. In Hussain-ara Khatoon vs. State of Bihar where the Supreme Court had to consider the conditions of a number of undertrials. who were in jail for a number of years, in many cases more than the sentences they could have got for crimes attributed to them, Justice Bhagwati ordered the following guidelines: a person's length of residence in the community, his employmerit status, history, and financial conditions, his family ties and relations, his reputation, his prior criminal record, certification by responsible citizens of the community, nature of offence charged and the apparent probability of conviction and the likely sentence."

Thus, it was held that if the court is satisfied that the accused has his ties in the community and there is no substantial risk of non-appearance, he may be released on personal bond. However, if in view of his background, his previous record, nature and circumstances of the offence, there is substantial risk of his non-appearance, he may not be released on personal bond.

**Speedy trial**

Speedy trial in criminal cases is a must. There is famous saying that justice delayed is justice denied. Suspects cannot be kept in suspense for long. Charges against them should either be confirmed or cleared. It is more so when undertrials remain incarcerated for a long period. Article 14(3-c) of the Covenant on Civil and Political Rights provides that suspects will be tried without undue delay. Article 3 of the European Convention provides that arrested person shall be entitled to trial within a reasonable time. Sixth amendment of the United States

Constitution states that "tht accused shall enjoy the right to a speedy trial." The Indian Constitution does not have constitutional provision with regard to a speedy trial. However, it has been held that any law which deprives any person of his life or personal liberty must be fair, reasonable and just. It has thus been held by the Supreme Court in the Hussain-ara Kbatoon case that law must ensure speedy trial. Any law which does not ensure reasonably quick trial cannot be called fair or just. Justice Bhagwati therefore considered reasonably expeditious trial as an integral and essential part of the fundamental right under Article 21. It was further held that, long duration detentions without trial are violative of Article 21 and as such undertrials were ordered to be released forthwith without fear of further trial. Speedy trial as an essential of Article 21 was reiterated in Kedra. Pehadiya case.

**Rule against ex-post facto laws**

It is a basic rule of natural law that no one may be punished for an act or omission which was not a crime at the time of its commission. This was the common complaint of World War II criminals. No act can be termed as criminal retrospectively. This is called as rule against ex-post facto laws. The rule was contained in Article 15 of the Covenant.

Article 20(l) of the Constitution recognises this rule. As it says:

> No person shall be convicted of any offence except for violation of a law in force at the time of commission of the act charged as an offence, nor be subjected to a penalty greater than that which might have been inflicted under the law in force at the time of the commission of the offence.

The international and national provisions are identical and there does not seem to be any dispute as to these rules. The law applies both to *ex-post* crime and *ex-post* penalty.

The Supreme Court had the opportunity to observe in following terms in respect of the principle:

> There can be no doubt as to the paramount importance of the principle that such *ex-post faclo* laws which retrospectively create offence and punish them are bad as being-highly inequitable and unjUSt.21

**Rule against double jeopardy**

There is yet another rule of natural law that a person cannot be tried twice for the same offence. Article 14(7) of the Covenant reiterates this rule of natural justice. Article 20(2) of the Constitution says that no "person shall be prosecuted and punished for the same offence more than once." In case of Sunil Batra, it was held by the Supreme Court that if the jail authorities detain a person, who is convicted to death sentences, in solitary confinement, it is violative of Article 20(2) of the Constitution. This was held because solitary confinement is a distinct punishment under section 73 of the Penal Code. There is some difference between Article 14(7) of the Covenant and Article 20(2) of the Constitution. While the Covenant incorporates the doctrine of *autrefois convict* as well as *autrefois acquit,* Article 20(2).provides for only *autrefois convict.* This means that there is a constitutional bar on repeated convictions only for tile same offence.

Article 20 does not bar second prosecution where the suspect has been acquitted. This is an anomaly indeed. The rationale of the rules is that once a person has been tried for a given offence, he cannot be tried again for tile same offence irrespective of the fact whether lie is convicted or acquitted.

Section 300 of the Criminal Procedure (1974) bars any further trial of a person who has already been tried and convicted or acquitted. This provision conforms to Article 14(7) of the Covenant. But it is not part of fundamental rights. Nevertheless, it can be reasonably said that Indian

Criminal jurisprudence ,accepts the principle of against Double Jeopardy.

**Presumption of innocence**

Indian criminal law also presumes the innocence of suspect unless it is proved that he has really committed the crime. Indian criminal jurisprudence goes still further by saying that in case of any doubt, the benefit of doubt will go to the accused. While the Indian law is quite clear and specific on the subject, police and prison practices have tended to reveal a different story. Illiteracy and ignorance of the people are sometimes taken advantage of by the law-enforcing agencies which are responsible for putting the suspects behind the bars.

Poverty aggravates their suffering with the result that either the detenues do not know their rights or even when they know they are too poor to pursue their rights and vindicate their innocence. Corruption, high rate of back-log of criminal cases, apathy towards poor and destitute suspects despite lip sympathy and lack of effective legal aid are contributory factors for condemning suspects to long spells of prison life despite their presumed innocence. Sustained efforts on the part of higher judiciary and State Governments are essential to change the attitude of police and prison staff as well as that of the magistrates, who primarily deal with the suspect in 95 per cent or more criminal cases.

**Prison treatment**

Of late, there has been awakening in public opinion regarding conditions of prison life which suspects and convicts have to bear while in custody. Until recently, prison law was considered a law unto itself where the jail superintendent was a monarch of whatever he surveyed in the four lofty walls of prison. No one could question his writ. Courts also exercised self-restraint and adopted a hands-off policy with regard to jail administration which was left to jail staff under the misconceived notion of maintaining highest discipline among prison inmates. It has been appreciated now that prison inmates still continue to be "persons" entitled to some rights, except the right of free movement and some other allied restrictions.

Courts have invoked principles of social justice to undo the wrongs which were hitherto perpetrated on prison inmates. Thus, in Sunil Batra's case, the Supreme Court has held that the prisoner has all the fundamental rights, though restricted by the fact of imprisonment. It was held that fetters are a barbarity and, like whipping, it must vanish. They offend human dignity. Fetters in an extreme case should be subject to quasi-judicial scrutiny.

The Supreme Court has held that solitary confinement has a degrading and dehumanising effect on prisoner. Constant isolation is unnatural and may cause insanity. It has been held that prisoners have the right to move, mix, mingle, talk and have company with co-prisoners. This cannot be curtailed except by law which is fair, just and reasonable." In Krishna Singh's case, Justice lyer rejected the subtle difference sought to be made by the jail administration between solitary confinement and separate cell. If the purpose is the same, it becomes an inhuman punishment, besides also being a double punishment.

Prisoners' conditions may be summarised in what Justice William Douglas said in 1974. A prison does not render one to be a nonperson whose rights are subject to the whim of the prison administration and therefore, the imposition of any serious punishment within the prison system requires procedural safeguards. Conditions have been most unsatisfactory in Indian prisons. Inspector General of Prisons of West Bengal once remarked that 10 per cent of inmates are lunatics who have been in prison for an average of 20 years. The Supreme Court recently ordered the release of eight prisoners from Hazaribagh jail who were said to be of unsound mind. Most of them had been there for over 25 years. One of them had been there since 1945. In yet another case, the Supreme Court ordered the release of juvenile prisoners, who were there for several years without any trial but, could not be released because of monetary compunctions. In 1979, Hussain-ara Khatoon's case depicted a sorry state of affairs of lady prisoners who were lodged in jails for a number of years. Some of them were in protective custody. They were all ordered to be released on personal bonds. Jails in India are an underworld where all types of offences are committcd with impunity under the patronage of the monarch. It is indeed a shame on the Indian prison system which defies social justice and inherent human dignity of every man.

It is heartening to note that things in prisons are promising to improve, but there is a lot to be desired. Prisons should be divided into two wings. One for undertrials and theotherfor convicts as provided under Article 10(2-a) of the Covenant. These two wings should be further divided. Juveniles as far as possible should never be lodged in prisons. They should be released on personal bond or parent's bond even when convicted. Women should not be in prisons until they have been finally convicted.

**Judicial protection**

Fundamental rights are of no value if there is no implementation or vindication of these rights. There must be protection against violation of such rights by State agencies. Implementation and vindication of human rights are integral parts of fundamental rights. Naturally, implementation or vindication can only be done by access to judicial protection. Courts have to be protectors of individual rights against State excesses or violations, particularly when the enforcing agencies become the violators of human rights. Article 32 seeks to empower the Supreme Court to enforce rights given to the people under Part III of the Constitution. The Court is thus empowered to issue writs of Habeas Corpus, Mandamus, Prohibition, Quo Warranto and Certiorari in the matter of enforcement of human rights. State High Courts have been given similar powers to issue the above writs for the enforcement of fundamental rights under Article 226(1) of the Constitution. Dr. Ambedkar considered Article 32 as the most important Article of the Constitution seeking to protect fundamental rights. It is gratifying to note that the courts in India have done a good job in protecting human rights. Thus, in the case of A.K. Gopalan vs. State of Madras, which was the first case under the Indian Constitution, involving fundamental rights, the Supreme Court declared Section 14 of the Preventive Detention Act as unconstitutional.

The Supreme Court held in 1950 that freedom of speech and expression included the freedom of press to propagate ideas and opinions. Indeed freedom of press is the integral part of democracy. In Keshavanand Bharti's case, the Chief Justice cited the U.N. Charter and U.D.H.R. which had influenced Part III and Directive Principles of the Constitution. He thought some rights were inalienable.

The other Judges upheld the importance of human rights in the context of the U.N. Charter, U.D.H.R. and the two Covenants. In Minerva Mills case, the Chief Justice laid great emphasis on Articles 14, 19 and 21 embodying principles of equality, six freedoms and right to life and liberty respectively. But he advocated harmony and balancing between human rights and directive principles. The Supreme Court has expanded the right of freedom of movement to include the right to travel abroad. This was held in the case of Satwant Singh where the court held that denial of passport is deprivation of freedom of movement and curtailment of personal liberty. The Court held that, as per Article 13 of the U.D.H.R., everyone has a right to leave any country, including his own. This was strengthened in Maneka Gandhi case where the court held that cancellation of passport was violative of Article 19 of the U.D.H.R. In Kharak Singh's case, the Supreme Court had held that there was no right to privacy under the Indian Constitution. This rigid stand was reversed in the case of Govind vs. State of Madhya Pradesh where the court read into Article 21 the right to privacy. It was further strengthened in Malak Singh's case where it was held that surveillance was violative of Articles 19(1-d) and 21 and intruded into right to privacy. The Supreme Court has greatly widened the scope of life and liberty in Article 21. Thus the Supreme Court has accepted Justice Field's famous remark that life does not mean mere animal existence. It means much more than just existence. Thus was held in Kharak Singh's case; right to life would mean to live with human dignity. This was further reinforced in Frances Mullin's case where the court held that right to life would "include the right to basic necessities of life and also the right to carry on such functions and activities as constitute the bare minimum expression of the human self."

The Court has condemned torture or inhuman treatment as against human dignity. The court has deprecated the practice of putting the prisoners in fetters for long durations or handcuffing the undertrials. In Frances Mullin's case, the Supreme Court held that personal liberty would mean to socialise with members of his family and friends. In Sunil Batra's case, it was held by the court that fetters deprive the person of "locomotion which is one of the facets of personal liberty."

In Maneka Gandhi case, the court held that procedure established by law would mean that law which seeks to impair personal liberty would be fair, just and reasonable. The Supreme Court has also come to the rescue of undertrials and convicts. It has held that indigent suspects are entitled to legal aid for defending themselves. This has been considered as one of the basic fundamental rights in respect of life. They are not to be subjected to acts of torture, inhuman or degrading treatment. In Bihar Blinding case, the Supreme Court has held that State is "under a constitutional obligation to provide free legal services to an indigent accused not only at the stage of trial but also at the stage when he is first produced before the magistrate as also when he is remanded from time to time." This is in consonance with Article 14 which guarantees equality before law. Both parties must be equal before law. Prosecution has competent legal advice.

The accused should have the same facility. In Prem Shukla's case, the court held that handcuffing of an accused while in transit from jail to court was a degrading treatment which violated Articles 5 and 10 of the Covenant on Civil and Political Rights. According to the court, any such law under Punjab Police Manual was unfair and unreasonable. Handcuffing was considered against human dignity and therefore, could only be justified as an exception. It violated Article 21 of the Constitution. In Hussain-ara Khatoon case, the Supreme Court discouraged the practice of undertrials remaining in prisons for long, sometimes longer than the prescribed maximum sentence for the crimes attributed to them. The court advised that if there is no substantial risk of non-appearance, he may be released on personal bond. Man's liberty should not be circumscribed by his poverty. It was held that speedy trial was part of Article 21.

The Supreme Court had occasion to consider the conditions of convicts in prisons in cases of Sunil Batra, Shobbraj and Frances Mullin. The court has held that convicts do not cease to be persons. They continue to be persons entitled to certain rights, although in a restricted way. Fetters and solitary confinement were discouraged by the court. In Mullin's case, it was held that detenue has a right to socialise with his family members and friends. The Court has tried to project socio-economic approach to legal issues before it. It has accepted public interest litigation as an instrument of rendering justice to weaker and indigent sections of society, who, otherwise cannot approach the court for implementation or vindication of their rights.

Thus, the Bhagalpur blinding case, the case of Undertrials as represented by Hussain-ara Khatoon, Agra Protection Home and ASIAD workers' cases represent the emergence of public interest litigation where welfare agencies sponsor litigation involving public issues. Even individual lawyers can champion the cause of weaker sections of society and file a writ for rendering socioeconomic justice through the courts.

The court has waived all formalities to render socio-economic justice. Public interest litigation has waived the principle of *locus standi.* Until recently only affected person could move the court for vindication of his rights or redressal in respect of violation of his rights. Sometimes, this was not possible, partly because of the cost involved in litigation in India which the victims could not afford. Ignorance of one's rights was another factor. Individual litigation was also time-consuming. It did not render prompt remedy or justice. Public interest litigation filled the gap and the court waived the plea of *locus standi.* Thus, any one can raise the legal issue of public interest without being personally involved in the matter. Hussain-ara Khatoon was the first public interest litigation case. A number of undertrials were rotting in prisons for a number of years without any trial or without trials coming to an end within a reasonable time. The petition was moved by a Supreme Court lawyer for writ of Habeas Corpus and release of those undertrials The court released the Undertrials on personal bond. The court held that free legal aid and expeditious trials were part of Article 21.

Since then a number of undertrials have been released. After this case, there have been quite a few cases involving public interest litigation which have rendered prompt relief to indigent victims of indulgent society. The latest was the ASIAD workers case where the court held that workers involved in ASIAD building construction should be paid minimum wages and children should not be engaged in hazardous work like building construction which was not included by Delhi Administration in hazardous occupations. Supreme Court gave a new year gift in December, 1982 when in a common cause petition by an Association of Central Government Pensioners, the court held that denial of liberalised pension rules to those having retired before April, 1979 was discriminatory and violative of Article 14 which guarantees equality.

The Chief Justice said that in view of the socio-economic values enshrined in the Constitution, it will not be fair to deprive the old pensioners of liberalised pension rules. Supreme Court has sought to protect the right to property against arbitrary deprivation or deprivation without due compensation. First, the Supreme Court held that a citizen cannot be deprived of his property without adequate compensation. After a series of constitutional amendments also, the court held that Government cannot pay an amount which is a sham in comparison to the value of the property. Forty-Fourth Amendment removed the right to property from fundamental rights part, hoping that it would create less difficulties for the Government in case of acquiring any property. However, any law which seeks to acquire property must be fair, just and reasonable. And law cannot be considered as fair, just and reasonable if it does not give appropriate compensation to the person whose property is sought to be acquired. The Supreme Court has ordered that Government action in public dealings should not be arbitrary. The court has sought to control misuse of executive discretion. This was held in International Airport Authority case where it said that State action should not smear of being arbitrary or unreasonable. Otherwise, the person who has been arbitrarily dealt with has a cause to complain and seek remedy.

In the matter of Directive Principles of State Policy, the Supreme Court has held in Keshavanand Bharti's case that in order to build egalitarian social order and welfare state, the State may bring about legislation to cater to the basic needs of a common man. The Supreme Court held in that case that the State can bring legislation to implement Directive Principles including Article 39(b) and (c) for the common good of the society. Nationalisations have been partly motivated to implement Article 39(b and c).

However, the court has power to ascertain whether the legislation is for implementation of the Directive Principles or otherwise. Supreme Court decisions have added a new dimension to the Directive Principles of State Policy which are not justiciable. However, the court has remarked that if the State has to cater to the needs of a welfare state, it can do so by implementing Directive Principles and the court will assist in the implementation of such principles.

Thus, in the ASIAD Workers construction case in 1982, it was held that children should not be given hazardous work like in construction of building. Besides, Minimum Wages Act should be implemented. In the pensioners case, the Supreme Court has held that there should be no differentiation between new and old pensioners, who should be treated equally and at par. In all fairness, it may be said that the Supreme Court bungled in the case of A.D.M., Jabalpur vs. Shukla in the matter of Habeas Corpus during the emergency period. It closed its doors to victims of emergency on the plea that it cannot question the action of State agencies.

During that period, the performance of some or the High Courts, particularly of Delhi, Bombay and Gujarat was judicious. The Supreme Court was then perhaps fear-ridden due to verbal threats contained in the arguments of the Attorney General. However, in view of the amends made thereafter by the Supreme Court, it is hoped that the highest court in India will uphold the rights of man in the socioeconomic background of the country even during emergency.

# 11

# Human Rights in South Asia and Beyond

Refugees by legal definition are subjects of general international Law. In popular usage, the, word Refugee is used in a wider context even to include the people involuntarily displaced within their own countries, sometimes even due to natural calamities. The term refugee in International law includes those persons compelled to leave ones own country to another to escape certain stated conditions. Absence of protection in ones own country and the tenuous nature of protection in the asylum country make refugee a subject of International concern. The protection of Human Rights of the Refugees who are without national protection and prevention of conflicts between the country of the origin of the refugees and the asylum country are also matters of international concern.

Historically the grant of asylum existed as an attribute of the sovereign who exercised the power discretionally which was not conducive to the development of a compendium rules or principles. The establishment of the Legue of Nations and subsequently the United Nations for the first time provided an

International mechanism to legally recognize and provide protection to the refugees as a category of persons in the International Law.

The early institutional definitions of refugee status included some of the key elements (a) being in a foreign country (b) and not having the protection of a national but there was vagueness as to the exact reasons for the fight which qualified a person for refugee status. The refugee definitions in the United Nations Relief and Rehabilitation Administration (UNRRA) and the successor organization, International Refugee Organization (IRO) were more precise and included the concept of fear of persecution as a ground of displacement attracting refugee status. A notable common feature in the early Refugee definitions was that they were often country specific such as "coming into from Germany" or "persons of Russian origin",

Post Second World War, the United Nations definitions of Refugee status, even though influenced by the earlier European definitions broadened the scope by removing 'temporal and geographical' limitations. International Law for the first time recognized the concept of the Refugee as warranting International Protection. The 1951, Statute of the United Nations High Commissioner for Refugees established a United Nations agency with full competence to deal with the Refugees. Meanwhile the 1949 Universal Declaration of Human Rights had firmly established the right to seek asylum as a Human Right when it declared in article 14 (1)"everyone has the right to seek and to enjoy in other countries asylum from persecution". The Humanitarian nature of the right to seek refuge in another country due to persecution for stated reasons thus, came to be included as the essential element of refugee definition.

The basic concept of Refugee laid down in the 1951

UNHCR Statute continued to be a key element in all subsequent Refugee definitions whether they took the form of United Nations Conventions such as the 1951 Convention of the Status of Refugees or its 1967 Protocol which removed the time and geographical limitations or (2) International Regional Instruments such as in 1969 Organization of African Unity (OAU) Convention governing the specific aspects of refugee problems in Africa or more recently in the context of European Union, the Schengen (1985) and the Dublin (1990) agreements which sought to harmonize European practices and procedures relating to Refugee matters.

In addition to the International and the Regional Conventions there were number of Inter governmental declarations that dealt with general or specific refugee problems in different geographical regions in the world. Thus the Executive Committee of the High Commissioners office (presently with 53 participating governments) has adopted resolutions annually on refugee related subjects such as voluntary repatriation, large scale influx, refugee women, refugee children, temporary refugee, and many other subjects arising out of refugee protection and assistance. Another group of Inter governmental declarations are found in 1966 Asian African Legal Consultative Committee (AALCC) Principles Concerning the Treatment of Refugees and its 1970 Accra, 1987 Bangkok addenda. The, Bangkok principles even though adopted by an inter governmental forum are only advisory in nature and had not been referred to even though South Asian countries, India Pakistan and Sri Lanka actively participated in the Bangkok deliberations. A more recent inter governmental declaration, concerning the treatment of refugees in the Latin American Region is the 1984 Cartagena Declaration.

1951 Convention or 1967 Protocol ratified by 136

states including the independent states of the former Soviet Union had assumed the character of a Universal Convention. Majority of the African countries have ratified both the UN Convention and the OAU Convention where as Latin American countries while ratifying the 1951 Convention had treated the refugee issues with the assistance of the expanded refugee definition in their own 1984 Cartagena Declaration. The countries of the European Union who are, all signatories to the 1951 Convention have rationalized their asylum practices and procedures with the Schengen 1985 and Dublin 1990 agreements while placing a strict interpretation to the 1951 Convention Definition of Refugees. The strict interpretation of the 1951 Refugee Definition by the European countries had been motivated by fears that liberal asylum practices would attract economic migrants from the developing world rather than genuine refugees fleeing persecution.

Ratification of International Refugee instruments even though enhances the International solidarity on humanitarian issues could be reduced to a mere symbolic gesture unless enabling municipal legislation is enacted. Exceptions are found in certain legal systems where ratifications of International Conventions renders them as part of, municipal law. Even in those situations in order to implement the ratified conventions it becomes necessary to enact legislation to setup national procedures and mechanisms. As example from the Asian Region we could mention the Philippines and the Peoples Republic of China both signatories to the 1951 Convention but so far had failed to adopt enabling national legislation. Refugee issues continue to be treated on an ad hoe basis within the overall framework of the fundamental principles contained in the International Instruments. The framers of the 1951 Convention themselves were not optimistic about a quick ratification of the convention by all the member states of the United Nations. They expected the process to be gradual but urged all nations even if they did not become contracting parties to respect the principles underlining the Refugee Conventions. Thus appendix (iv) 1951 Convention: - "Express the hope that the Convention relating to the, Status of Refugees will have value as an example exceeding its contractual scope and that all Nations will be guided by it in granting sofar as possible to persons in their territory as refugees and who would not be covered by, the terms of the convention. The treatment for which it provides"

The countries of the South Asian Region some of which Were affected by massive movements of refugees played no role in the deliberations leading to the adoption of the 1951 United Nations Convention on Refugees. Among the 26 countries who participated in the drafting and adoption of the 1951 Convention there was not a single South Asian country. For that matter, no country from Asia was represented in the initial deliberations. India and Pakistan who experienced the largest movements of refugees in the history after the partition in 1949 viewed the exercise relating to the enactment of 1951 Convention as European origin. This perception had continued to influence the policy makers not only of India and Pakistan but also in rest of the South Asian countries.

The countries in South Asia have during the past fifty years dealt with an estimated 3540 million refugees relying on traditional principles of asylum founded in their historical, religious and cultural practices. The principles underlining the traditional practices had by and large confirmed to the standards found in International Refugee Law. This is evident from the absence of severe international criticism of South Asian asylum practices. It is in the above background that the National Model Law on Refugees was discussed and approved by the -Informal Consultations on Refugees and Migratory Movements in their 1997 Dacca Sessions. The Informal Consultations which had the benefit of active participation of eminent jurists and opinion makers in South Asia as well as UNHCR expertise -consensually recognized the importance of translating, the traditional practices of asylum in the region into tangible National Laws based on a common model. This was considered a prerequisite before proceeding to initiate discussions on a normative regional declaration or convention on refugees. The National Model Law incorporates the fundamental elements of 1951 Refugee Convention and its 1967 Protocol as well as elements from the expanded refugee definitions of the 1969 OAU Convention and the 1984 Cartagena Declaration. National Model Law had also drawn from 1966 Bangkok Declarations on Principles Concerning the Treatment of Refugees of- the AALCC. The various conclusions of the Executive Committee of the High Commissioners Office on different aspects of refugee protection, such as minimum standards of treatment, the principle of non-refoulement, voluntary repatriation, special needs of refugee women and children and special situations of mass influx have found their way into the National Model Law making the proposed Model, comprehensive and modem.

A brief comparative analysis of some of the key concepts on refugees incorporated in Model National Law with the analogous provision in the International Refugee Instruments would provide useful guidance to the law makers of the South Asian Region. The key concepts identified for discussions are :-

1. Definition of a refugee

2. 'Exclusion Clauses

3. Non-refoulement
4. Voluntary Repatriation as a durable solution
5. Special needs of refugee women and children
6. Role of the UNHCR

**Definition of Refugee**

— any person who is outside his or her country of origin, and who is unable or unwilling to return to, and is unable or unwilling to avail himself or herself of the protection of that country because of a well-founded fear of persecution on account of race, religion, sex, nationality, ethnic identity, membership of a particular social group or political opinion, or,

— any, person who owing to external aggression, occupation, foreign domination, serious violation of human rights or other events seriously disrupting public order in either part of whole of his or her country of origin, is compelled to leave his or her place of habitual residence in order to seek refuge in another place outside his of her country or origin.

The above definition of a refugee in the National Model Law had responded to the criticism levelled by the South Asian countries on the limitations of the "fear of persecution" based Refugees definition in the 1951 Convention and its 1967 Protocol. National Model Law Refugee definition while retaining the "fear of persecution" based Convention definition in its first limb has expanded it to include "ethnic identity and sex based persecution". It has been the South Asian experience that the many of the refugee outflows were the result of ethnic turmoil and as such it is relevant to include ethnic persecution as a ground for refugee status. The Model Law notes that the membership of a particular social group includes gender based persecution but could have been more appropriate if sexual orientation was included as a basis of a social group. Inclusion of sex based persecution, as an additional ground of persecution is an improvement from the provisions in the International Refugee Instruments where "sex" is not explicitly mentioned as a ground which can attract persecution. At a time when a global attention is focused on the principle of equality of treatment of women, violation of human fights of women should form a distinct ground warranting inclusion as a refugee.

The second limb of the National Model Law Refugee definition, expands the scope of refugee status from a fear based of persecution to include modem day phenomenon of generalized violence and gross violation of Human Rights. Model Law provision had been inspired by the expanded refugee definition in the OAU Convention and the 1984 Cartagena Declaration. 1951 Convention Refugee definition had also come for criticism for limiting persecution only to the State actors. Experience of Africa, Latin America, Asia and currently in the Balkans show that the people also flee their countries due to generalized violence and violation of Human Rights by State as well as non-State actors. State inability or unwillingness to prevent violation of Human Right or break down of Law and Order in the whole or part of the country could compel human beings to flee the country to seek refuge in other countries. Any definition that does not include these categories as persons deserving International Protection and assistances is grossly inadequate. 1969 OAU Convention was the first to incorporate the expanded refugee definition which was followed and further modernized in the 1984 Cartagena Declaration by inclusion of "massive violations ' of human rights" as a ground for inclusion as a refugee. The National Model Law while retaining fundamental elements of the 1951 Refugee Definition including the hallowed requirement for a person to cross the frontier of his country of origin has incorporated expanded grounds under which flight can attract refugee status. Experience flows in some South American countries which have porous and indefinite border may still throw up complex questions regarding determinations of refugee status.

*Exclusion Clauses*

A person shall be excluded from refugee status for the purpose of this Act if:

— he or she has committed a crime against peace, a war crime or a crime against humanity, as defined in the international instruction drawn up to make provision in respect of such crimes;

— he or she has committed a serious non- political crime outside the country of asylum prior to his or her admission into this country as a refugee.

The exclusion clauses in the Model National Law are a refined version of analogous exclusion clauses found in International and Regional Refugee Instruments. However, International instruments include in the exclusion clauses "acts contrary to the purposes and principles of the United Nations"—which has been omitted from the Model National Law. During the past 47 years of the operation of the 1951 Convention there had been no reported cases of exclusion by the operation of the clause regarding acts contradictory to the principles of the United Nations. However, with the establishment of the UN tribunals against, the war crimes in former Yugasolvia and Uganda and the establishment of International Criminal Tribunal, convicted persons may attract the application of UN specific exclusion clauses.

The Model National Law in the foot note to the

exclusion clauses clarifies that Committing of political crimes do not ipso facto qualify a person to become a refugee but on the contrary a politically motivated violation of criminal law can disqualify a person from refugee status. This interpetation of the National Model Law appeared to be overtly restrictive when compared with the interpretation placed on the comparable exclusion clauses in International and Regional Refugee Instruments. A political activist whose freedom of association is illegally restricted by the agents of the State when defending his/ her fundamental freedom commits a crime against law enforcement agencies may not qualify for refugee status on the basis of the interpretation of National Model Law. A person whose fundamental rights are violated and whose only method of escape was to resort to violence could have qualified for refugee status under International Refugee Law.

*Principle of non-refoulement*

— No refugee or asylum seeker shall be expelled or returned in any manner whatsoever to a place where there are reasons to believe his or her life or freedom would be threatened on account of any of the reasons set out in sub-section (a) or (b) Section 4.

— The benefit of the present provision may not, however, be claimed by a refugee or asylum seeker where there are reasonable grounds for regarding him or her as a danger to the security of the country or who has been convicted by a final judgment of serious crime and constitutes a danger to the community.

The term Non-refoulement derived from the French language is used in the context where the State is restrained from returning a refugee to a country where he / she is likely to face persecution or threat to life or freedom. The principle on Non-refoulement has received the sanctity of Jus Cogens in International Law. The principle of non-extradition of political offenders had existed as an international legal concept for few countries. However, non-refoulement of refugees as an international law concept even though comparatively recent in origin has now assumed general acceptance as a fundamental principle of refugee law. The provision of Model National Law are consistent with similar provisions in international regional refugee instruments and judicial interpretation of the scope of application of the principle in different countries who are signatory to the 1951 Convention.

*Voluntary repatriation*

The repatriation of refugees shall take place at their free volition expressed in writing or other appropriate means which must be clearly expressed. The voluntary and individual character of repatriation of refugees and the need for it to be carried out under conditions of safely to the country of origin shall be respected.

The 1951 Refugee Convention and its 1967 Protocol provides for International Protection and gets out obligations of contracting States towards refugees but had failed to provide except for naturalization other possible solutions to the problem of refugees. 1951 Statute of the Office of the United Nations High Commissioner for Refugees, in paragraph 8c, enjoins the High Commissioner to assist government and private efforts to "promote the voluntary repatriation or assimilation within new National Communities". The OAU Convention was the first inter governmental convention which by its Article v highlighted voluntary repatriation as the most desirable durable solution and emphasized the voluntary nature of such repatriation. The Bangkok principles in Article 4 dealt with the subject under the caption of the right to return. The Bangkok principles placed emphasis on the obligation of the country of origin to receive returning refugees and failed to treat voluntary repatriation as a durable solution to the problem of refugees. (IRO). In the context of South Asia when over 10 million Bengali speakers fled the war of independence of Bangladesh in 1971 General Assembly recognized voluntary repatriation as the only "satisfactory solution" G.A. Res. 2790 (XXVI) Dec.1971. Incorporation of voluntary repatriation as a durable solution in the National Refugee Laws of South Asian countries with guarantees of safe, dignified and voluntary return could ensure respect for individual human rights of the returning refugees. Such provisions could also greatly facilitate and promote the durable solutions to the problem of refugees.

### *Standards of treatment of refugees*

The minimum standard of treatment of refugees has been a subject of debate during the past fifty years. The 1951 Refugee Convention stipulates number of social and economic rights as well as the right to naturalization which are hardly feasible in the developing world. Further more, questions have been raised on the over emphasis placed on refugee rights and not on refugee obligations towards the country of asylum. In an apparent attempt to meet this criticism the National Model Law in paragraph 14 makes provisions for rights and duties of refugees as follows

Every refugee so long as he or she remains within this country, shall have the tight to:

i. fair and due treatment, without discrimination on grounds of race, religion, sex, nationality, ethnic identity, membership of a particular social group or political opinion.

ii. receive the same treatment as is generally accorded to

aliens under the Constitution or any other laws and privileges as may be granted by the Central or State Government. .

iii. receive sympathetic consideration by the country of asylum with a view to ensuring basic human entitlement.

iv. be given special consideration to their protection and material well being in the case of refugee women and children.

v. choose his or her place of residence and move freely within the territory of the country of asylum, subject to any regulations applicable to aliens generally in the same circumstances.

vi. be issued identity, documents.

vii. be issued travel document for the purpose of travel outside and back to the territory of the country of asylum unless compelling reasons of national security or public order otherwise require.

Every refugee shall be bound by the laws and regulations of the country of asylum

Provisions in paragraph 14. iv. National Model Law for special consideration of women and children is a unique feature not found in any other refugee instrument. It is estimated that over 70% of worlds refugees are women and children. Refugee women are rendered vulnerable during flight as well as in the refugee camps. Concerns have been raised on sexual violence perpetrated on refugee women in a number of UNHCR Executive Committee Resolutions. (39 XXXVI Refugee Women and International Protection), (64 XLI Refugee Women and International Protection), (73 XLIV Refugee Protection and Sexual Violence). The above resolutions dealing with refugee women and International Protection have set out guidelines for special protection of these vulnerable section of refugee population.

The refugee children without having the basic facilities for education and development in refugee camps in asylum countries are precariously placed. The Convention of the Rights of the Child ratified by all the countries in the South Asia has special provisions for the protection of refugee children. (Article 22). UNHCR Executive Committee had adopted resolutions on Refugee Children to ensure access to the basic education and provide food security. (No.59 (XL) P. 1989), (No 47 (XXXVIII) 1982). Many refugee children are often unaccompanied minors needing special care and protection. The provisions in the Model Law for special considerations of women and children assume significance in this context.

*Determination of refugee status and role of UNHCR*

The National Model Law provides for a comprehensive mechanism for determination of refugee status of asylum seekers. The appointment of a senior level official as Commissioner of Refugees for determination of refugee status in the first instance and the establishment of a Refugee Committee as an appellate authority consisting of a retired High Court Judge as Chairperson designated in consultation with the Chief Justice are salutary guarantees of due process in refugee status determination. The provision set out in section 12 of the National Model Law to ensure due process during determination of refugee status include the right to be heard directly or through a representative or a legal practioner and when necessary to have the assistance of an interpreter are comparable with the rights of due process available to a citizen of a country. The obligation cast on the Commissioner ofRefugees to give reasons in writing when rejecting a refugee status application would ensure transparency, accountability and provide an opportunity for the rejected asylum seeker to appeal to the Refugee Committee.

It is in the context of the determination of refugee status that the National Model Law introduces a role for UNHCR. National Model Law section 12 c. states "the asylum seeker, if he or she wishes, shall be given an opportunity, of which he or she should be duly informed, to contact a representative of UNHCR". Guarantee of access to UNHCR could ensure application of International standards in the determination of refugee status. The provision also indirectly envisages a legitimate role for UNHCR in the National refugee status determination process. The provisions for UNHCR involvement in paragraph 12 could be considered inadequate when contrasted with the following provisions for cooperation with UNHCR provided in 1951 Refugee Convention in article 35.

*Cooperation of the national authorities with the United Nations*

The Contracting States undertake to co-operate with the Office of the United Nations, High Commissioner for Refugees, or any other agency of the United Nations which may succeed it, in the exercise of its functions, and shall in particular facilitate its duty of supervising the application of the provision of this Convention. In order to enable the Office of the High Commissioner or any other agency of the United Nations which may succeed it, to make reports to the competent organs of the United Nations, the Contracting States undertake to provide them in the appropriate form with information and statistical data requested concering:

(a) the condition for refugees,

(b) the implementation of this Convention, and

(c) laws, regulations and decrees which are, or may hereafter be, in force relating to refugees

Above cooperation provision are closely followed in the 1969 OAU Convention in its Article viii and provisions in article 14 of the 1984 Cartagena Declaration. The only Declaration related to refugees that has judicially avoided reference to cooperation with UNHCR is the 1966 Bangkok Principles which was in fact formulated with participation of UNHCR.

National Model Law is an advanced piece of Model Legislation incorporating refugee related legal development since the adoption of 1951 Refugee Convention of United Nations. The Model Law has benefited from the Legal developments in Africa, Latin America as well as the Resolutions and deliberations in the inter governmental Executive Committee -of the High Commissioners programme. The only area of omission in the National Model Law is the absence of direct or indirect reference to the principle of international burden sharing. South Asian countries have desisted ratification of international refugee instruments in view of the social and economic responsibilities that may result from such ratifications even though there are provisions in the Convention for the reservations of such articles. South Asia arguably considered the poorest geographical region in the world, would need international assistance to deal with the burdens imposed by refugees who are-subjects of international law. International burden sharing should go hand in hand with international humanitarian cooperation.

**The Model national law on refugees a comparative review**

***Introduction***

Following the decision at the Third Regional Consultation on Refugee and Migratory Movements in South Asia held in Delhi in November, 1996, to prepare a Model National Law on refugees, a working group was set up under the chairmanship of Mr. Justice P.N.

Bhagwati to undertake the drafting of a model law. The text of a draft model law was submitted to the participants of the meeting in Dhaka the following year.

The Model Law has eighteen paragraphs which cover broadly nine substantive areas:

— The refugee definition
— Exclusion from refugee status
— Non-refoulement
— Procedures for refugee status determination
— Cessation of refugees status
— Rights and Duties of Refugees
— The situation, of mass influx
— The situation of refugees unlawfully in the country of refugee
— Voluntary repartriation of refugees

**The refugee definition**

The definition in the Model Law is very much wider than that found in the 1951 Convention Relating to the status of Refugees (hereinafter referred to as "the 195 1 Convention"), the OAU Convention Governing Specific Aspects of Refugee Problems in Africa (hereinafter referred to as "the OAU Convention") and in the Principles Concerning Treatment of Refugees adopted by the AALCC in Bangkok in 1966 (hereinafter referred to as "the Bangkok Principles").

Firstly, the grounds on which a "well-founded" fear of perscution are based, are much broader in the Model Law than in the other three instruments; it includes "sex" and "ethnic identity", both of which are not included in any of the other three instruments. Secondly, the Model Law definition includes as refugees, the so-called "OAU Convention" definition which includes persons who "owing to external aggression, occupation foreign domination or other events seriously disrupting public order..." are compelled to leave their countries. This broader definition is not contained in the 1951 Convention nor in the Bangkok Principles. Thirdly, the Model Law definition also includes persons who leave their countries owing to "serious human rights violations", an idea taken from the Cartagena Declaration on Refugees' and which is not found in any of the other three instruments.

*Exclusion from refugee status*

The exclusion provisions in the Model Law are more restrictive than those contained in the 1951 Convention or in the OAU Convention. As regards the 1951 Convention, in addition to the two categories of crimes referred to in the Model Law, it also excludes from international protection any person who "has been guilty of acts contrary to the purposes and principles of the OAU".

The Bangkok Principles contained exclusion clauses similar to the 1951 Convention listing three categories of crimes as basis for exclusion. Further, it may be noted that while the 1951 Convention and the OAU Convention allows exclusion on the basis that "there are serious reasons for considering that" the individual has commited one of the crimes mentioned, the Model Law omits this phrase and thus permits exclusion only if the individual"... has committed" one of the crimes mentioned, thus seemingly requiring a higher standard of proof than is required in the 1951 Convention or in the OAU Convention. The Bangkok Principles contain the same wording as the Model Law in this aspect.

*Non-refoulement*

The non-refoulement provision in the Model Law is wider in scope than that in the 1951 Convention, but more restrictive than the OAU Convention. In the Model Law, non-refoulement is applicable to asylum-seekers as well as refugees, thus incorporating the principle of "non-rejection at the frontier"'. The 1951 Convention provision on non-refoulement, on the other hand, refers specifically to "refugees" only and this has been interpreted by States generally to exclude the principle of non-rejection at the frontier. Like the Model Law, the non-refoulement provision in the OAU Convention and in the Bangkok Principles also specifically covers asylum seekers, the OAU Convention refers to "No person shall be subjected to measure such as rejection at the frontier..." while the Bangkok Principles refer to "No one seeking asylum... shall be subjected to measures such as rejection at the frontier..." The Model Law non-refoulement provision has wider coverage by using the term "place" in lieu of such terms as "frontiers of territories", "territory' and "State or country", which are terms used respectively in the 1951 Convention, the OAU Convention and the Bangkok Principles. The word "place" is seemingly wider as it could be interpreted to include any area on land, whether this -be a State or not, a frontier or not, as well as any area at sea.

The Model Law is also wider in using the phrase "where there are reasons to believe his or her life or freedom would be threatened" as opposed to the more definitive phase, "where his life of freedom would be threatened ... "as contained in the 1951 Convention and similar phrases in the OAU Convention and the Bangkok Principles.

The exception to non-refoulement is similar to that in the 1951 Convention. The 1951 Convention, however, qualifies the term "serious crime" with "particularly", thus requiring the commission of an extremely serious crime for the application of the exception to nonrefoulement. The OAU Convention does not have any exception to non-refoulement while the Bangkok principles excepts non-rejection at the frontier on basis of "overriding reason of national security or safeguarding the population".

It may further be noted that the 1951 Convention contains provisions covering specifically expulsion of refugees. These provisions prohibit expulsion of refugees save on exceptional grounds of national security or public order and only after due process of law the refugee should be allowed a reasonable period to seek legal admission into another country. A similar provision exists in the Bangkok Principles. Such a provision does not exist in the Model Law.

*Procedures relating to refugee status determination*

The Model Law sets out the procedures for refugee status determination and more specifically, provides that the request of asylum seekers should be referred to the Commissioner of Refugees whether such requests be received at the border point or inside the territory of the country. It also provides that no restrictions should be imposed on the asylum seekers pending the determination of refugee status, except "those that are necessary in the interest of sovereignty and integrity of the State or public order". None of the other three instruments contain provisions relating to treatment of asylum seekers (except non-rejection at the frontier as noted above) or to procedures for refugee status determination; the type of procedures being left essentially for States to adopt although UNHCR and the Executive Committee have developed some minimum procedural safeguard for such procedures. There are provisions in the 1951 Convention which prohibit signatory States from applying restrictions to movements, but these relate to refugees and not asylum seekers.

*Cessation of refugee status*

In regard to the cessation clauses, while the 1951

Convention and the OAU Convention contain essentially five grounds for cessation, the Model law sets out essentially four grounds, omitting the reference to refugees "who having lost their nationality, voluntarily re-acquire it", as a ground for cessation. The Bangkok Principles also does not contain this particular ground and uses the term "returns permanently" in place of "re-establishment" in relation to a refugee who has returned to his country origin.

***Rights and duties of refugees***

*Non-discrimination* - The 1951 Convention and the OAU Convention both contain provisions relating to non-discriminatory treatment of refugees, differing in the stipulated grounds. The grounds in the Model Law are more aligned to the OAU Convention, although the latter does not refer to "sex or ethnic identity". The 1951 Convention refers only to "race, religion or country of origin" as grounds warranting non-discrimination of refugees.

*Treatment as aliens* - In so far as the Model Law provides generally that the standard of treatment of refugees is to be the same as that accorded to "aliens", this provision more in line with the Bangkok Principles. In contrast, the 1951 Convention contains extensive provisions on the various standards applicable in relation to different fields of civil, social and economic rights, some the same as that accorded to aliens, some the same as that accorded to nationals as the country, and some, the most favourable treatment accorded to foreign national. The OAU Convention does not contain any specific provisions relating to civil, economic and social rights of refugees, however, in stipulating that the OAU Convention is "the effective regional complement in Africa of the 1951 United Nations Convention on the Status of ' Refugees", it is clear that the standard in the 1951 Convention are also applicable in the OAU Convention context. Therefore, presumably, the standards of civil, economic and social rights as contained in the 1951 Convention are also applicable in the OAU Convention context.

*Ensuring basic human entitlements*- This is a broad provision not found in any of the other instruments:

*Special consideration for the protection and well being of refugee women and children* - This provision is not found in any of, the other instruments. However, the Final Act of the 1951 Convention refers to the principle of family unity recommending that governments take the necessary measures for the protection of the refugee's family, especially with a view to ensure the unity of the refugee's family and the protection of refugees, who are minors, particularly, unaccompanied children and girls.,

*Freedom of choice of residence and of movement* - The 1951 Convention contains similar provisions and presumably this is applicable in the OAU Convention as well. There are no such provisions in the Bangkok Principles.

*Identity papers* - The 1951 Convention is more restrictive in obligating the issuance of identity papers only to refugees who do not have valid travel documents presumably, this is also applicable in the OAU Convention. The Bangkok Principles do not contain such a provision.

*Travel documents* - There are similar provisions in the 1951 Convention and in the OAU Convention. In regard to the latter, the travel document is that of the 1951 Convention. The Bangkok Principles do not provide for travel documents.

*Refugees bound by the laws of the country of asylum* - Similar provisions are contained in 1951 Convention, although worded as a "duty" on the part of the refugees to conform to laws of the country. In addition, refugees are also obliged to conform to "measures taken for maintenance of public order". The OAU Convention contains provisions obligating signate States to prohibit refugees in their territory from attacking any other member states by "activit likely to cause tension.." In the Bangkok Principles, there are no provisions expressly impos a duty on the part of the refugees to conform to the laws of the country, however, there provisions which prohibit refugees from engaging in activities which endanger the national security of the country of refuge, or activities which are contrary to the principles and of the United Nations.

*Mass influx*

This is a unique provision not found in any of the other international instruments.

*Refugees unlawfully in the country of refuge*

This provision is similar to that contained the 1951 Convention. Presumably, this is applica in the OAU Convention. There is not such provision in the Bangkok Principles.

*Voluntary repatriation*

There is no voluntary repatriation provision in the 1951 Convention where the focus is assimilation and naturalisation of refugees. The Bangkok Principles makes broad reference 1 refugee's right to return to his own country, if he freely chooses to do so and the duty of country of origin to receive him.

The OAU Convention, on the other hand, contains extensive provisions relating to volunt repatriation. As in the case of the Model Law, the emphasis is on the voluntary character safety of the return. There is, however, no reference to the "individual character" of the repatriai not to the requirement that a refugee expresses his desire to return "in writing" or "oj appropriate means" as is stipulated in the Model Law. In addition, the OAU Convention oblige countries of origin to facilitate the resettlement of returning refugees and to "grant them rights and privileges of nationals of the country" and provides that refugees who volunta return to their country should not be penalised for having left the country for any of the reas which had given rise to the refugee situation. In addition, there is also reference to the cou) of origin as well as voluntary agencies and international and intergovernmental organization giving every possible assistance to facilitate the return. Furthermore, the OAU Convention, provides that "Whenever necessary, an appeal shall be made through national information in( and through the Administrative Secretary-General of the OAU, inviting refugees to return h( and giving assurance that the new circumstances prevailing in their country of origin will en, them to return without risk and to take up a normal and peaceful life without fear of b( disturbed or punished, and that the text of such appeal should be given to refugees and cle explained to them by their country of asylum".

As may be noted, the Model Law is very broad in its scope of international protection. Not only does it contain a refugee definition which goes beyond the definitions found in the 1951 Convention, the OAU Convention and in the Bangkok Principles, it also caters for a situation of mass influx which permits asylum seekers to reside for a requisite period of time in the asylum country without their individual status being determined, thus ensuring that international protection is accorded to all those who need it. Furthermore, the exclusion clauses are far more restrictive than those found in the other instruments reviewed. Additionally, the scope of nonrefoulement is also wider than the 1951 Convention, covering asylum seekers as well.

The Model Law also sets out procedures for refugee status determination which, by and large satisfy the requisite minimum standard propagated under Executive Committee Conclusion No. 8. The standard of treatment for refugees advocated in the Model Law is the same as that accorded to aliens. Although this opens to question whether the refugee would have rights, such as the right to work and to elementary education, the country of asylum is exhorted to give sympathetic consideration to "ensuring basic human entitlements".

The special reference made to the protection of women and children is exemplary. In terms of durable solutions, the Model Law focuses on voluntary repatriation setting out the basic requirements of voluntariness and safety of return. While this aligns with the OAU Convention and the Bangkok Principles, it contrasts with assimilation and naturalisation provided for in the 1951 Convention.

# Bibliography

Article I(I) of the Declaration on the Right to Development. I IN General Assembly Resolution 41/128 of 4th December, 1986.

Aziz Basha vs. Union of India, A.I.R. 1968, S.C. 662 at p. 674 S 30.

Basu, M. *Introduction to the Indian Constitution* (New Delhi: Rejhi Publishing, 1960).

Bell Whitaker, *The Biharis in Bangladesh* (London: Minority Rights Group, 1982), as, cited in Weiner, "Rejected Peoples...", op. *cit,* 11. 7 Pakistani sources however claim that more than 500,00 Biharis are already living ill Karachi and that it has no obligations to accept any more of these Pakistanis' from Bangladesh.

Chimni B.S. "*The Legal Conditions of Refugees in India*" journal of Refugee Studies, Vol. 7.

Elementary and Secondary Education Act, Public Law No. 93-389, 512, 88 Stat. 464, 571 Aug. 21, 1974, as amended by Public Law No. 93-568, *see*. 2, 88 Stat. 1855, 1858 Dec. 31, 1974.

Gaur K.D, "Poor Victims of Uses and Abuses of Criminal Law and Process in India", Journal of the Indian Law Institute (JILI) (New Delhi), vol. 35, (Part II) (1993), 'Conclusion'. *See* some of the case law which he cites to support his conclusions.

Government of India, Ministry of External Affairs, *Bangladesh Documents* (New Delhi 1972); Richard Sisson and Leo F.

Rose, *War and Secession: Pakistan, India and the Creation of Bangladesh* (Berkeley University of California Press, 1990)

Govt. of India, Ministry of Labour and Rehabilitation, Branch Secretariat, Administrative Instructions for Transit Relief Camps for Refugees from East Bengal, Calcutta, (1971).

In Nagendar Sing, *Human Rights and International Cooperation* (New Delhi: S. Chand & Co., 1969).

Indeed, the problem of trafficking in women is endemic in the whole of South Asia. According to an estimate, during the last ten years over 200,000 women and children were brought to India just for onward "dispatch" to other countries. The Hindustan Times, 2nd January, 1997.

Jois, M.R., *Human Rights and Indian Value* (National Council of Teacher Education), Revised Edition, New Delhi, 1998.

Kuldip Nayar, *"No Decision Yet on Lanka Tamils"*, the Statesman, 6th October, 1992.

Lok Raj Baral, *Regional Migrations, Ethnicity and Security*, The South Asian case, (1990).

Manfred Woelilcke, *"Environmental Refugees"*, *Aussenpolitik, No. M,* 1992, pp. 287-296, Bharat Dogra, "Developmental Refuges: Displaced Forever", *Frontier,* August 31, 1991; Myron Weiner, "Rejected Peoples and Unwanted Migrants in South Asia", *Economic and Political Weekly.*

Mathew Thomas explores this point in his Ph.D. Dissertation on *"Political Economy of Ethnic Conflict in Bhutan"*, to be submitted at the School of International Studies, Jawaharlal Nehru University, New Delhi.

Most of the Statistical information is provided unofficially by the Ministry of Home Affairs, Rehabilitation Division, Government of India, New Delhi.

Myron Weiner, Rejected Peoples and Unwanted Migrants—The Impact of Migration of the Politics and Security of South Asia (1991).

Myron Weiner, *Sons of the Soil: Migration and Ethnic Conflict in India,* (Prineton, New Jersy: Princeton University Press, 1978); T.S. Murthy, *Assam: The Difficult Years,* New Delhi: Himalayan Books, 1983).

Narayanswamy M. R., *Tigers of Lanka: Front Boys to Guerrillas*

(New Delhi: Konark Publishers, 1995). Also Dagmar Hellmann-Rajanayagam, *Tile Tamil Tigers: Armed. Struggle for Identity,* (Stuttgart: Franz Steiner, 1994).

Partha Nath Mukherji, *"The Great Migration of 1971"* vol. IX, No. 10.

Prasun Sonwalkar, 'Exodus of Bangladeshis to India', The Times *of India.* 6 December, 1991; Amulya Ganguli, 'Bangladeshi *Lebnsraum',* Times if *India,* 13 July 1992, as cited in Sandy Gordon, "Resources arid Instability in South Asia" *Survival.* Vol. 35, No 2 Summer, 1993.

Ramesh Thaper vs. State of Madras (AIR) 1950 S.C. 124. In recent decision on Levy of Import Duty on newsprint, the Supreme Court has observed that freedom of press is "heart of social and political intercourse." *The Times of India, 10* December, 1984.

Ratanlal R. and Thakore D. K., *Law of Crimes* 22d ed. -(Bombay: N. M. Tripathi & Co. and Bombay Law Reporter, 1971), p. 1376. Generally, *see* Samirendra Ray, *Judicial Review and Fundamental Rights* (Calcutta: Eastern Law House, 1974).

Ratilal vs. State of Bombay, A.I. R. 1954, S.C. 388. It was held, in this case that while State can validly impose law, the administration must remain in the hands of religious denomination.

Saxena J.N., "Legal Status of Refugees: Indian Position", Indian Journal of Int. Law, Vol. 26, No. 3 & 4, 1986.

***See*** Amrik Singh, "Human Rights and the Rule of Law", *Mainstream,* Vol. XXXIII No. 22.

***See*** Kanan Gahrana, "Human Rights: A Conceptual Perspective", *Indian Journal of International Law, Vol. 29,* Nos. *3* and *4, July-Dec. 1989.*

***See*** Report of Amnesty International—"Bangladesh", Unlawful Killings and Tortures in the Chittagong Hill Tracts", September, 1986.

***See*** Universal Declaration of Human Rights, 1948; International Covenant on Economic, Social and Cultural Rights, 1966; and International Covenant on Civil and Political Rights, 1966.

***See***: *Allid. Hussain Saheb v. Chartered Bank,* A.I.R. 1964 (1 Mad. 1012) for discussion of Secrecy in Banking; Indian Evidence Act, 1872, sees. 121 to 129, 132, on Privileged Communications, sees. 24, 25, 26, 29 on Confessions, sees. 33 of Special Marriage Act, 1959; sees. 53 of Indian Divorce Act, 1869 (in camera proceedings); sees. 96, 95, 127-A, 128, Representation of Peoples Act (Secrecy of Ballot).

Seervai H., *Constitutional Law of India* (Bombay: N.M. Tripathi & Co., 1967).

Shama Sastri R., *Kautilya's Arthasastra* (Mysore: Raghuveer Press, 1951).

Singh M.P., *"Position of Aliems in Indian Law,"* Heidelberg Colloquim on *"The Legal Position of Alliens in Nation and international Late"*, September 1985.

Sir Sivaswamy Aiyer, *Evolution of Hindu Moral Ideals,* (Calcutta University Press, 1935); Sri Aurobindo, *The Foundations of Indian Culture,* (New York: Sri Aurobindo Library, 1953).

There are reports of tile LTTE helping in the establishment of Tamil National Retrieval Troops (TNRT), and taking them for training in subversion and sabotage to Jaffna. *The Hindustan Times.* July 17, 1995.

There have been a number of useful studies oil this issue. For the latest one ***see*** 1). Sahadevan, India *and Overseas Indians: The Case of Sri Lanka* (Delhi Kalinga Publications, 1995). For early Sri Lankan perspective oil this problem *see,* Shelton Kodikara, Indo-Ceylon *Relations Since Independence,* (Colombo: Ceylon Institute of World Affairs, 1965).

Trikamial R. Desai, *The Indian Easements Act,* IIth ed. (Ahmedabad: C. C. Vora, 1956). Generally, ***see*** Vasudha Dhagamwar, *Law, Power and Justice: Protection of Personal Rights under the Indian Penal Code* (Bombay: N. M. Tripathi, 1974).

Urmila Phadmis, *Ethnicity and Nation-Building in South Asia* (New Delhi: Sage 1990). Urmila Phadnis, S.D. Muni and Kalim Bahadur (eds.) *Domestic Conflicts in South Asia* (New Delhi: South Asia Publishers, 1986).

# Index